Regional Economic Diversity

Regional Economic Diversity

Lessons from an Emergent India

POORNIMA DORE

and

K. NARAYANAN

OXFORD
UNIVERSITY PRESS

OXFORD
UNIVERSITY PRESS

Oxford University Press is a department of the University of Oxford. It furthers the University's objective of excellence in research, scholarship, and education by publishing worldwide. Oxford is a registered trade mark of Oxford University Press in the UK and in certain other countries

Published in India by
Oxford University Press
22 Workspace, 2nd Floor, 1/22 Asaf Ali Road, New Delhi 110 002, India

First Edition published in 2022

ISBN–13 (print edition): 978–0–19–013059–6

ISBN–10 (print edition): 0–19–013059–8

ISBN–13 (eBook): 978–0–19–099297–2

ISBN–10 (eBook): 0–19–099297–2

DOI: 10.1093/oso/9780190130596.001.0001

Typeset in Minion Pro 10.5/14
by Newgen KnowledgeWorks Pvt. Ltd.

Printed in India by
Rakmo Press Pvt. Ltd.

To Lakshmi and Kartik Dore
for their unwavering quest of the greater good

and to the Late Smt. P.V.Lakshmi for her enduring spirit.

What They Said ....

"A highly significant piece of work on regional economic development, this handy and versatile book delves into regional patterns of growth and the implications of such growth of socio-economic development. Based on ingenious data analysis, the author has identified regional clusters which appear to drive growth in India and makes a strong case, given the diversity within states, for the need to address growth at the sub-state level using an "aspirational regions" approach. Should we focus our attention and the efforts to specialization on diversification? Are regions in India embarking on growth trajectories which converge or diverge? These are the two most consequential questions which the book seeks to answer and in the process, provides a wealth of information from the perspective of investment and industry, regional planning and employment generation as well as granular regional growth patterns.

I strongly recommend this book owing to the pioneering analysis undertaken and the quality recommendations which have been made, These crucial insights and recommendations would help guide policy makers, academics are well as industrialists in not just India, but also across developing countries in the world to decipher, aid and influence the trajectory of regional development and in doing so, provide an impetus to national development."

—Amitabh Kant, Chief Executive Officer,
National institution of Transforming India (NITI Aayog)

"Doing Sub-national economic analysis has been a challenge in India primarily due to issues of data constraints. Which is why most analysis has been limited to inter-state comparisons. This book attempts to explore the possibilities of doing more disaggregated analysis at the level of National Sample Survey (NSS) Regions. The National Sample Survey has been conducting sample surveys with stratification at the level of NSS regions for almost 50 years. This allows in principle the ability to do analysis at a more granular level than that of states over long periods of time. The authors explore the possibilities of such an approach in this book. It would be a valuable resource to all scholars interested in doing detailed regional analysis."

—TCA Anant, Former Chief Statistician of India,
Member – Union Public Service Commission of India (UPSC)

"The book reflects on the spatial dimensions of development, juxtaposing the empirical artefacts in the backdrop of the theoretical underpinnings on which the unexplorable components in India are enormous. The dynamics of divergences across regions poses new challenges which can be mitigated through innovative interventions without disturbing the gains associated with concentration. The book is unique not only in terms of the approach it follows, but also the methods it deploys in handling the researchable issues. The economic geography angle which has not been pursued much by the researchers in the country, comes out sharply in the course of analysis, making the work more realistic and reasonable. It rightly argues that the variables which account for the differences in the typology of regions in two different time periods must be unravelled. The depth that it cultivates will surely substantiate the logic of evidence-based research for policy making. The volume is indeed an expression of novelty."

—Arup Mitra, Professor of Economics,
Institute of Economic Growth

"This pioneering book should be read by everyone interested in economic development in India. Two innovative economists – Dr. Poornima Dore, the Head of Data Driven Governance at Tata Trusts, and Prof. K. Narayanan at IIT-Bombay – demonstrate that National Sample Survey (NSS) region is the best level at which to understand the dynamic processes of agglomeration, and sectoral and regional diversity. Agglomeration or a location's ability to attract the right combination of industry and people to promote its development trajectory, is usually measured at the state level. Using the NSS region, which Is a sub state level but above the district level, the authors measure change over a seven-year period and produce a number of significant and remarkable findings that will be of great interest to policymakers, investors, and institutions such as the Reserve Bank of India. Students and scholars interested in development economics will also find this book to be full of valuable insights."

—Holli A. Semetko, MSc PhD (LSE), MBA (Emory)
Asa Griggs Candler Professor of Media and International Affairs
Professor of Political Science
Emory University

"This is a competent analysis of at the micro-level on an economic subject, which is usually viewed at the macro-level. Hence its use for future policy-making is great, a worthy read."

— R Gopalakrishnan, Author and Corporate Advisor
Ex-Director, Tata Sons Ltd

"This book/volume is a stellar contribution to the evolving discourse/ emphasis on foregrounding 'agglomeration' economies while formulating policy for growth in light of the endemic/entrenched intra-state development disparities in India.

Dore and Narayanan's analytical framework offers an interesting/novel unscrambling of the dialectic of localizing (specialization) economies and urbanizing (diversification) economies to also assess the inter-regional and inter temporal trends and patterns of development. The case for using the NSS **region** in preference to specific states as the basic administrative unit of analysis and intervention, is persuasively buttressed with extant data to highlight the key determinants of differences across regions in India between 2004-05 and 2011-12.

The need to develop regional, even sectoral clusters, keeping in mind the extent of uneven manufacturing distribution even **within** the same state requires a granular exposition of the concomitants of a robust regional economy. This the book does with credible gravitas.

The policy implications of these research findings for both the private and public sectors in terms of sectoral planning, fiscal incentive design and employment generation are far reaching. Policy makers, think tanks, industrialists' administrators and researchers will see in the book an invaluable resource do help explore dimensions of economic structure and access to finance, skills and markets and their role in regional development.

This is a bold attempt to break through the obfuscations and straight-jackets of the conventional frames and foreground processes for developing **specific sectors** of competitive advantage. The book's alternative prism/lens of '**specialized diversification**' offers a creative framework indeed—and one that invites interventions and engagements at myriad levels of theory and praxis !"

—Meenakshi Gopinath
Chair, Centre for Policy Research
Principal Emerita, Lady Shri Ram College

Table of Contents

Preface and Acknowledgements

This book owes its existence to our early experiences of trying to make sense of the regional economy and a gradual realization that there are others like us, at the cusp of industry, government, and academia, who in their individual or institutional capacity have been looking for answers.

Why do some regions experience very high growth, while others do not? How do firms take decisions on the choice of location, and are there diminishing returns to scale beyond a point? What leads to concentrations of population and high-density pockets? At a broader level: What is more conducive to the economic development of a nation—specialization or diversification? Are regions within a developing economy experiencing divergence or convergence as they embark upon a high-growth path? Can we make sense of the Indian experience in a way that provides learnings for other economies? Do state-level patterns of development mask the vast variation at the regional level, particularly for countries that are large and diverse? How do we assess the role of economic diversity and measure regional value added when such data is not readily available? And, what are the key determinants of differences across regions and over time?

This book is the culmination of our work over the last 7–8 years on analysing such patterns of development in the Indian subcontinent. During this period, we have had the benefit of the feedback of several noted scholars and practitioners. Surajit Bhattacharyya, Rama Pal, and Sarmistha Pattanaik of IIT Bombay and especially research Co-advisor Sanjiv Phansalkar of Vikas Anwesh Foundation, with sharp questions and valuable feedback, enriched the early stages of our analysis during seminars at IIT Bombay. Parts of this work have been presented at various forums, including the 10th International Conference of the Forum for Global Knowledge Sharing at the National Institute of Advanced Studies (NIAS) in Bengaluru in November 2015. We thank Professors K.L. Krishna, N.S. Siddharthan, Y.S. Rajan, B.L. Pandit, and S.R. Hashim for their experienced insights that strengthened this work. Subsequent invitations to deliver the Gokhale Endowment Lecture hosted at the University of Madras in October 2018 and for a seminar at Nagoya University in Japan in January 2018 resulted in deliberations for which we would like to thank K. Jothi Sivagnanam and Aya Okada. We are fortunate to be part of eminent institutions, namely the Tata Group and the Tata Trusts, that have contributed to the global growth story across sectors and geographies, and IIT Bombay, which is a premiere seat of higher academic learning. Special thanks to the late Mr. A.N.Singh, R. Venkataramanan, N.Srinath, Sanjiv Phansalkar, Prabhat Pani, and Devang Khakkar for the opportunities to give our best to the ambitious goals of these institutions. Our travels to remote parts of the country, our engagements with decision-makers across the spectrum, and our exposure to students have kept us grounded to the real problems that people face and the real questions on people's minds. We have been encouraged by subject matter experts such as Arup Mitra and Holli Semetko, who, along with their detailed comments and feedback on this work, insisted that we must think of converting these insights into a book. We are also grateful for well-wishers and respected academicians such as Amitava Mukherjee, Mukund Rajan, Partha Mukhopadhyaya, S. Chandrasekhar, and Ramkumar Kakani who have underscored the importance and timeliness of this subject and egged us on to complete the book. Special thanks to the team at Oxford University Press, especially Dhiraj Pandey, for believing that this is a story worth telling and helping it reach a wide audience, Daniel Gill and Sanjay Arora for facilitation, and Gopinath TA and Ayshwarya R. for taking care of every detail to make it happen. Thanks to Sindhuja Kasthala for her help with the maps to enhance the reading experience. We thank the stalwarts who have endorsed this book and the esteemed specialists who took the time to review and recommend this for publication.

We thank our fellowship of colleagues, friends, and most importantly our family for bearing with us while we took on this arduous journey of book writing. Poornima Dore would like to thank Sourav Roy for being her eternal co-traveller on all such radical adventures from night-outs to print-outs-together our wild journeys become worthwhile. Devika Dore Roy for giving 'life' a new meaning and growing with this book, Kartik Dore for inculcating a love for precision and humour, and Lakshmi Dore for the inspiration to embrace literature and authenticity. Sumita Roy and

Saroj Kumar Roy have been rock solid. K. Narayanan would like to thank Parvathy Narayanan for her unstinted support in accomplishing his academic tasks, and his sons Aravind and Arihant for always setting the bar high.

We believe that this book would be of interest to business leaders from the perspective of industrial location, investment, output, and market opportunities. It would also capture the attention of government administrators and policymakers for regional planning, fiscal incentive design, and employment generation. We hope that our findings and insights help to strengthen the statistical system, so that in the years to come we have a richer information base to tease out and track some of the finer patterns of regional economies. Several issues which are key focus areas for investors as well as multi-lateral funding, namely financial inclusion, digital literacy, job creation, and boosting cities as engines of growth, depend upon the regional economy's ability to absorb and respond to policy stimuli. Learnings from Indian regions have valuable lessons not just for India but also for other countries. We also hope that the broader academic community, including faculty and students of management, economics, geography, and development find it interesting to study the underlying patterns of growth drivers at a regional level.

We hope that you, the reader, get as involved reading this volume as we did in putting it together.

Dr. Poornima Dore
Dr. K. Narayanan

Saroj Kumar Roy have been rock solid. K Narayanan would like to thank Parvathy Narayanan for her unstinted support in accomplishing his academic tasks, and his sons Aravind and Ashwin for always [illegible] the [illegible].

We believe that this book would be of interest to business leaders from the perspective of industrial location, investment, output, and market opportunities. It would also capture the attention of government administrators and policymakers for regional planning, fiscal incentive design and employment generation. We hope that our findings and insights help to strengthen the statistical system so that in the years to come we have a richer information base to take our study further and capture some of the richer patterns of regional economies. Several issues which are key focus areas for investors as well as multilateral funding agencies namely regional inclusion, digital literacy, job creation, and boosting cities as engines of growth depend upon the regional economy's ability to absorb and respond to policy stimuli. Learnings from Indian regions have valuable lessons not just for India but also for other countries. We also hope that the broader academic community including faculty and students of management, economics, geography and development find it interesting to study the underlying patterns of growth drivers at a regional level.

We hope that some of the readers get as involved reading this volume as we did in putting it together.

Dr Poornima Dore
Dr K Narayanan

The book represents the views of the authors exclusively, which are not necessarily shared by the publisher.

Foreword

Most economists argue about the validity of GDP as an adequate measure of development. But we do generally agree that measurement is an important place to get started. In my own teaching and researching career, I have come across numerous indices that attempt to capture holistic development. The value of space or location, however, as an important vector, has emerged only since the mid 90's; as the focus on economic geography, and hence the region as a unit of development, has gained prominence.

What is an ideal measure of output at the regional level? Given that there is no agreed measure of regional output in India, can the same be extrapolated using NSS region level data? I encountered the first specimen of this approach, in 2015 at NIAS, where Poornima presented her calculations from the paper that she and Narayanan had submitted to the Forum for Global Knowledge Sharing. I have interacted with Poornima during the annual conferences of the Forum and her research looking at challenges in development at the sub-regional level always interested me. She currently works as is Director – Analytics, Insights and Impact at the Tata Trusts and previously used to head their Data-Driven Governance vertical. She has established herself as an expert in impact finance as well as research based on real-time data, and has a rare/unique worldview that covers both business and public policy. Narayanan has been my student in Delhi School of Economics back in the mid-1980s, and has since taught a course on Indian economic development at University of Delhi and IIT Bombay for many years. He has been interacting closely with me during the last 35 years and this research in particular is very close to what he wanted to pursue. He has published widely co-authoring with his students in diverse field of economics. His research work in the field of applied econometrics and developmental issues are well received in the academic community.

Regional diversity in development has been a bone of contention among several scholars and the debate continues. I am delighted to see this work evolve over the years and now take the form of a book which can reach a wider audience, since this issue needs the serious engagement of a wider set of stakeholders—it must not stay within the confines of academia.

The patterns of employment generated are of vital importance to business and policy makers alike—as we grapple with situations of low employment levels and economic deceleration. Equipping our workforce with adequate skills and access to finance is critical if they are to achieve their economic potential. In this context, a deeper understanding of regional differences and patterns is essential. It is useful to look at our policies of specialization, in the context of this books findings on diversification being a driver of the Indian economy. The role of cities and markets, and the need to invest in smaller cities, are aspects that require serious reflection and planning.

I also think the book makes an important point about the need for granular data to enable regional planning. As an econometrician, I have seen researchers and policy makers repeatedly hit roadblocks when data is not accurate, updated or plainly unavailable. The authors here address this by constructing variables where necessary and come up with alternate measures. At the same time the book makes a convincing case to collect and release official data sets at the regional and unit level to enable the kind of robust quantitative analytics that future economic planning will demand. The government and technical agencies including multilaterals like the IMF and World Bank need to facilitate the capacities to manage and credible and periodic information for planning and budgeting.

I encourage you to read this book, as a synthesis of academia, practice and policy. It is a valuable step in making the dynamics of the regional economy accessible, understandable while highlighting the period of 2004-05 to 2011-12 in India as a case in point. The approach and findings have lasting relevance in the decades to come as we look at policy debates on diversification, divergence and economic disparities.

K. L. Krishna
Former Director, Delhi School of Economics
Former Chairman, MIDS, Chennai, and
Former President, The Indian Econometric Society.

List of Illustrations

Tables

Figures

Maps

List of Abbreviations

ASI	Annual Survey of Industries
DA	Discriminant Analysis
DV	Diversity Index
FDI	Foreign Direct Investment
GDP	Gross Domestic Product
GSDP	Gross State Domestic Product
IBGE	Brazilian Institute of Geography and Statistics
JNNURM	Jawaharlal Nehru National Urban Renewal Mission
MGNREGA	Mahatma Gandhi National Rural Employment Guarantee Act
MPCE	Monthly Per Capita Consumption Expenditure
NCO	National Classification of Occupations
NIC	National Industrial Classification
NSDC	National Skill Development Corporation
NSDP	National State Domestic Product
NSDPPC	National State Domestic Product Per Capita
NSS	National Sample Survey
NSSO	National Sample Survey Organization
OECD	Organization for Economic Corporation and Development
OLS	Ordinary Least Squares
PIA	Pesquisa Industrial Annual
R&D	research and development
RBI	Reserve Bank of India
RVA	Regional Value Added
RVAPC	Regional Value Added Per Capita
SCB	Scheduled Commercial Bank
SD	Standard Deviation
SDP	State Domestic Product
UN	United Nations
UPS	Usual Principal Status
UPSS	Usual Principal Secondary Status
VA	Value Added
VIF	variance inflation factor
WPR	workforce participation rate

1
Introduction
Statistics beyond states

India has been one of the fastest growing economies in the last two decades. While some countries have explicitly focused on encouraging growth poles as a strategy for accelerated economic development, in the case of India, the official policy position on economic development over successive five year plans has been to boost growth while reducing regional disparities. Questions regarding whether we have succeeded in our planned objectives and to what extent is growth evenly across regions within the country and over time have been the focus of empirical assessment among scholars as well as policymakers.

A region's ability to experience growth is largely determined by its ability to attract either industry or people. This phenomenon is known as 'agglomeration' and promotes concentration of firms, development of industrial hubs, policies towards special economic zones (SEZs), flows of labour and capital, as well as the formation and growth of cities. An analysis of such regions or 'clusters' of regions is important since the wealth of nations seems increasingly to be related to the competitiveness of the regional economy, the presence of productive clusters, and the capabilities of its constituents towards both efficient production and consumption. It is also important to foster the understanding of such regional dynamics given that the success of several policy efforts towards financial inclusion, digital literacy, leveraging the demographic dividend, and boosting cities as engines of growth depends upon the regional economy's ability to absorb and respond to such policy stimuli.

In India, the states serve as an important starting point to understand these variations and are also the best studied units thus far. India has 28

Regional Economic Diversity. Poornima Dore and Krishnan Narayanan, Oxford University Press. © Oxford University Press India 2022. DOI: 10.1093/oso/9780190130596.003.0001

states and 8 union territories. Each state has a character of its own, and there are some common characteristics which make certain groupings possible among and within states, giving credence to the authors' efforts to make a statement on the characterization of the regions within. There are very few select studies examining the pattern of intra-state disparities of development in India, covering different periods of time. This book is a preliminary step in this direction and seeks to analyse all Indian regions at the sub-state level and provide insights at a granular level, which can be very valuable.

Contextual Landscape

The subject of regional growth is, therefore, of interest both to the private sector from the perspective of industrial location, investment, and output as well as to public sector enterprises, the government or policymakers, for the purpose of economic growth, regional planning, fiscal incentive design, and employment generation. In the Indian context, there can be tremendous implications due to three important factors:

Manufacturing and Its Contribution to GDP

If we consider the experience of other developing economies such as China, India, and Southeast Asia, we find that the GDP share of agriculture has decreased sharply for all countries, including India. However, we find that with the increase in the share of services, the share of manufacturing has also grown almost proportionately for these countries and forms the dominant component—almost 40 per cent—of their GDP. Even for countries where services are dominant, manufacturing forms a close second. This is not so in the case of India, where the contribution of manufacturing to the GDP has stagnated at 16 per cent, raising questions about India's development model, including its sustainability, especially for generating adequate employment. In order to achieve the targeted share of 24 per cent of GDP, or finding alternate pathways to sustainable growth, leveraging agglomeration economies will be essential.

Employment and High-End Skills

Given the age structure of India's working population, successive five year plans have sought to increase the rate of job creation to create 100 million additional jobs by 2025. The services sector has been the major contributor to job creation in recent years, through information technology, transport, communications, and real estate (Mehotra et al. 2014). Post 2010, there is further momentum with the emergence of newer forms of services such as e-retailing, fintech, the digital revolution, logistics, tourism, and legal services. This phenomenon has been documented by a number of studies across OECD countries at the industry level which find within-sector shifts in the composition of employment towards skilled labour as the level of the technological complexity of operations increases. Rajan (2006) holds the view that in India's case, skill levels of the workforce have been responsible for the differential growth of various regions. The neglect of infrastructure has meant that the only way to stay competitive is to focus on high value added–high skill industries.

Demography and Increasing Urbanization

The current urban population is expected to double over the next 20 years. Statistics indicate that 31.1 per cent of India's population lives in cities (Census 2011) and by 2040 the overall urbanization rate will go up to 43.3 per cent (UN 2014). If 40 per cent of the overall population is likely to fall into the category of youth (as defined by the age group of 15–30), it goes without saying that at the least a similar proportion, if not more, would be visible in urban areas. This adds up to about 1.4 billion youth in urban India by 2040 (Economic Survey 2018–19). In other words, there will be an unprecedented level of youth population in cities due to the projected increase in urbanization coupled with demographic transition. The three components of urban growth are said to be: natural growth of the population, rural to urban migration, and reclassification of rural areas as urban (Kundu 2011). Given this, it is possible to broadly categorize the youth bulge into two segments:

1. Domicile: The youth born and brought up in cities as is reflected by the general rate of population growth and demographic trends.
2. Migrants: As urban India is also characterized by a high degree of permanent as well as seasonal migration, this segment consists of the youth who come to the city in search of a living or for other reasons.

It is, therefore, important to understand the forces of concentration and dispersion which result in a region's ability to attract labour and capital. The nature of employment patterns at a regional level determines the extent to which an industry needs to provide for education, training of the new entrants into the labour force, as well as public and private sector investments linked to the emerging regional centres. Each of these—sectoral shares, employment creation, and urbanization—are all closely linked with the concentration of economic activity. This is succinctly put in the industrial dispersal report of 1980 which stated that 'Public policy cannot ignore the advantages of agglomeration and hence the aim of policy must be to develop viable growth centres in backward regions' (GoI 1980).

The erstwhile Planning Commission of India, the present NITI Aayog, successive chief economic advisors to the prime minister, and a host of agencies have been pushing for planned growth and exploring ways to spur economic development across the 28 states and 9 union territories while reducing regional disparities. Having a federal structure and a central financial regulator (the Reserve Bank of India [RBI]), a regionally relevant design and implementation of economic policies, with an active coordination between the Centre and the rest, is of paramount importance. All citizens, individually and collectively, get impacted by these policies and their final implementation at the grassroots level. The actual results on the ground and the ability of a region to experience growth are determined by several factors, including existing natural advantages, the ability to attract enterprise, access to a willing and competent workforce, access to funds both to purchase and to invest, and connectivity to markets and information. Some of these factors may already be present in a region, waiting to be harnessed, while the rest will need to be strategically augmented.

Important Debates

What drives growth and what can growth lead to? Does growth require a nation/region to build on its natural competitive advantage to the exclusion of all else, or should it diversify its risks to be an all-weather player? Also, what is the impact of growth over time—does it lead to a convergent state, where all nations/regions move to a higher equilibrium in time; or is the growth journey bound to create a divergence and increase inequalities over time. This book is situated right in the midst of these two debates:

Specialization vs Diversification

One of the long-standing debates is whether specialization or diversification is more desirable for regional growth? The Marshallian view (Marshall 1890; Arrow 1962; Romer 1986) maintains that when industries belonging to a particular sector collocate, they generate economies of scale within the industry. Such localized economies as represented by specialization are of prime importance for economic development. This explains the incentives that governments offer towards the formation of Special Economic Zones (SEZs), technology parks, and industrial hubs. The Jacobsian school of thought (Chinitz 1961; Jacobs 1969) opines that the collocation of industries belonging to different sectors is indicative of an outward shift of the production possibility frontier and, hence, urbanization economies as represented by sectoral diversification should take primacy.

International studies on agglomeration economies and their linkage with the process of economic development picked up momentum during the third quarter of the twentieth century and continue even today. Most of these studies examine the phenomenon of specialization and division of labour, and seek to explore the causes, indicators, and impacts of agglomeration economies as observed empirically. They reveal that the specific impact of such factors varies substantially by industry and, to some extent, by country. Specialization is found to be the key driver in Korea and Indonesia (Henderson et al. 2001; Deichmann et al. 2005), whereas in

India, diversification appears to be more significant (Lall and Mengistae 2005; Lall and Chakravorty 2007). Sectoral diversity (in other words, urbanization economies) appears to allow significant cost savings for individual firms in India and is the only economic geography variable to do so consistently. Further analysis is required to understand why the results from India differ from those of Korea and Indonesia. In addition to the nature of the data, such differences could also be due to variations in the definition or measurement of indicators. Besides that, India is a much larger country with pronounced regional variations. A direct comparison with other south-Asian economies may, therefore, not be appropriate. Mitra (2011) points towards the need for greater empirical evidence in the context of a developing country such as India.

Convergence vs Divergence

Another important debate is between convergence and divergence. The convergence argument is centred primarily on the inverted 'U' hypothesis (Kuznets 1955; Williamson 1965), which states that if one takes a historical view of economic development, nations are seen to initially experience increased disparities, which narrow over time as nations move ahead on the development continuum. Those in higher brackets need to keep reinventing themselves to stay on top and maintain high growth rates—there is very little space to manoeuvre or engage in inter-industry shifts for high-income populations. The bottom line is that while in the short run inequalities may increase, in the long run there is a move towards convergence.

The divergence argument draws its genesis from Young (1928, 531) who postulates that 'the economic growth process under the condition of increasing returns is progressive and propagates itself in a cumulative way'. Young draws from both Smith (1776) and Marshall (1890) to say that the link between division of labour and the size of the market can also be the reverse, that is, the size of the market can be determined by the volume of production. This results in a mutually reinforcing impact, also called positive feedback loops, further specified by Myrdal (1957) in his theory of cumulative causation. In other words, the rich become richer, while the poor become poorer, and regions or communities tend to move further apart.

Our book examines regional economy and the Indian experience through the lens of these two debates. There are two specific components of regional economy that we believe are very important, namely economic structure and levels of access.

1. *Economic structure* is defined by the size and composition of the regional economy. This involves the size of the market of goods and services, the labour pool available, colocation, and the degree of agglomeration economies that the region can leverage.
2. *Levels of access* refers to the access to finance, human resource, and markets. These are the three critical factors that are essential for a robust regional economy. This would cover the banking footprint, access to high-end skills, and proximity to urban centres, all of which can help to realize the growth aspirations of the region.

This framework of analysis can be applied in the Indian context to develop empirical evidence. The Indian development landscape has been studied over the years by several noted scholars such as Basu and Srivastava (2004), Lall and Chakravorty (2007), Kundu (2011), Dreze and Sen (2013), Panagaria et al. (2014), Chandrasekhar and Sharma (2014), Sridhar (2017), and Hasan et al. (2017). These studies have been empirical and have looked at growth and equity, economic geography, and investment patterns with a focus on specific parameters such as state-level indices, GDP growth, industrial productivity, and urban development. The literature available on development at sub-state levels, especially around questions of economic structure and access, is very sporadic, which is what has served as an important motivation for the creation of this book.

A review of the research landscape reveals the following:

1. Most books on regional development have focused on the administrative unit of the state or the city. Given the size and diversity within each state in India, there is a case for going one step below to identify homogeneous units at a *sub-state level*. Several international studies are based on very granular levels of analysis and hence can claim to be more robust or representative.
2. While the impact of agglomerative factors on profit, cost, output, productivity, and so on, have been explored, there is scope to

develop a more detailed understanding of the importance of *sectoral diversity* in regional economy, since it has emerged as a variable of significance in India.

3. Such phenomena have typically been examined at a specific point in time (static). Since agglomeration by definition is a *dynamic process*, there is merit in studying it over a period of time or in comparing the results across two time periods, to see if there is a move towards convergence or divergence.
4. There is a need to *develop a stronger database* that captures details of the economic structure and access to finance and skills at a regional level, since most published data is available only at the country or state level. While the Census of India data does capture details up to the village level, this is available only once every 10 years. Also, several indicators are not part of the census questionnaire. Currently, different data sets in India capture assorted indicators at different levels of granularity.

Issues Covered in this Book

This book aims to address a set of four core questions covering the following dimensions:

1. Are the patterns of development more dynamic at the regional level compared to the state level? Do certain regions showing similarities cluster together, and is it possible to create a typology of clusters?
2. What is the extent of sectoral diversity at the state and regional levels and is this diversification a function of scale (as represented by size) or skills (as represented by the skill sets of the workforce)?
3. How can we measure differences in output at the regional level? How are output levels influenced by the level of sectoral diversity, urbanization, and other factors? Are such linkages straightforward?
4. What were the key determinants of differences across regions in India between 2004–5 and 2011–12? What factors related to economic structure and access to finance and skills explain these changes over time?

Highlights of This Book

Most regional science literature speaks of homogeneity as an important principle in defining a region. The very geographic, cultural, and economic diversity of India is a challenge to comprehend, even more so for central policy formulation, as also for their implementation by the states. The very size of some of its states, in terms of land area and population, is larger than most European countries. Administratively, each state is broken up into a number of districts, with a total of 736 districts in the country. For the purpose of regional analysis, therefore, the state is too broad a level and the districts are far too many. For our purpose, thus, we adopted the framework followed by the National Sample Survey (NSS), through which several *homogenous and geographically contiguous districts within each state are brought together to form an NSS region*. Each state can have 1–6 NSS regions within, depending on its size. This provides an effective base for our assessment—by breaking up each state into units, we look at India as a set of over 75 regions.

Second, an important contribution is to bring all indicators to this common homogenous denominator, which is the NSS region. While it is without a doubt a cumbersome effort to construct or compile any requisite data set at the NSS-region level, it is very useful to assess whether comparable indicators are the same across regions or undergo any shifts, and if so, how can policymakers take such shifts into account. The NSSO Employment Unemployment Surveys (EUS) have been the main source of comprehensive *labour market information* in India. We draw from the NSSO EUS data for the 61st round (2004–5) and the 68th round (2011–12), and triangulate with other data sets on output and population from the *Handbook of Statistics on Indian Economy 2004–5* and *2011–12* published by the RBI, *Basic Statistical Returns of Scheduled Commercial Banks in India 2005* and *2010* published by the RBI, and the *Census of India 2001* and *2011*. Most studies at the sub-state level rely on the Annual Survey of Industries (ASI), which has data at the level of the firm and, therefore, largely deals with the formal sector. For an inclusive understanding of the Indian economy, it is important to put equal emphasis on the informal sector as well, since it accounts for the bulk of the regional economy. As our analysis is based on the NSS data from the household perspective, we are able to capture both the formal and the informal sectors.

Third, another unique feature of this book is that we adopt a different approach to analyse the data. Several variables are constructed at the NSS-region level, namely the diversity index (DV), regional value added (RVA), share of high-end skills (SKILLIV), and so on. These are described in detail in Chapter 3 and are used across the analytical assessments in Chapters 4 to 7. Access to labour and finance is also represented in a different way; several studies have looked at education levels as a measure of the quality of workforce, or at foreign direct investment (FDI) approvals for access to finance. If one deliberates on what it will truly take for a region to become a growth hub, the share of professional skills and regular employment give a more granular representation of the access to good quality labour. Similarly, the banking footprint in a region is captured in terms of the number of offices present and the credits or deposits made at the branch office level to assess finance, since we opine that a robust regional economy is one where last mile access to finance is better.

Finally, this book throws light on the trends and patterns of agglomeration and regional diversity through a descriptive analysis at the regional level for 2004–5 and 2011–12. We examine the strength of the diversification argument by analysing sectoral shares and the composition of the economy at the regional level. We also quantify regional outputs (RVA) for the first time in India and tease out the differences at the sub-state level to spot the highest and lowest performing regions in terms of output. The divergence hypothesis is also tested and the key aspects of economic structure and access that seem to explain the differences between regions over a period of time are identified. Since the regional story is so dynamic, we also check if the regions tend to form certain groupings or clusters, enabling a typology of such regions relevant for policy action.

This book is organized into the following chapters:

Chapter 2 provides the conceptual and analytical framework for the book by outlining the *spatial dimensions of structural change*, drawing from eminent economists and geographers. These concepts are closely linked with empirical studies which help trace the pattern of agglomeration and regional development. Sectoral diversification is found to be a significant factor in the Indian experience and various studies point towards the need for greater empirical evidence on agglomeration in the context of developing countries.

In **Chapter 3**, the definition and rationale of the 'region' as a unit of analysis is discussed along with the various components of *economic structure and access*, and a detailed methodology of calculating regional value added, sectoral shares, the diversity index, and so on, is explained. A deep discussion on data sources at the regional level as well as the analytical techniques that they lend themselves to, which we use in later chapters, are touched upon here.

Chapter 4 attempts to describe and characterize the broad *trends and patterns of regional development* in India along with preparing a typology of clusters of all regions. Moving from the pan-India story to state-level analysis, it maps out the trends in geographic distribution at a regional level.

Chapter 5 provides a detailed analysis of the economic structure of a region and whether *sectoral diversity* is driven more by the size or the level of skills of the labour force. A diversity index is constructed to represent the economic structure of a region. An enquiry is then made into whether size and diversity are truly associated and whether measures of diversity and size are interchangeable. The labour matching aspects of agglomeration are examined, followed by a deep dive into the role of skill levels in determining the sectoral mix. As the workforce grows and there is a greater concentration of firms, the average worker is able to find an employer that is a better match for its skill. This forms the labour matching aspect of agglomeration.

Chapter 6 focuses on *regional value added* and examines the differences between and determinants across the two time periods: 2004–5 and 2011–12. Estimates of regional contribution to the net domestic product, covering the output of both the organized and unorganized sectors, have been calculated for all NSS regions. A pooled cross-sectional regression is carried out to examine how some of the factors outlined in the agglomeration literature, including access to finance and skills, contribute to making regions engines of growth.

Chapter 7 tests the *divergence hypothesis* to see if the regions have moved closer to each other or farther apart over the two time periods, 2004–5 and 2011–12, and identifies the variables that actually account for these differences. A detailed discriminant analysis is carried out for a set of variables across both time periods, the results of which reveal certain distinguishing factors and interesting insights.

Chapter 8 undertakes a cluster analysis to identify possible *clusters that evolve across regions* over the study period. While it is not possible to discuss all clusters of all regions in detail, six regions of Maharashtra are illustrated as a case in point to explain the similarities and differences between clusters and regions.

Chapter 9 summarizes and concludes the book, emphasizing the *implications for theory, practice, and policy* that arise as a result of the analysis carried out in the various chapters of the book, which can influence regional development planning and its implementation. There are specific takeaways and proposed recommendations at institutional and administrative levels which can be of interest to policymakers, bureaucrats, academicians, industrialists, and, in fact, to any individual in India or another developing country, who seeks to understand, improve, and influence the trajectory of regional development.

2
Spatial Dimensions of Structural Change

What makes people, companies, or even governments choose one region over another? Highly varied sizes and activity arrangements arise at the regional and local levels, with some locations having a concentration of a few industries while others being highly diversified (Fujita and Thisse 1996). What influences the spatial distribution of economic activity? These are questions of interest in today's context of regional planning and rapid urbanization.

Understanding Agglomeration

For any discussion on spatial development, we need to first understand the concept of agglomeration. The phrase was first coined by Weber (1909) as 'an advantage or cheapening of production or marketing which results from the fact that production is carried on at some considerable extent at one place, while a deglomerative factor is cheapening of production which results from the decentralisation of production'.

Marshall (1890) is typically credited as the first scholar to explain the economies of agglomeration in terms of the interaction between labour markets, integration between suppliers and producers, and finally knowledge spillovers. In reality, this theme has been touched upon by Smith (1776) and von Thunen (1826) as well. There is a close relationship between the principles of specialization, division of labour, and technical progress and how they relate to societal conditions over time. This, in turn, has a spatial expression as well, which establishes the pattern of 'agglomeration'.

Regional Economic Diversity. Poornima Dore and Krishnan Narayanan, Oxford University Press. © Oxford University Press India 2022. DOI: 10.1093/oso/9780190130596.003.0002

For the purpose of this book, agglomeration can, at a broad level, be said to mean the concentration of production on one hand and the concentration of populations on the other. Interestingly, the period upto 1990 has been marked by very limited literature on the spatial aspects of economics. This brings us to an important question: Why has agglomeration not received adequate attention within economics during the interim period? Krugman (1991) hypothesizes that the 'constant returns–perfect competition paradigm' is unable to cope with the growth of large urban agglomerations. Traditional economics is built on the assumptions of perfect competition and diminishing returns. Agglomeration involves spatial competition which is, by nature, oligopolistic and involves interactive decision making (Fujita and Thisse 1996). Hence, economics has lacked a model that actively tackles both increasing returns and imperfect competition. Increasing returns cause activities to concentrate in locations with greater market access. This is a distinctive feature of the new economic geography literature that factors in both of these aspects which govern models of location choice. These models explain why the spatial concentration of economic activity occurs in the first place.

It is important to understand that agglomeration economies are actually external economies, in that their benefits are not under the control of any single actor or firm. It is only when multiple firms (of either the same or of different industries) act together that agglomeration economies can be realized (Meyer 1977). It has, in fact, been put forward as one of the key factors which determine the concentration of production and populations owing to two kinds of advantages:

1. Advantages to firms or households that arise by way of locating close to firms in similar industries.
2. Advantages to firms or households that arise by way of locating in or near densely populated areas

This is substantiated by the fact that across geographies, certain regions account for a large proportion of employment, output, and investment, and are also densely populated. How does economic theory explain this spatial concentration and distribution of economic activity? Why do we observe persistent economic disparities between geographic units and what are the underlying factors or assumptions that govern this phenomenon?

Structural Change

Let us situate these questions within the broader paradigm of structural change:

We observe changes in economic structure, as most developed countries have historically experienced a certain sequence of changes in their economic structure, starting with a predominance of agriculture, then shifting in favour of industry and, subsequently, services. The process of industrialization and diversifying away from agriculture has a significant impact on the structure and evolution of the regional economy. It is also closely linked with the formation of cities and growth centres, characterized by the movement of both economic activity and populations. This shift from agriculture to manufacturing and then services is explained by demand-side as well as supply-side theories.

On the *demand side*, it is argued that the shift from agriculture to industry takes place as a result of low-income elasticity of demand for agricultural products and high-income elasticity of demand for manufactured goods (Fisher 1939). For any given change in income, the demand for agricultural goods may rise to some extent, but the degree to which the demand for manufacturing goods will increase is expected to be higher. This is because the food needs of people are limited. The process of economic development is marked by the move towards higher levels of per capita income. Hence, as income levels increase, it is expected that the demand for manufacturing goods will also increase, leading to a shift in the production structure towards manufacturing. With further development in manufacturing, demand is generated for services such as trade, transportation, finance, communications, and others—the share of which expands over time.

Supply-side theorists contend that the reason for the shifting pattern is that agriculture is subject to diminishing returns. As additional units of input are invested in land, the subsequent level of production and income is not as high as before. As a result, it is unable to maintain increasing levels of production and income. Manufacturing, on the other hand, experiences increasing returns and, therefore, becomes the engine of growth (Kaldor 1967). The key role of manufacturing in growth is explained by Kaldor through his three famous laws, emphasizing strong causal relations between growth of manufacturing and growth of GDP, between growth of manufacturing output and growth of productivity in manufacturing, and between rate of growth of manufacturing and growth of productivity in other sectors. These three laws link the growth of an economy to the process of sectoral shifts. It may be noted that such theories look at the economy largely as a function of two sectors, namely agriculture and manufacturing, since they were conceived at a time when industrialization was at its peak and the services revolution was yet to take off. Most developed countries have since observed a rise in the share of services as the next stage of growth.

So far, we have looked at the demand and supply-side. Enter a third dimension—space. The process of structural change has a spatial dimension that needs to be factored in. Agglomeration economies accentuate such shifts, at both sectoral and regional levels through localization economies (Marshall 1890) and urbanization economies (Jacobs 1969). In case of the former, similar industries (or sectors) are seen to cluster together due to forward and backward linkages. Technological developments facilitate and economically necessitate the geographical concentration and scale-oriented production, leading to larger requirements of transport, storage, and communication. Cutting down on transport costs by concentrating production in fewer locations that are closer to the input and output markets helps to reap economies of scale as well as lower fixed costs (Krugman 1991). Urbanization economies come into play with the development of related market areas and cities with a mushrooming of business activities in both formal and informal sectors over time (Jacobs 1969), thus resulting in several different sectors locating close to each other, causing people to migrate, regions to specialize, and competitive advantages to emerge.

These structural shifts manifest themselves through changes in the regional pattern of output as well as employment, albeit in varying degrees. For instance, in the United Kingdom, with the declining share of agriculture in the national product from 32 per cent in 1801 to 6 per cent in 1901, its employment share also declined from 35 per cent to 9 per cent. Economists such as Lewis (1954) attribute this to the transfer of surplus labour from the traditional sector (agriculture) to the capitalist sector (manufacturing). In this situation, employment expands as capital accumulation takes place. Capital formation, in turn, increases the rate of savings and, thereby, growth. Lewis (1954) emphatically makes the point that economic development of an underdeveloped country not only involves but even requires a shift of surplus labour from agriculture to industry. The magnitude of such a shift and the consequent structure of the regional economy, of course, depend on the technology changes, the rate at which industrial development takes place, and, therefore, the labour absorbing capacity of the developing industry.

Kuznets (1955) argues that the changing structure of demand as a result of increasing per capita income levels induces changes in the structure of production. At the same time, changes in the technological conditions of production, the increasing scale and concentration of production, and institutional arrangements necessitated by changes in the location of production and population also have a significant influence on the pattern of these changes. In other words, while differences in the income elasticity of demand do play an important role, the differential growth of productivity in different locations is responsible for changes in the sectoral composition of output and employment.

Thus, we find that the concentration and distribution of production and population in terms of location—the concept of agglomeration—is of great importance in the discourse on regional development. It finds its expression not only in the location of firms but also in the composition of the economy and the choices of households on matters of residence and employment.

Literature on agglomeration can be drawn from location theory, new economic geography, and urban studies. We divide the underlying theories into two broad schools of thought: the perspective of the firm (concentration of production) and the perspective of the household (concentration of population). Each of these schools serves to explain the growth of a region either in terms of the concentration of production in certain locations due to choices exercised at the firm level, or in terms of the concentration of population in certain regions due to choices exercised at the individual or the household level. The firm and the household are also not mutually exclusive and can be seen to have inter-relationships within the region. It can also be said that the firm generates demand-side conditions for jobs, while the household provides supply-side inputs of labour (including skills), capital, and entrepreneurship. In the reverse flow, the household and other firms act as markets and consumers for the firm, while the firm and the household act as suppliers of goods and services.

The firm and the household are two important decision-makers in the context of regional economy. Hence, it is useful to look at both these perspectives while examining the literature which explains such choices. Our main purpose is to sift through this literature to identify factors which explain the trends and patterns of regional development. This book is built around the population perspective and we use household-level data to analyse the same. Regions that focus on, say, health services and computer manufacturing are expected to have a much greater per capita educational attainment than regions that focus on food processing, primary metals, furniture, and textiles. Different types of regions will demonstrate different equilibriums and efficient per capita levels of output, given by the private and social returns to local investment in the human capital of each region.

Spatial Distribution of Economic Activity

While the factors governing different contexts may be unique, it is possible upon examining these theories to arrive at some broad principles from the literature which explains the economic rationale for such geographic and spatial concentrations, considering both perspectives. The key causes of agglomeration economies, as discussed in the strands of literature outlined previously, can be organized in the following way (Nourse 1968; Lall and Chakravorty 2007):

1. Market access and transport cost
2. Specialization (localization economies)
3. Inter-industry linkages
4. Diversification (urbanization economies)

We will explain this classification and build a case for an in-depth study of the fourth point, that is, diversification, in order to understand the regional differences in development in the Indian context.

Market Access

Krugman (1991) hypothesizes that low-cost access to a market is a huge incentive for firms to choose a particular region, as this constitutes an increase in revenue with lesser cost investments. Hence, if transportation costs are low, it contributes to low-cost market access and hence spurs agglomeration. As more firms gravitate towards a location, either the wage rate goes up or labour inflow takes place. In any case, wage income in the region increases. If transportation costs are very high, a dispersion of activities is experienced. On the other hand, if the transportation cost is minimal, firms may be very randomly distributed. In fact, Fujita and Thisse (2002) have propounded that when the spatial mobility of labour is low, agglomeration takes place only at intermediate levels of transportation costs. In other words, the relationship between spatial concentration and transportation costs seems to follow an inverted U-shaped curve.

Greater market access leads to greater demand, which in turn pushes for scale economies and low-cost technologies. Cutting down on transportation costs by concentrating production in fewer locations that are closer to input and output markets helps to reap economies of scale as well as lower fixed costs. Here, distance, availability of transportation services, and quality of transportation networks all play a critical role in determining access. In addition to the lowering of costs, improved accessibility also reduces the geographic barriers to interaction, thus influencing other aspects such as labour supply, network effects, information sharing, opportunities to collaborate, and so on (Lall, Shalizi, and Deichmann 2004). Thus, access to markets is a significant driver of agglomeration.

Specialization (**Localization Economies**)

Localization economies arise when firms of a particular industry or sector collocate and, as a result, the region becomes specialized in that sector. These are externalities that 'enhance the productivity of all firms in that industry' and are also known as MAR externalities, having arisen from the theories of Marshall (1890), Arrow (1962), and Romer (1986). This includes benefits such as sharing of labour, information, and networks which are of relevance to the industry in question. To elaborate, labour would include the skilled labour which is trained for that particular industry. Co-location of such firms gives them access to a labour pool of workers who are trained in that trade. Knowledge sharing of trade-related innovations and the best practices is more likely when firms are located close to each other, given that face-to-face interaction is possible and inter-firm transfer of labour is highly likely. The same holds true for linkages within the industry which can be leveraged for the joint sourcing of raw materials and outsourcing of common non-core activities. At a policy level, such networks also help in the strategic coordination of firms to lobby with policymakers.

On the demand side, localization economies can occur on the output side when products are not perfect substitutes but have subtle quality differences. Some examples are furniture and jewellery stores, car dealerships, and so on. In such cases, competitors tend to locate close to each other. This leads to a reduction of information asymmetry to the consumers as they are able to save travel time and compare across products in one place. Thus, by attracting price- and quality-sensitive shoppers, firms are able to increase their overall revenues. These are also called 'thick market' externalities. It is possible that the benefits of such externalities can be offset by other costs such as those of increased transportation due to congestion or by higher wages and rents due to the excess demand for labour and land in the face of increased competition between firms (Rosenthal and Strange 2001).

The argument in favour of own industry concentration follows the logic that when a local industry is specialized, there are greater cost savings. A corollary to this is that externalities primarily occur within a particular industry. Another way to look at this is that if an industry faces MAR externalities, firms are likely to locate in a few places where the industry is already concentrated.

Inter-industry Linkages

When own industry concentration is coupled with the production of intermediate goods, it leads to an additional set of economies. High concentration of firms creates a demand for large quantities of intermediates, and a high concentration of intermediates, in turn, attracts more firms to produce them (Myrdal 1957). This circular causation helps to bring down sourcing costs for the buyer as well as transportation costs for the supplier. Inventory costs can also be brought down through just-in-time production. In addition, suppliers get access to a ready market, hence demand generation is not a constraint.

In addition, these linkages create important information transfer mechanisms. Interaction between firms creates opportunities to exchange ideas on improving product quality, reducing cycle time, tapping fresh markets, and introducing product modifications. It is also argued that decisions of firm location based on buyer–supplier linkages can reap agglomeration economies even without high factor mobility. This is because productivity improvements are possible directly through a reduction in transaction costs via forward and backward linkages (Venables 1996). Thus, the presence of local supplier linkages serves to increase the efficiency of firms as well as enhance the products of buyer industries, thus inducing agglomeration. This is particularly true in case of industries which depend heavily on high-quality intermediates, such as automobiles or pharmaceuticals. In this manner, inter-industry linkages serve also to reinforce the localization process.

Diversification (Urbanization Economies)

So far, we have covered economies arising from access to specific markets or being located close to similar or related industries. There are a set of economies that are said to arise from the sheer size and sectoral diversity of a region. The size of the region is indicative of the available market, labour pool, and so on. The greater the population density, the greater the demand for various goods and services, which, in turn, results in a mushrooming of diverse business activities. This leads to the general development of infrastructure, along with transportation and superior communication facilities. It also results in the setting up of schools, hospitals, and other public services, in addition to specialized financial and professional services. Access to all of these creates a huge impetus for firms belonging to different industries to collocate. Studies reveal that an increase in city size has substantial productivity benefits (Sveikauskas 1975; Tabuchi 1986; Ciccone and Hall 1996). Size is closely related to diversity, as larger regions may support a wider range of activities. Smaller regions may specialize in a few manufacturing or administrative activities, while larger ones tend to support an array of productive activities that require buyers and sellers to be co-located. We will test this assumption in our study and see whether it holds well in the case of India. The importance of urbanization economies arising from diversity has been expounded in the work of Chinitz (1961) and Jacobs (1969). The existence of diverse industries leads to a proliferation of new ideas and technologies, as diverse knowledge sources come together and interact with each other. This boosts innovation and can lead to the development and testing of new technologies. Such benefits of diversity accrue to all firms in the agglomeration irrespective of the industry.

The key element here is the heterogeneity of activities made possible in larger regions, which increases the range of products for the consumers as well as producers via two routes: the first is through access to a wider array of goods and services for the firm and the consumer, and the second is through technological spillovers which expand the production possibility frontier and raise the level of output (Abdel-Rahman 1988)

In summary, all the factors mentioned so far that cause agglomeration are closely interlinked and may occur individually or in combination. It is difficult to analyse the relative importance of these factors because separating out the effects of each is an onerous task (Beaudry and Schiffauerova 2009). The Marshallian view is that localization economies are of prime importance, while the Jacobsian school of thought opines that urbanization economies and industrial diversity take primacy. Since this debate is the primary focus of our study, the empirical literature review, which follows, analyses the relative importance of localization and urbanization economies.

Empirical Experiences

We now take a look at the findings of empirical studies undertaken to assess the impact of the factors discussed in the previous section. In keeping with the theoretical approach, we can classify the empirical studies through two perspectives—impacts on the firm and impacts on the region:

1. Firm-level impacts (by way of increased productivity, reduced cost, higher profitability, and, on a related note, locational choice)
2. Region-level impacts (primarily by way of increase in population or output, formation of new cities and decay of older ones, increase in pollution or congestion costs)

Both of these effects are very important from a policy perspective. In this section, we will look at certain empirical studies which have analysed the extent to which these linkages actually hold and share the results obtained. As reflected in our review, firm-level impacts have received greater emphasis historically as compared to the broader regional impacts, which is something this book seeks to address. Most of the firm-level impacts at an aggregate level do have a regional impact, and hence the two are closely related.

Productivity Enhancement

There are several empirical papers that study the impact of agglomeration economies on productivity. In a study of the Korean industry, Henderson et al. (2001) estimate scale economies using city-level industry data for 1983–9 and 1991–3, and assess the impact of localization as well as urbanization economies. They find that a doubling of local employment leads to productivity increases of 6 to 8 per cent. In other words, localization economies are found to be significant, while urbanization economies are not, except in the case of high technology industries. Interestingly, the impact of localization economies was lowest in traditional manufacturing and highest in heavy industry and transportation. They also find that agglomeration is driven towards locations with high market access, that is, locations where low transport costs permit cheap supply to markets through quality transport networks.

In another study of the Indian industry, Lall and Mengistae (2005) use survey data for the year 2003 from the World Bank's Investment Climate Survey of India. This survey covers manufacturing units sampled from the top 3 to 4 cities from 12 of India's 15 largest states. The paper looks at the impact of various factors on productivity and hence location choice, including factors such as domestic and foreign market access as well as localization economies. They find that own industry concentration has a significant effect on productivity differences between locations, and this is observed to be the highest in the case of technology-intensive sectors. They also argue that in locations that suffer from natural disadvantages, the government can compensate for such factors by creating a better business environment to correct the divergence caused by agglomeration economies.

Cost Reduction

Another approach is to ascertain the impact of agglomeration economies on cost. Do these economies help to reduce cost? If so, to what extent and, therefore, how do they impact the choice of location and regional growth? While studying firm-level data from Brazil, Lall et al. (2004) analyse the impact of factors such as localization, inter-industry linkages, and urbanization on the total cost of a firm. This cross-sectional study estimates a cost function that includes a mix of micro firm-level variables along with measures of economic policy, infrastructure, and the region's economic geography by using data for the year 2001 from the Pesquisa Industrial Anual (PIA), which is collected and compiled by the Brazilian Institute of Geography and Statistics (IBGE).

They find that there is considerable heterogeneity in the results, depending on industry and firm size. For instance, localization and urbanization economies in industries such as transportation and printing are seen to have significant cost-reducing effects. On the other hand, standardized industries, such as garments and textiles and non-durables, experience high congestion costs which push up wages and rents, thus outweighing the benefits of agglomeration and resulting in increased cost. At the same time, these industries show a high degree of market access. This implies that such industries may tend to concentrate in smaller or specialized areas but have access to large markets.

A similar estimation strategy has been employed in Lall and Chakravorty (2007) for estimating the impact of agglomeration economies using firm-level data for Indian industry using plant-level data for 1998–9 by the Annual Survey of Industries (ASI). The principal finding of this study is that industrial diversity (in other words, urbanization economies) provides significant cost savings for individual firms and is the only economic geography variable to do so consistently. The estimated cost elasticity is 46 per cent for chemicals and as high as 83 per cent for electrical/electronics, suggesting high-cost benefits to diversification. This raises questions on policy initiatives that focus on the development of specialized clusters because localization economies seem to have few cost benefits and, in some cases, are seen to have positive coefficients, which implies an increase in costs. The findings clearly point towards a greater policy focus on the encouragement of mixed-industry clusters rather than single-industry clusters. We draw on some of these findings to build on the theme of sectoral diversity, which represents urbanization economies.

Increase in Profitability

A third approach is to consider the impact of agglomeration economies on profitability. In a study of the Indonesian manufacturing sector, Deichmann et al. (2005) conduct a cross-sectional study using 2001 establishment data from the Indonesian Survey of Industry. They explore how firm-level profits are influenced by variables representing localization economies, urbanization economies, inter-industry linkages, market access, as well as observed geographical indicators and unobserved local characteristics. They find that localization economies are significant in certain industries such as high technology and natural resource-based industries, as opposed to industries such as garments and textiles.

This is possibly because certain industries are heavily dependent on similar firms for the sharing of technical knowhow, the latest technology, as well as a joint sourcing of raw materials, which helps to reap higher profits. They also find that access to suppliers plays a significant role in the choice of location, especially in sectors such as food and beverages, chemicals, and rubber. Their simulations on the effectiveness of public intervention suggest that increases in infrastructure endowments in lagging regions may not be able to promote a balanced regional development and may attract firms from sectors which already have a high degree of concentration. Public policy may not be able to counter the effect of agglomeration economies. This makes it all the more critical to understand the underlying trends and patterns related to agglomeration while designing public policy measures.

Regional Diversity

A study undertaken in Brazil sets up a model of a city, estimating the demand and supply-side to arrive at an equation on city sizes and their growth. It constructs a data set for 1970 to 2000 for 123 agglomerations by combining various urban municipios in Brazil (da Mata et al. 2007). City size in this case is represented by the total population of the city. The study finds that reductions in intercity transport costs have a fairly strong effect on the growth rates of the city population: a 10 per cent decrease in the intercity transport cost of a unit increases the growth of city population by 1.4 per cent over a decade. This finding ties in with Beeson et al. (2001) who analysed census data for the United States of America (USA) from 1840 to 1990 and found that access to transportation networks was an important long-run source of growth.

Henderson et al. (2001) in their study on Korea find that inter-industry linkages are closely associated with growth. The coefficients of the number of formal-sector firms to formal-sector workers are significant: Having a higher number of firms relative to workers stimulates competition and encourages interaction and knowledge sharing between firms. The positive relationship between this and city growth conveys that strong inter-industry linkages can act as a driver for city growth, as better linkages attract more firms and workers and result in an increase in the city size. In another paper on China, Au and Henderson (2006) estimate the net urban agglomeration economies and plot value added per worker against city employment in an inverted U graph. In other words, they find that agglomeration benefits increase with city size up to a point and then drop. Higher peaks are observed for service-oriented cities and lower ones for manufacturing.

A large portion of studies in India explaining regional variations in development have been carried out at the state level. Over the years, certain studies (Awasthi 1991; Dehejia and Dehejia 1993) have documented regional diversity, outlining the run up to and the relevance of reforms in India's economic history. From Independence till the early 1960s, industrialization was concentrated in three presidencies—with 56 per cent of all licenses being issued to firms in Maharashtra, West Bengal, and Tamil Nadu. The period that followed up to the 1980s witnessed industrial decentralization and a declining regional inequality. The period from the mid-1980s onwards has been characterized by an increasing regional inequality, with a significant decline in the eastern states accompanied by a rise in the income shares of the western states. What has emerged over the years appears to be a default case scenario. Absence of the spatial dimension in planning in India has been criticized by several scholars (Awasthi 1991). The Indian approach is said to have been underlined by a belief in the 'redemptive mystique' of large industry, an 'emulative desire' to follow the demographics of other developed countries, and 'a village fetish' (Johnson 1970). Basu and Maertens (2007) examine the low growth pattern of the agricultural sector and highlight that the rising inequality since the 1990s—between states and also between rural and urban areas—is a concern.

There are a few studies in India that capture the spatial dimension of the concentration of certain aspects at a more granular sub-state level in the post-reform period. Chandrasekhar and Sharma (2014) analyse the spatial concentration of jobs in 2011–12 and construct a location quotient to identify what kind of economic activities are concentrated in which regions, as well as a Thiel index to assess the extent of inequality in the distribution of jobs. There are some noteworthy studies that have critically examined aspects such as trends in urbanization, differences between rural and urban workforce participation rates, and whether larger cities contribute to greater workforce participation at a macro level (Kundu 1997, 2011; Thomas 2013). Another study covers the spatial concentration of urbanization by analysing district-level census data of 2001 (Denis et al. 2012) and finds that urban growth is observed to a greater measure in the periphery and smaller cities, and paints a picture of urbanization that is 'dispersed and diverse to an important degree'. Sridhar (2017) examines economic change and specialization in India's cities using location quotients and shift share for 1997–2001 and finds similar evidence of diversification at the city level.

Mitra (2011) also finds that smaller cities seem to be the growth drivers. His work speaks of the nexus between industrialization and urbanization but finds that its poverty reducing effects are fairly limited, thereby warranting active policy intervention. He observes that the dearth of meaningful census data on sectoral shares limits the ability to make statements relevant to the economic structure. Thereafter, he goes on to use the primary survey data of four cities to build his point and constructs a well-being index. Mukim and Nunnenkamp (2012) draw on the data on FDI approvals for 1991–2005 and find a strong concentration of FDIs between states and also within states in specific districts. The economic geography variables include a Herfindahl index to capture economic diversity, market access, and population. They employ a discrete choice model at the district level to assess the determinants of foreign investors' location choices using cross-sectional data from different sources for 2001.

Output levels and productivity have been studied extensively in both India (Goldar 1986; Kathuria et al. 2010) and abroad (Moomaw 1981; Tabuchi 1986). The problem of regional definition becomes crucial whenever attempts are made to obtain the estimates of regional income and production. Such estimates are often essential because policy objectives are commonly set in terms of achieving a stipulated per capita income or production level for a region (Meyer 1963). Studies pertaining to certain other developing countries such as Brazil, Indonesia, and so on, provide some level of regional granularity by using metropolitan-level data (da Mata et al. 2007) or post office codes (Deichmann et al. 2005). Noted Indian studies have primarily been conducted at the state level (Bhat and Siddharthan 2012; Drèze and Sen 2013; Panagariya et.al. 2014). As discussed, the few pertinent studies in India at the district level are based on the Annual Survey of Industries (ASI), which collects plant-level data and is, therefore, focused more on the organized manufacturing sector (Veeramani and Goldar 2005; Mukim and Nunnenkamp 2012). A few exceptions (Kathuria et al. 2010) combine the data sets of ASI with NSSO to give a regional picture, but their focus is more on total factor productivity.

Globally, academicians have underscored the urgent need for deep research on regional variations since it has become increasingly clear that there may be diverse pathways to development in different regions, pathways which need to be analysed and better understood (Dunford et al. 2016). With the notable exceptions mentioned earlier in this section, there exist limited studies which specifically examine the empirical evidence on agglomeration in the Indian context and even lesser on urbanization economies denoting regional diversity and the nature of economic activities within sub-sectors at the NSS-region level. The absence of output data at the regional level makes this a difficult task.

Salient Points Thus Far

We find that while agglomeration economies can play a role in determining outcomes at both the firm level and the household level, it is an under-researched area, particularly in the Indian regional context. Although this relationship seems otherwise obvious and intuitive, it is only since the 1990s that spatial and geographic dimensions of economics have started being actively researched globally, owing to the complications of increasing returns and imperfect competition.

We find that the impact of such factors vary substantially by industry and, to some extent, by country. Localization economies are found to be the key driver in Korea (Henderson et al. 2001), whereas in India, urbanization economies appear to be more significant (Lall and Mengistae 2005). Interestingly, for high technology sectors in particular, the results appear to be reversed. In Korea, urbanization economies are found to be significant only in high technology sectors, while in India, mainly localization economies are found to be significant for high technology sectors. The Korean study seems to tie in more with the theory, given that technology-oriented sectors are more likely to benefit from technology spillovers as a result of diversity and hence have significant urbanization economies.

In Indonesia (Deichmann et al. 2005), agglomeration seems to be driven by localization in technology-oriented sectors. This cross-sectional study yields results similar to the Indian case (Lall and Mengistae 2005) and is explained by the logic that high-tech firms benefit from spillovers from other firms within the same industry rather than from diverse industry firms. Further analysis is required to understand why the results from Korea differ from those of India and Indonesia. In addition to the nature of the data, it could also be due to the variations in definition or the measurement of indicators. Also, India is a much larger country with pronounced regional variations, as our study will highlight. A direct comparison with countries such as Korea and Indonesia may, therefore, not be appropriate.

Each of these factors can be measured using a variety of indicators such as network distance, own industrial employment, input–output coefficients, Ellison-Glaeser index, and Hirschman Herfindahl index to name a few. Choice of variable can have a significant impact on the results, hence it is important to select the indicator with care. For instance, while many studies have used own industry employment as a measure, this may not reflect the industry concentration very well. The variable may take a high value either due to a large number of people being employed by a single firm or due to a moderate number of people being employed by several firms. To that extent, such studies may not capture the true interaction effects which are responsible for agglomeration economies. On a related note, while urban population can be used to represent city size, which can then be closely related to diversity, it does not essentially represent diversity itself.

The review of the domain reveals that there are serious gaps in the research on Indian conditions pertaining to some of the following issues:

1. There is a clear need for studies at the sub-state level that capture the impact of agglomeration on regional economy, in the context of a developing country such as India. Given the immense variety within regions, there is an absolute need to understand the patterns and see if regional groupings occur. Do the regions appear to gradually move closer to each other or are there indications of cumulative causation at work?
2. Since most other studies are from the firm perspective and have a manufacturing bias, variables representing labour are typically in terms of employment, wages, or education levels, while capital-related variables are either in terms of fixed capital or FDI approvals. Although these variables are useful to regional variances, there is scope to build on more direct measures of access to labour and finance from a holistic regional economy perspective.
3. There is a need to understand the nature of work undertaken by the population and the availability of skilled labour in order to enrich the existing literature on agglomeration which emphasizes the role of labour matching.

4. The role of urbanization and million-plus cities in the categorization of regions is critical as various theories have references to cities and the role of urbanization in regional growth. This is an important aspect of understanding the typology of the region and the division of labour in the context of a rapidly urbanizing economy.
5. Sectoral diversification (arising out of urbanization economies) has been found to be a significant factor in the Indian experience. The extent of this specific phenomenon has not been empirically analysed from the perspective of regional development in terms of the variations across regions.
6. The regional picture is incomplete, in the absence of official estimates on regional output, which limits the ability to draw conclusions about regional growth and productivity. While there are comprehensive studies on manufacturing and service sector growth for the formal sector, data issues limit the scope of research on the informal sector, which accounts for 90 per cent of employment in India.

As a response, this book proposes a framework to gauge the factors might account for differences across regions in India in the past decade, particularly in the context of economic structure and levels of access.

Analytical Framework

It is useful to analyse data from the perspective of two theoretical debates that have heavily influenced our understanding of the regional economy, namely:

1. Diversification and Specialization (Marshall vs Jacobs)
2. Divergence and Convergence (Myrdal vs Kuznets)

We develop a framework (Figure 2.1) to study the causal factors determining agglomeration, adapting from Nourse (1968) and Pearce and Davis (2000) to put these factors under two broad heads: economic structure and access to finance, skills, and markets.

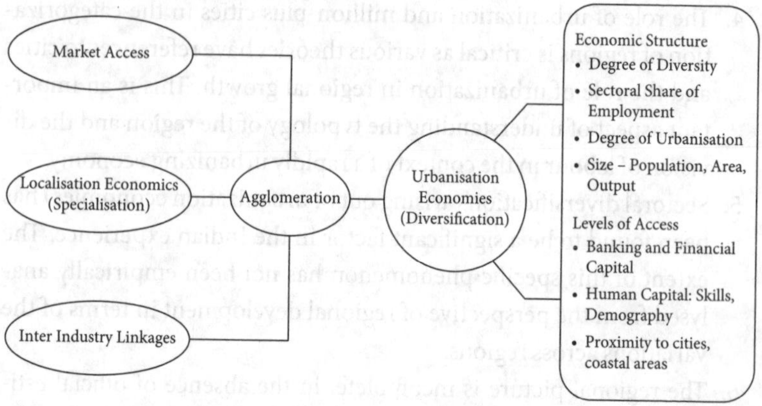

Figure 2.1 Analytical Framework
Source: Authors' own adaptation of 'Pearce and Davis (2000)'

Let us take the initial endowments, both in terms of resources and institutions, as given. If that is so, the economic rationale of the concentration of production and population hinges on the four broad aspects of market access, localization economies (specialization), inter-industry linkages (forward and backward), and urbanization economies (diversification). The trends and patterns can be defined by two critical aspects:

1. The economic structure as defined by the size and composition of the regional economy. This determines which industries or sectors flourish in the region by way of sectoral shares, what is the size of the market of goods and services, and what is the size of the labour pool available to cater to the growing demands of production as given by area, population, and population density. It also determines the extent to which multiple sectors collocate and show a willingness to learn from each other, thereby pushing out the production possibility frontier for the region.
2. The levels of access; with respect to factors that impact the dynamism of the regional economy, namely access to finance, human resource, and markets. The network of bank branches, the number of bank accounts, and the level of deposits and credits at the branch level help to give a well-rounded picture of the degree of access to finance at the household level. Proximity to urban centres and

coastal areas determines both the inflow and outflow of goods and services and is also indicative of transportation costs. The share of regular employment and high-end skills defines the quality of jobs and the human resource available to realize the growth aspirations of the region.

These factors together contribute to the pattern of agglomeration. Let us now proceed to examine some of these issues in the subsequent chapters. This framework of analysis can be utilized to build a model which allows one to develop empirical evidence in the Indian context with a primary focus on agglomeration economies and their role in the context of diversification.

3
Economic Structure and Access

What to Measure?

The objective of this book is to study the patterns of agglomeration and regional economic diversity in India with data. Some of this involves econometric methods and is intended to: (1) analyse the trends and patterns of agglomeration and regional diversity through a descriptive analysis at a regional level, (2) identify the key factors that explain the differences between regions over a period of time, (3) examine the determinants of such factors with specific reference to sectoral diversity and regional value added, and (4) identify possible clusters across regions. Chapter 2 has provided the substantive theoretical and empirical perspectives along with the spatial framework for analysis. The present chapter purports to elaborate three dimensions of the empirical design that follows, namely (i) the database and the corresponding adjustments, (ii) the selection, definition, and construction of variables discussed in the book, and (iii) the analytical techniques adopted in various chapters. The subsequent sections of this chapter correspondingly deal with the said three aspects.

'Region' as the Unit of Analysis

The first step is to identify the unit of analysis and define what we mean by 'region' for the purpose of this book. Traditionally, three different approaches have been used in defining regions (Meyer 1963). The first stresses on *homogeneity* with respect to a combination of physical, economic, social, or other characteristics such that locations depicting similarities along such specified lines come together to form a region. The second emphasizes the so called *nodality* or *polarization*, usually around some central urban place, and the summation of all settlements around

Regional Economic Diversity. Poornima Dore and Krishnan Narayanan, Oxford University Press. © Oxford University Press India 2022. DOI: 10.1093/oso/9780190130596.003.0003

this place forms a region. The third approach is *programming* or *policy-oriented*, concerned mainly with administrative coherence or identity between the area being studied and the available political institutions for taking policy decisions. In reality, the three traditional definitions of regional type are not mutually exclusive. In fact, most regional classification schemes in practice appear to be variations of the homogeneity criterion, which is the one we choose to follow.

We apply the homogeneity criteria as we take a deeper look at the Indian regional economy and choose the classification adopted by the National Sample Survey Office (NSSO). India is administratively divided into 29 states and 8 union territories, which are classified into 736 districts pan India. The NSSO, for the purpose of its surveys across the country, divides each state into regions based on homogeneity related to agro-climatic conditions, demography, geographical contiguity, and so on. These regions have been identified at the sub-state level in consultation with different central ministries, the Planning Commission, the Registrar General, and State Statistical Bureaus by grouping contiguous districts having similar geographical features, rural population densities, and crop pattern. In other words, each state is divided into National Sample Survey (NSS) regions, each of which is a set of homogenous districts within the state. Union territories and smaller states are denoted by one NSS region each. This is the classification that we choose to adopt, and hence throughout this book we refer to these regions as NSS regions. For instance, Goa is a single NSS region, Tamil Nadu comprises four and Uttar Pradesh is divided into six NSS regions. This allows us to study regional economy from an interesting intermediate lens—one step below the state and one step above the district.

The NSSO conducts quinquennial surveys on employment and unemployment to assess the volume and structure of both. The genesis of the current format of quinquennial surveys dates back to the 27th round in 1972–3, as a result of the M. L. Dantwala committee report. We use the NSSO Employment Unemployment Survey data for the 61st round (2004–5) and the 68th round (2011–12) to analyse agglomeration patterns in India. A multi-stage stratified sampling design has been adopted by the NSSO for the 61st and the 68th round surveys that form the basis of our data set, and hence make it representative of the regions under consideration. The rural and urban areas of the country are taken as adopted in the latest population census, for which the required information is available with the Survey Design and Research Division of the NSSO. By assigning weights to extrapolate our results at the NSS sample level, we also get population estimates for each region. More details about the NSS sampling methodology are available in the reports for each year published by the Government of India (2006a; 2013a). The NSSO conducts these surveys periodically and the 68th round is the latest round (using a comparable pattern) of data available. This has in more recent years taken the form of the Periodic Labour Force Survey (PLFS) , which is a useful approach but not directly comparable to the data sets we analyse. The selected years are also equidistant from 2007–8, which was the year of the global meltdown. Given the time periods we have considered, it is expected that the impact of any short-term factors related to the meltdown which might affect the regional economy would be reduced, if not eliminated.

The country is divided into 78 NSS regions in the 61st round and 88 NSS regions in the 68th round. This is due to addition of fresh regions in the 68th round by either culling out districts from existing regions (such as West Bengal) or including regions which were left out in the earlier sample (Ladakh). For the purpose of our study, we consider 75 NSS regions in period 1 and 85 NSS regions in period 2, giving us 160 observations over the two time periods under study.[1] The full list of regions provided in Appendix 1 and 2, is drawn from the Appendices to the NSS reports of both time periods, published by the Government of India (2006b; 2013b).

Factors Influencing Economic Structure and Access

There are several factors which are significant to the robustness of the regional economy. In the analytical framework described in Chapter 2, we identify economic structure and levels of access as important parameters. Let us now delve into greater detail with respect to some critical ones. Several variables have involved specific construction or compilation at the

[1] Three regions, namely Lakshadweep, Daman and Diu, and Dadra and Nagar Haveli have not been considered by us for this study due to lack of data on several indicators during the compilation of data sets.

NSS region level, since all data is not readily available at this level of granularity from the existing data sets. We will also outline the logic and methodology of construction of each variable that represents these factors.

Workforce Participation

The size of the labour pool is one of the first and most direct indicators of economic activity. For each individual, the NSS survey collects information on place of residence, which we use to study the spatial distribution of various parameters. We use the usual principle status (UPS) approach, where the broad activity status of a person—namely employed, unemployed, and 'not in labour force'—is decided by major time investment over a reference period of one year. Thus, a person is classified as belonging to labour force, if she/he had been either working or looking for work during the longer part of the 365 days preceding the surveys (Krishnamurty and Raveendran, 2008). We measure this as a proportion of the total population in the 15–60 age group to calculate the workforce participation rate (WPR).

Regular Employment

Employed persons are further bifurcated into three broad activity groups according to their status of employment. These broad groups are: (i) self-employed, (ii) regular wage/salaried employees, and (iii) casual labour. For the purpose of our analysis, we include a variable REGEMP which captures the share of regular wage employment as a proportion of total employment. This helps us understand the nature of the labour market and also the size of the informal sector.

Sectoral Shares

For the persons who are part of the workforce, one would like to understand which sectors they are employed in. This gives us the sectoral mix of economic activity in the region and how it is distributed across agriculture, manufacturing, services, and so on. Every economic subsector is assigned a code as per the national industrial classification (NIC), which seeks to provide a basis for the standardized collection, analysis, and dissemination of industry (economic activity) wise economic data for India.

We tabulate the details for those in the workforce by region and by industry using the NIC codes at 2-digit level (Table 3.1). This comes to a total of 14 sectors. The NIC codes for 2004–5 and 2011–12 are different since the 61st round follows the NIC 1998 classification and the 68th

Table 3.1 Sectoral Split as per NIC

Sector Code	Broad Category	NIC 2-digit	Sector Name
AGRI	Agriculture	A	Agriculture, Hunting, and Forestry
		B	Fishing
MFG	Manufacturing	C	Mining and Quarrying
		D	Manufacturing
		E	Electricity, Gas, and Water Supply
CON	Construction	F	Construction
SVS	Services	G	Wholesale and Retail Trade; Repair of Motor Vehicles, Motorcycles and Personal and Household Goods
		H	Hotels and Restaurants
		I	Transport, Storage, and Communications
		J	Financial intermediation
		K	Real Estate, Renting, and Business Activities
		L	Public Administration and Defence, Compulsory Social Security
		M	Education
		N	Health and Social Work
		O	Other Community, Social, and Personal Service Activities
		P	Private Households with Employed Persons
		Q	Extra-Territorial Organizations and Bodies

Source: National Industrial Classification (NIC) (2008).

round follows the NIC framework of 2008. We have carried out a sector-by-sector comparison and adjusted the values so that data of both periods are comparable and in sync with NIC 2008.

We then calculate the percentage employment shares for each industry by state. For certain segments of our empirical analysis, we go one step further and calculate sector shares at the NSS region level, such that E is the share of employment in sector j in region r.

$$Ejr = \frac{\textit{Persons employed in Sector } j}{\textit{Total Persons employed in the Region or state } r} * 100 \qquad (1)$$

These shares across the 14 sectors are used in the calculation of the diversity index, elaborated in the next section. We further compile the sector-related data into four core sectors as per Table 3.2. Table 3.2 gives the composition of the four core sectors based on the NIC codes. The percentage share in each core sector is represented by the variables AGRI,

Table 3.2 Mapping Occupational Classifications to Skill Levels

Code	Type	Skill Level	Degree	Education
0–2	Professionals	IV	Post-graduation	>15 years formal education
3	Associate technicians	III	First university degree	13–15 years formal education
4	Clerks	II	Secondary education	11–13 years formal education
5	Service	II	Secondary education	11–13 years formal education
6	Skilled agricultural workers	II	Secondary education	11–13 years formal education
7	Crafts and other trade-based work	II	Secondary education	11–13 years formal education
8	Plant operators and assemblers	II	Secondary education	11–13 years formal education
9	Elementary occupations	I	Primary education	Up to 10 years and/or informal skills

Source: National Occupational Classification Report (2004).

MFG, CON, and SVS in the analytical chapters 4, 6, and 7. In Chapter 6, CON and SVS are further combined to form the tertiary sector represented by TERT.

Diversity Index

How diverse is the regional economy? Is it dependent on one or two sectors, or is it more widely distributed? As discussed in Chapter 2, the debate between specialization and diversification is of great significance and the extent of sectoral diversity needs to be understood better. Sectoral diversity is said to provide a summary measure of urbanization economies, given that such benefits accrue across industries and to all firms in the agglomeration (Jacobs 1969). Firms tend to cluster in regions which are more diverse, with the heterogeneity of economic activity resulting in greater variety of output. To capture diversity, a standard measure, similar to the Hirschman Herfindahl index, is used to represent the degree of concentration of employment within a region (Henderson et al. 2001).

We construct a diversity index as per Lall and Chakravorty (2005) by converting the percentage employment shares by industry for the 14 sectors calculated in the previous section into ratios. These are then squared, and the summation of these squares forms the Hirschman Herfindahl index "Hr," which gives an index of concentration.

The diversity index is given by: $DV_r = 1 - H_r$ (2)

$$\text{Where, } H_r = \sum_j \left[\frac{E_{jr}}{E_r} \right]^2$$

Such that H_r is the sum of the squares of employment shares of all industries j in region r.

DV takes values in the range of 0 to 1. A score nearing 1 indicates that multiple sectors drive the economy, while a score closer to 0 indicates that the regional economy is driven only by one or two key industries. In other words, a higher value of DV represents greater sectoral diversity in the concerned region.

Access to High-End Skills

Does a region have access to professionally skilled workers? This goes a long way in determining the location choices of industry, facilitating long-range planning and being indicative of whether the region is able to attract good quality talent. This is a very important factor, especially if one looks at development from the capabilities perspective. Most analyses in the Indian context have looked at proxy measures to represent skill levels, which has given mixed results. In a study by Maiti and Mitra (2010), the enrolment ratio turned out to be insignificant, possibly because the enrolment ratio is not a good proxy for skill formation. Other studies use the percentage of persons having received secondary and higher education (Bhat and Siddharthan 2012) to represent skill levels. We adopt a more direct approach to capture skill intensity, with more recently available data in the Indian context. We measure high-end skills as the percentage of the workforce engaged in occupations that require level IV skills (see Table 3.2).

For each worker surveyed by the NSS, information on the type of occupation in which individuals are engaged is collected using the 3-digit classification of the national classification of occupation (NCO). In this classification system the grouping of occupations is based on the fundamental criteria of 'the type of work performed'.

In the 61st round of the NSS, occupations have been classified as per the NCO of 1968 so that all workers engaged with the same type of work are grouped together irrespective of the industrial classification of establishments where they are engaged. In 2004, the NCO was revised to include various subsectors and separate elementary jobs as a complete category. These occupational classifications were further linked to skill levels for the first time in 2004.

This incorporates the concept of skill level with respect to the performance of various jobs in addition to the concept of the type of work performed, which was the basis of the 1968 classification of NCO. This classification now lends itself to very interesting analysis possibilities. The 68th round of the NSS applies this revised NCO 2004. We adjust the values of the 61st round to make it compatible with NCO 2004. We then analyse the resultant data to look at the differences between states and also within industry subsectors in order to assess the skill levels of the workforce and the nature of the occupations they are engaged in.

Code 1 covers all senior and corporate managers across all industries as well as legislators. Codes 2 and 3 cover engineering, science, health, medicine, teaching, finance, tax, and other professionals. Code 4 covers office clerks, cashiers, material recording clerks, and library clerks. Code 5 includes housekeeping and restaurant services, security, domestic work, salespersons, and models. Code 6 covers skilled agricultural and fisheries workers. Code 7 comprises the occupations that are building and material relate, precision and metal related, food processing and textile related, and those related to printing and crafts. Code 8 covers operators in power, gas, mines, metals, chemical processing, assembly lines and textile, as well as drivers and ship deck crews. Code 9 covers street vendors, shoe cleaners, agricultural and construction labourers, transport labourers, garbage collectors, and so on.

It now becomes possible to connect the occupational division codes with the skill level and educational qualifications to assess the regional distribution of different types of jobs and skill levels. Table 3.3 maps the occupational classification with the corresponding skill levels. We tabulate the proportion of persons having NCO codes 0–2 as SKILLIV.

$$SKILLIV_r = \frac{\textit{Persons engaged in occupational categories } 0,1, \textit{and } 2}{\textit{Total persons employed in the region or state}} * 100 \quad (3)$$

This is a measure of the proportion of the workforce with high-end skills.

Regional Value Added

An assessment of the size of the economy involves a measurement of the gross domestic product (GDP) or value added (VA). Official estimates of VA are only available at the state level. Hence, how does one work towards providing further granularity at the regional level? This is a unique contribution of this study, in that this is the first time an attempt has been made to construct VA at the NSS region level and use it for regional analysis in India.

Table 3.3 Definition of Variables

Variables	Variable Name	Measurement	Data Source
Regional value added	RVA	Constructed by applying relevant regional weights to state level output	Handbook of Statistics on Indian economy 2004–5 and 2011–12, RBI; 61st and 68th round of the NSSO surveys
Regional value added per capita	RVAPC	Regional value added/total population of the region	
Population	POPN	Total Population of the region	Census of India 2001 and 2011
Geographical area	AREA	Total Area of the Region in km square (summation of district level values)	Census of India 2001 and 2011
Population density	POPDEN	Population of the Region/ Total Area of the Region	Census of India 2001 and 2011
Disposable income per capita	MPCE	Monthly per capita Expenditure	61st and 68th round of the NSSO surveys
Share of agriculture	AGRI	Proportion of total workers engaged in Agriculture	Classification based on NIC codes of industrial classification as followed by the 61st and 68th Round NSSO surveys. The 14 categories at 2 digit level are further collapsed into the four core sectors.
Share of manufacturing	MFG	Proportion of total workers engaged in Manufacturing	
Share of construction	CON	Proportion of total workers engaged in Construction	
Share of Services	SVS	Proportion of total workers engaged in Service sector	
Share of Tertiary Sector	TERT	Proportion of total workers engaged in Construction and Service sector combined	
Diversity index	DV	$DV_r = 1 - H_r$ denoting the sectoral mix on a scale of 0 to 1	Constructed based on sectoral shares for 14 categories based on NIC codes from the 61st and 68th Round NSSO Surveys
Bank branch offices	OFF	No. of bank branch offices	Basic Statistical Returns of Scheduled Commercial Banks in India, 2005 and 2010, RBI.
Bank accounts	ACC	No of bank accounts in '000	
Credit per branch	CRE	Volume of credit outstanding in Rs. Cr./ No of branch offices	
Deposit per branch	DEP	Volume of deposits in Rs. Cr./ No. of branch offices	

(continued)

Table 3.3 *Continued*

Variables	Variable Name	Measurement	Data Source
Workforce participation rate	WPR	Proportion of population engaged in work as per usual principal status	61st and 68th Round NSSO Surveys
Urbanisation share	URB	Proportion of total population living in urban areas	
Variables	Variable Name	Measurement	Data Source
Share of High-end Skills	SKILLIV	Proportion of total workforce with level IV skills in occupations coded 0 to 2	61st and 68th Round NSSO Surveys based on NCO codes 2004.
Share of Regular Employment	REGEMP	Proportion of total population engaged in regular work	61st and 68th Round NSSO Surveys
Coastal Dummy	Cd	Takes the value of 1 if coastal boundary is present and 0 if otherwise	Assigned by author
Million-plus Dummy	MNd	Takes the value of 1 if the region contains a million plus city, else 0	List of cities treated as individual stratum in 68th Round NSSO Survey

For state-level measurement of VA, we take the National State Domestic Product (NSDP) data as provided by the Reserve Bank of India (RBI) for 2004–5 and 2011–12 in its *Handbook of Statistics on Indian Economy*. This means that we have to meaningfully extrapolate state-level VA into a regional framework by applying relevant weights. A new method was introduced by Mitra and Mehta (2011) to convert state domestic product values to reflect city-level output, since all official estimates of output are available only at the state level. In this study we take this a step further by applying this methodology to construct the regional value added (RVA) for NSS regions.

This method draws from the UN Habitat guidelines for measuring urban data which provide an approach for calculating VA in a situation where micro-level data points are not available. It involves extrapolation of data at a national or state level by applying appropriate weights. This method assumes that the unit level share of output is proportionate to the employment share. There is, however, a difference in productivity across regions, which accounts for the differential contribution to VA. This difference is said to be captured in the wage rates. One limitation is that there might be differences in productivity, originating from the differences in technology used. While the RVA variable in itself does not account for it, we seek to address this by including skill intensity as one of the independent variables, which, we expect, has a significant impact on the level of RVA. Mitra and Mehta (2011) follow the UN guidelines to arrive at city output such that

$$City\ Output = Urban\ Domestic\ Product * \frac{City\ Employment}{Urban\ Employment} * \frac{City\ Wage}{Urban\ Wage} \quad (4)$$

Since ours is a similar case where the regional output is not available, we apply this method to calculate RVA, our measure of regional output, and find that the conditions for arriving at city output hold true at the regional level too.

$$Regional\ Domestic\ Product\ or\ Regional\ value\ Added\ (RVA) = State\ Domestic\ Product * \frac{Regional\ Employment}{State\ Employment} * \frac{Regional\ Wage}{State\ Wage} \quad (5)$$

We take the official NSDP per capita (NSDPPC) values provided by the RBI for 2004–5 and 2011–12 in its *Handbook of Statistics on Indian Economy* and multiply them by state population to arrive at the state domestic product. We apply population figures extrapolated from the NSS population weights for the construction of this variable in order to maintain consistency, since employment figures are drawn with NSS as the base. When we calculate wage data to capture productivity differentials, we find that the data on wages in the Indian context is incomplete. NSS captures wages for regular workers and casual workers, but earnings of the self-employed are not collected. In a country such as India, where a very large proportion of workers are self-employed, this is a serious lacuna. As an alternate to the wage ratio, we follow Mitra and Mehta (2011) and consider that the ratio of the workforce participation rates at the regional and state level reflects the wage ratio. The rationale for this is that a region with a higher wage ratio, that is, better work opportunities relative to the state average, is likely to reflect in higher labour flows and hence a higher workforce participation rate in the region.

$$Regional\ value\ Added\ (RVA) =$$
$$State\ Domestic\ Product * \frac{Regional\ Employment}{State\ Employment} * \frac{Regional\ WPR}{State\ WPR} \quad (6)$$

In order to capture the details of economic activity at the individual level, we need to first identify those persons who are part of the workforce. These individual-level details are then aggregated by region, with the help of the usual principle activity status data to calculate workforce participation rate, as already explained.

We apply this methodology in the regional context at the NSS region level to calculate VA in absolute terms represented by RVA as well as in per capita terms represented by regional value added per capita (RVAPC).

Access to Finance

Does an individual have better access to finance in Gadchiroli or Gorakhpur? A region's access to finance determines the availability of capital, both for industrial and other business activities, as well as for household requirements and consumption. A robust banking footprint and volume of fund flow are good markers of the dynamism of the local economy. We measure access to finance in terms of bank penetration and the volume of business per branch. The numbers of bank branch offices (OFF) and accounts (ACC) in the region provide a measure of the penetration and institutional access. The presence of bank branches is critical as it determines the ability of individuals as well as businesses and other institutions to access credit and engage in a robust savings behaviour, thus enabling savings and capital formation. The volume of deposits per branch (DEP) and the volume of credit per branch (CRE) are measures of the quantum of finance available at the regional level. The *Basic Statistical Returns of Scheduled Commercial Banks in India* is a periodic report published by the RBI. This includes all private, foreign, and nationalized banks operating in India and covers almost the entire banking footprint across the nation. This data is available at the district level for 2005 and 2010, which we have compiled at the NSS region level for each district by mapping it to the concerned region. This appears to be the first time this data set has been used at the NSS region level to capture access to finance, and hence this is an important highlight of this book.

Degree of Urbanization

Higher urbanization of a region typically represents higher industrialization, greater concentration of people, and an increased availability of multiple services and markets. In India, an 'urban' area is defined as having (i) a minimum population of 5,000, (ii) at least 75 per cent of the male main working population engaged in non-agricultural pursuits; and (iii) a density of population of at least 400 persons per square kilometre. Thus, urbanization is defined in terms of population density and economic activity. The Indian landscape, like most other developing economies, is dotted with the formation of small towns, higher concentration in cities, and a shift as people migrate out of rural areas in search of jobs and related opportunities. The NSS maps every individual to a place of residence at a regional level, which is either rural or urban as per this definition of 'urban'. We, therefore, calculate the urban population in a region and represent it as a percentage of the total population of the region. This gives us the share of urbanization.

$$URB_r = \frac{\textit{Persons living in Urban Areas in the Region}}{\textit{Total Population of the Region}} * 100 \qquad (7)$$

Proximity to Markets

Access to markets determines how easily you can sell what you produce and buy what you wish to consume. One avenue is the export market which can be denoted by coastal proximity or ports. Another is the domestic market, which is dominated by the larger cities. While local markets also provide a very important measure, there is limited publicly available information on local markets. Thus, we look at coastal proximity with a coastal dummy variable in our analysis to note the presence or absence of a coastal boundary. We further introduce a dummy variable in Chapter 6 to capture the presence or absence of million-plus cities in the region. For this, the listing of 27 million-plus cities as provided in the sampling frame document of the 68th round of NSS is used (Government of India 2013c). These cities have been identified as having a population of more than one million based on the census of 2001, and hence this list is applicable to both periods of our analysis.

For all of the factors discussed so far, in addition to the data sourced from the national sample surveys, state-level output in absolute and per capita terms at constant 2004–5 prices is drawn from the *Handbook of Statistics on Indian Economy* published for 2004–5 and 2011–12 by the RBI (2005a, 2012). The NSDP is used at state level for comparisons and NSDPPC is used for the construction of regional value added. Data related to financial access are drawn from the *Basic Statistical Returns of Scheduled Commercial Banks in India*. Since the latest year for which this is available is 2010, we refer to the 2005 report for 2004–5 and the 2010 report for 2011–12 (RBI 2005b, 2010). For data on geographic area, population, and so on, we refer to data from the *Primary Census Abstract of the Population Census of India* which is collected on a decadal basis and published by the Registrar General and Census Commissioner (2001, 2011). For the purpose of our analysis, we refer to the census data of 2001 for 2004–5 and to the census data of 2011 for 2011–12.

Analytical Techniques

While we are on the subject, let us take a minute to outline the analytical techniques we apply in the following chapters. The details may be of interest to some, while others may like to focus on the main premise and findings in each chapter. While the details of each method and the results are explained in the respective chapters, our effort through this book is also to simplify and make regional analysis more accessible, and so we take this opportunity to introduce to our wider readership the techniques applied and what they aim to achieve.

Multiple Regression Analysis

The measures we construct to capture diversity and regional value added emerge significant in explaining the differences over time and are very important for us to understand the changing regional economy. It is important to study the possible factors determining these two critical variables. Chapter 5 focusses on analysing the determinants of sectoral diversity. We apply an ordinary least squares (OLS) regression on the cross-sectional data for 2004–5 and 2011–12 to estimate the determinants of diversity and test for causality at the state level. We then carry out a pooled estimation using data over the two periods of 2004–5 and 2011–12. This is followed by taking a deeper look at the regional level by carrying out a multivariate cross-sectional analysis and then a pooled estimation in order to assess which factors have changed and the extent to which these changes explain the change in diversity. The detailed methodology as well as the results of these four models are presented in Chapter 5. In Chapter 6, we go a step further and seek to analyse the determinants of regional value added as well as regional value added per capita using cross sectional as well as pooled analysis. We also apply regional dummies for the top 10 regions ranked by output in absolute as well as per capita terms. This is done to ascertain whether the top 10 regions behave differently as compared to other regions. There are eight models in all, explained in detail in Chapter 6.

Discriminant Analysis

Discriminant analysis involves the determination of an equation which predicts whether a particular case is part of a group or not. It is used in situations where the dependent variable is categorical and the independent variables are at interval level, or where the dependent variable has more than two categories. Discriminant analysis is of two types—descriptive discriminant analysis and predictive discriminant analysis. The former is used to describe and explain differences between groups. The latter is used to leverage these differences in allocating observations to the groups. In our case we look at the two periods of 2004–5 and 2011–12 as the two groups. Thus, the group allocations are already complete.

Hence, descriptive discriminant analysis helps us identify critical variables which drive the differences in agglomeration over time. The methodology of discriminant analysis is explained in detail in Chapter 7 and is applied to assess which of the variables in the study best explain the differences across the two periods.

Cluster Analysis

Cluster analysis is a method used to identify natural groupings. One may not know a priori which groups the observations fall into, and cluster analysis can help identify if there are patterns which result in automatic groupings. While cluster analysis by itself does not provide reasons or explanations for such groupings, it is a good starting point to identify inherent patterns within the data. Since we study a large number of regions—75 NSS regions in 2004–5 and 85 NSS regions in 2011–12—we use this method to identify regions that are similar to each other but different from other regions. We seek to assess whether regions within the same state may actually exhibit a stronger similarity to regions of other states, and hence seek to understand the patterns of such clustering over 2004–5 and 2011–12. The detailed methodology and logic for cluster formation is explained and applied in Chapter 8 to discover which regions cluster together over time.

4
Trends and Patterns of Regional Economic Development

It is important to understand the spatial concentration and distribution of economic activity against the backdrop of structural change, wherein progress is said to involve a gradual diversification of the economic base across sectors. Historically, all developed countries have experienced a sequence of changes in their economic structure, starting with a predominance of agriculture, then shifting in favour of industry and, subsequently, services, both in terms of output and employment. This is explained by factors such as low-income elasticity for agricultural goods on the demand side (Fisher 1939) and increasing returns to scale on manufacturing (industry) on the supply side (Kaldor 1967).

The Indian Experience

The Indian experience is different from that of other developing countries, as there seems to be a clear move away from agriculture and towards services in terms of contribution to the GDP, coupled with a stagnation of industry. A structural change in employment is also taking place in India but slower than that of output. In 2011–12, the share of agriculture stood at 47 per cent of the total employment, while contributing to 14 per cent of the GDP; industry and construction accounted for 25 per cent of the total employment, while contributing to 28 per cent of the GDP; and services employed 29 per cent of the workforce and contributed to 58 per cent of the GDP (Mehrotra et al. 2014, 1). This implies a situation of lower productivity and higher employment potential of industry in India. The reverse is true in the services sector. While its share in the GDP has been remarkably high, its share in employment is quite low and has been

Regional Economic Diversity. Poornima Dore and Krishnan Narayanan, Oxford University Press. © Oxford University Press India 2022. DOI: 10.1093/oso/9780190130596.003.0004

growing at a slower pace (Thomas 2012, 46). This means that high-productivity jobs have grown but with low employment potential.

There is a clear and definite need to understand these patterns at the state and regional levels. Sachs, Bajpai, and Ramiah (2002) analyse the differentials in growth across 14 states and 6 union territories in India using the data of gross state domestic product (GSDP) per capita from National Accounts Statistics for 1950–1 to 1966–7. They find a substantial variation between states in terms of per capita state product. A similar analysis at the sub-state level has not been possible due to the absence of data. Chandrasekhar and Sharma (2014) examine whether certain sections of industry are concentrated in certain regions by using the NSSO data for 2011–12 and dividing each state into rural, urban, and million-plus cities. The services sector seems to find uniform representation across states but with greater emphasis on million-plus cities and urban areas, as expected, while construction appears to be the most unequally distributed. Thomas (2012) finds that more than 20 per cent of the increase in urban jobs was generated in Maharashtra, making it important to examine the sectoral mix within such states and between sub-regions of the state to understand how these patterns have changed over time.

The present chapter attempts to gauge and assess the broad trends and patterns of regional economic development in India with a focus on sectoral shares in employment over 2004–5 and 2011–12, both at the state and the NSS region levels. The core purpose is to see how the states and the regions compare with each other and whether there are significant differences in their rate of progress.

Trends at All India and State Levels

While traditionally the sectoral mix at a global level is discussed in terms of three key sectors—agriculture, industry, and services—we add another dimension by representing construction as a separate sector. The reasons are twofold:

a. From 2000 onwards, India has experienced an unprecedented growth in construction. With investments in infrastructure on the rise, our analysis at the 14-sector level indicated that construction deserves specific attention in our study.

b. There are schools of thought which consider construction as part of manufacturing, whereas others include it as part of services. The inclusion in one or the other gives a very different sectoral picture.

We have analysed the National Industrial Classification (NIC) data at the 2-digit level for all sectors of the economy captured through the 61st and the 68th rounds of the NSS, which amount to 14 sectors, and compiled these into 4 distinct sectors, as per Table 4.2, which are: agriculture (AGRI), manufacturing (MFG), construction (CON), and services (SVS).

From Figure 4.1, we find that the share of agriculture has fallen below 50 per cent for the first time, with a significant section of the workforce moving away from agriculture and towards other sectors. Manufacturing shows a single percentage point increase from 13 to 14 per cent. As expected, the share of services goes up from 25 to almost 30 per cent of employment.

The most significant increase is in the share of construction; almost doubling from 6 to 11 per cent. Construction emerges as the

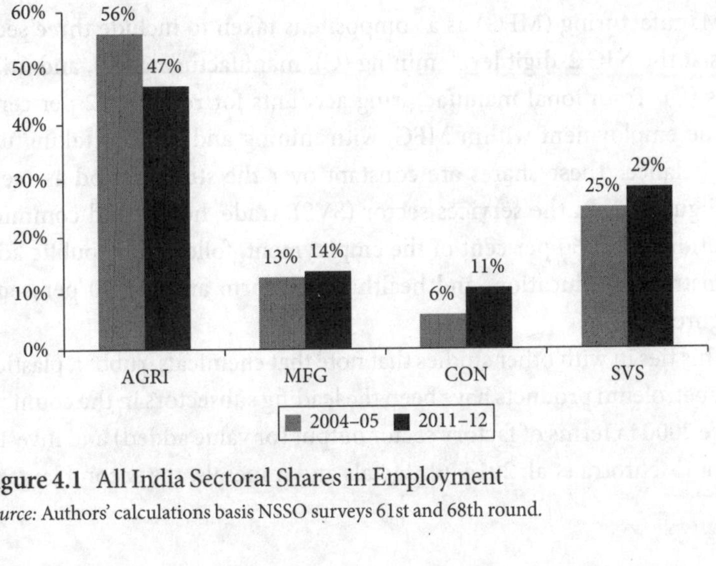

Figure 4.1 All India Sectoral Shares in Employment

Source: Authors' calculations basis NSSO surveys 61st and 68th round.

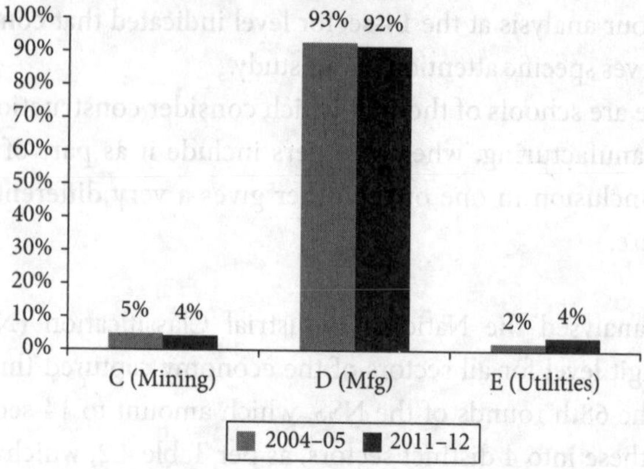

Figure 4.2 Share of Sectors within Manufacturing (MFG)
Source: Authors' estimates based on NSS various rounds.

single largest employer in this decade, providing jobs to about 50 million (Mn) people. Employment in construction almost equals that in manufacturing in terms of absolute numbers, with about 59 Mn being employed in all subsectors within manufacturing (Mehrotra et al. 2014, 10). This justifies the separate representation of the construction sector, so as not to skew the results on trends and patterns. The effort is to avoid drawing faulty conclusions by extending to the general manufacturing or services sector results which are quite unique to the construction sector.

Manufacturing (MFG) as a composite is taken to include three sectors at the NIC 2-digit level: mining (C), manufacturing (D), and utilities (E). Traditional manufacturing accounts for roughly 92 per cent of the employment within MFG, with mining and utilities taking up the balance. These shares are constant over the study period as seen in Figure 4.2. In the services sector (SVS), trade, hotels, and communications form 60 per cent of the employment, followed by public administration, education, and health which form another 20 per cent (Figure 4.3).

This ties in with other studies that note that chemicals, rubber, plastic, and petroleum products have been the leading subsectors in the country since 2000 in terms of factory sector output (or value added) and investment (Mehrotra et al. 2014, 6). Metals and minerals, the second largest

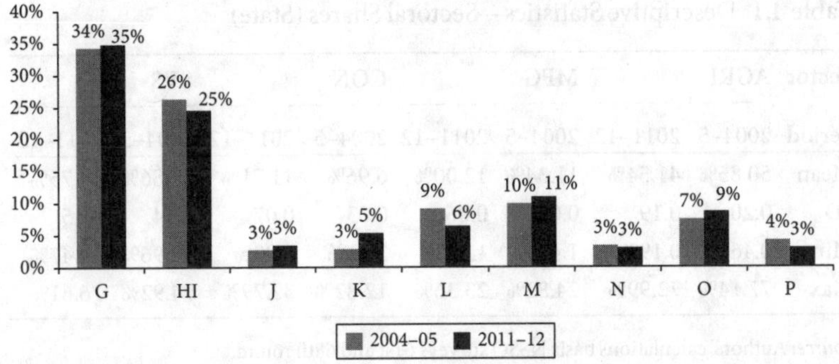

Figure 4.3 Percentage share of Sectors within Services (SVS)
Source: Authors' calculations basis NSSO surveys 61st and 68th round.

industry group in terms of factory sector value added, also attracted major factory sector investments into the country during 2003–6. However, when it comes to factory employment, the prominent industries have been textiles, garments, leather goods, food products, and tobacco products. Thus, even within the organized manufacturing sector, the industries that attracted major investments and produced the bulk of value added have been different from the industries that absorbed a sizeable chunk of the labour force. Wearing apparel, textiles, furniture, non-metallic mineral products, and wood products, mostly all labour-intensive industries, are the subsectors that really reflect the fluctuations in employment. While absolute output has grown in these sectors, it has not grown much in terms of the relative share of output in these sectors to total manufacturing value added. This implies that it is the low-productivity small scale enterprises that are driving employment in these sectors.

For the rest of our analysis we consider the composites of MFG and SVS, as some of the individual shares of the component sectors within MFG and SVS are very small.

We now take a look at the structure of the economy at the state level by analysing the shares of the four sectors within each state and union territory. We calculate the proportionate shares of each of the four sectors in the state economy over the two periods under study. We also compute the descriptive statistics across states as provided in Table 4.1.

Table 4.1 Descriptive Statistics—Sectoral Shares (State)

Sector	AGRI		MFG		CON		SVS	
Period	2004–5	2011–12	2004–5	2011–12	2004–5	2011–12	2004–5	2011–12
Mean	50.85%	41.54%	11.34%	12.00%	6.96%	11.71%	30.86%	34.75%
SD	0.20	0.19	0.06	0.06	0.03	0.07	0.14	0.15
Min	0.46%	0.19%	1.49%	1.42%	2.31%	3.29%	12.96%	14.47%
Max	77.14%	72.99%	24.82%	23.36%	12.82%	32.79%	74.92%	76.61%

Source: Authors' calculations basis NSSO surveys 61st and 68th round.

Agricultural Share at State Level

A marked reduction in the share of agriculture becomes apparent when we consider the average sectoral share across states. The mean share of agriculture has come down from 50.85 per cent to 41.54 per cent. While the standard deviation across states has not changed much, we find that there is a sizeable reduction in both the maximum and minimum shares of agriculture. A state-wise breakdown (Figure 4.4) underscores the uniform decline in the share of agriculture across the board, reconfirming that even the agrarian states are diversifying into other sectors. Delhi had the lowest share at 0.46 per cent which has come down to 0.19 per cent. If we eliminate the union territories, then Goa had the lowest share at 22 per cent in 2004–5, which has come down all the way to 4 per cent. Chhattisgarh, which saw the highest share of agriculture during both periods, witnessed a reduction from 75.6 per cent to 72.9 per cent. Even Punjab, the granary of India which stood at 37 per cent, now has only 27 per cent of its workforce engaged in agriculture. This is true for some of the hitherto agrarian states such as Uttarakhand as well.

Manufacturing Share at State Level

In terms of the pan India average, we find that the share of manufacturing has marginally increased from 11 per cent to 12 per cent across states (Figure 4.5). At the same time, the states' maximum and minimum shares

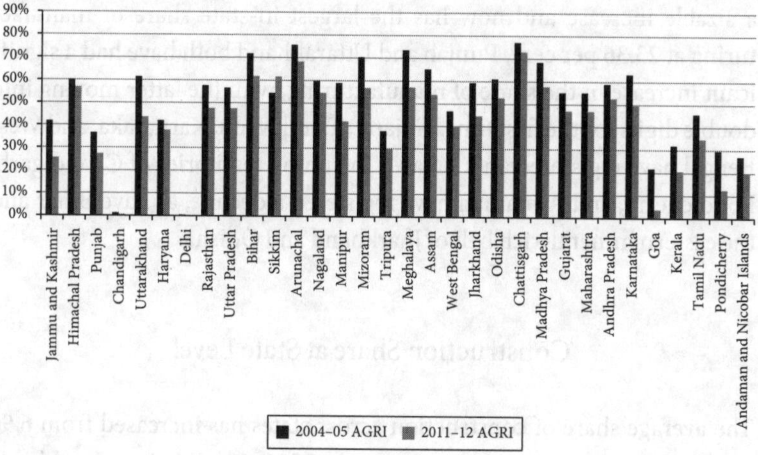

Figure 4.4 Share of Agriculture in State Employment
Source: Authors' estimates based on NSS various rounds.

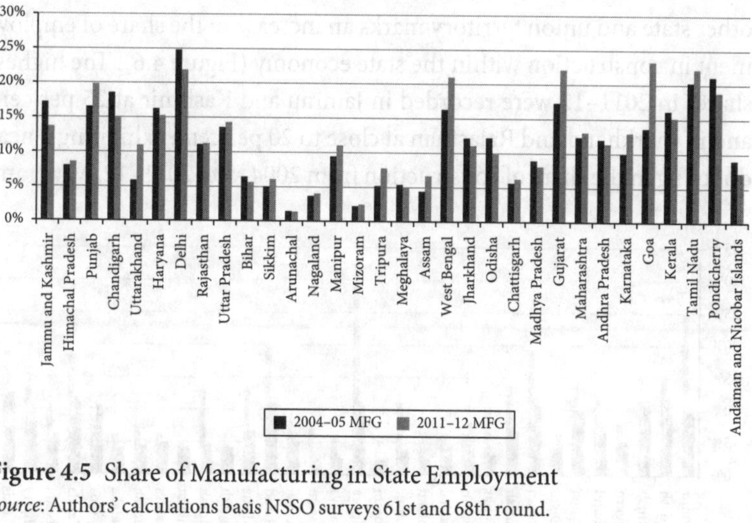

Figure 4.5 Share of Manufacturing in State Employment
Source: Authors' calculations basis NSSO surveys 61st and 68th round.

of manufacturing have fallen marginally. Delhi, which had the highest share in 2004–5 at 24.8 per cent, is now at 21.9 per cent. Arunachal Pradesh continues to have the lowest share of manufacturing, and this has further declined from 1.49 per cent to 1.42 per cent. The state-level picture reveals a marked increase in the shares of certain states. Goa experienced a sizable increase and now has the largest in-state share of manufacturing at 23.36 per cent. Punjab and Uttarakhand both have had a significant increase in the share of manufacturing, with the latter moving into double digits for the first time. Gujarat, Tamil Nadu, Karnataka, and West Bengal have registered an increase. The union territories of Chandigarh, Pondicherry, and Andaman have registered a decline, as have Bihar and the eastern mineral-rich belt of Jharkhand and Odisha.

Construction Share at State Level

The average share of construction across states has increased from 6.96 per cent in 2004–5 to 11.71 per cent in 2011–12. This is a sizeable increase on a small base. The standard deviation has almost doubled from 0.03 to 0.07, indicating that this increase is quite unequally distributed across states. We find that with the exception of Delhi and Goa, every other state and union territory marks an increase in the share of employment in construction within the state economy (Figure 4.6). The highest shares in 2011–12 were recorded in Jammu and Kashmir at 25 per cent and in Jharkhand and Rajasthan at close to 20 per cent, exhibiting a near doubling in the share of construction from 2004–5 to 2011–12. Mizoram,

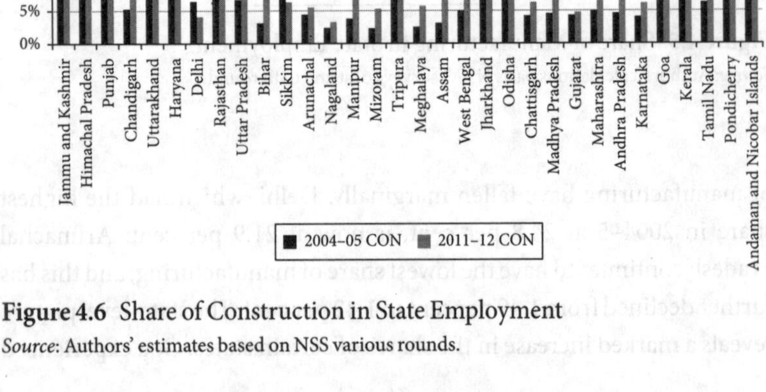

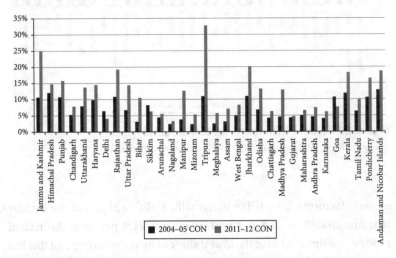

Figure 4.6 Share of Construction in State Employment
Source: Authors' estimates based on NSS various rounds.

which had the lowest share of construction at 2.32 per cent in 2004–5, went up to 5 per cent in 2011–12. Nagaland had the lowest share of construction in 2011–12 at 3.29 per cent. The state with the highest share of construction during both periods is Tripura which witnessed an increase of almost 2.5 times over this period, from 12.82 per cent to 32.79 per cent. Thus, the pattern followed by the construction sector is very different within the Northeast region itself, with both the highest and the lowest shares in the country being found in its states.

Services Share at State Level

The average share of employment in the services sector registered an increase from 30.86 per cent to 34.75 per cent across states over the two periods. This is fairly modest when compared to the share in output that is attributable to the services sector. At the same time, a steady increase is observed across states. Figure 4.7 reveals that there is an almost uniform increase in the share of the services sector. Chandigarh has the highest share across both periods at over 70 per cent, followed by Delhi. This could be due to the significant presence of government administration

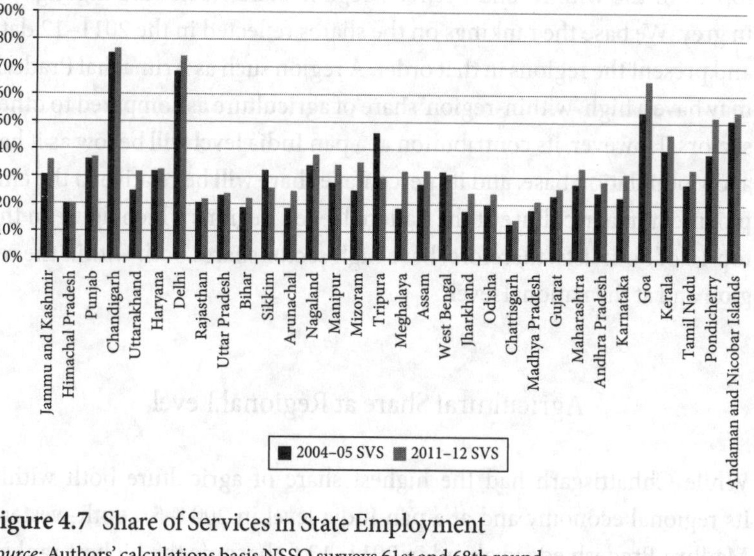

Figure 4.7 Share of Services in State Employment
Source: Authors' calculations basis NSSO surveys 61st and 68th round.

and public service jobs in union territories. If we look at other states, Goa tops the list and goes up from 54 per cent to 64 per cent from 2004–5 to 2011–12. Chhattisgarh continues to have the lowest share of employment in services at 12.96 per cent in 2004–5, which goes up to 14.47 per cent in 2011–12.

Trends at Regional Level

We now deepen our analysis and study these trends at the NSS region level. Each state is broken up into several sub regions defined by the NSS, as elaborated in Chapter 3, and the total number of regions analysed pan India are 75 in 2004–5 and 85 in 2011–12. Details of the sectoral shares for all regions are provided in Appendix 3 for 2004–5 and in Appendix 4 for 2011–12. Here, we summarize our results and focus our discussion on the top 10 and the bottom 10 regions for each of the four sectors. We explore the ranking of shares both within and between the regions. The 'within-region' shares table captures the proportion of sector i in region j as a percentage of the overall employment in region j. The 'between-region' shares table captures the proportion of sector i in region j as a percentage of the overall employment in sector i. Regions which overlap among the top 10 in the within- and between-region shares tables are highlighted in grey. We base the rankings on the shares reflected in the 2011–12 data and present the regions in that order. A region such as Arunachal Pradesh may have a high 'within-region' share of agriculture as compared to other sectors. However, its contribution at a pan India level will be low as it has a low population base, and its percentage share will be relative to the employment in agriculture at the national level. Regions which figure in the top 10 of both lists, therefore, have high sector shares both within the region and at the national level.

Agricultural Share at Regional Level

While Chhattisgarh had the highest share of agriculture both within its regional economy and at a pan India level in 2004–5, south-western Madhya Pradesh edged ahead in 2011–12 to become the highest ranked

Table 4.2 Top 10 Regions—Agriculture

Within-region shares: AGRI				per cent share		Between-region shares: AGRI				per cent share	
Rank 2011	No	State	Region	2004–5	2011–12	Rank 2011	No.	State	Region	2004–5	2011–12
1	235	Madhya Pradesh	South Western	75%	73%	1	93	Uttar Pradesh	Eastern	6.09%	5.53%
2	221	Chattisgarh	Chattisgarh	77%	73%	2	101	Bihar	Northern	4.22%	5.05%
3	292	Karnataka	Inland Eastern	74%	71%	3	91	Uttar Pradesh	Northern Upper Ganga Plains	4.07%	4.93%
4	274	Maharashtra	Inland Central	73%	70%	4	282	Andhra Pradesh	Coastal Southern	3.74%	4.42%
5	276	Maharashtra	Eastern	66%	69%	5	221	Chattisgarh	Chattisgarh	3.69%	4.02%
6	121	Arunachal	Arunachal	76%	68%	6	294	Karnataka	Inland Northern	3.66%	3.56%
7	101	Bihar	Northern	75%	62%	7	102	Bihar	Southern	2.80%	3.00%
8	111	Sikkim	Sikkim	54%	62%	8	274	Maharashtra	Inland Central	2.63%	2.76%
9	102	Bihar	Southern	67%	62%	9	272	Maharashtra	Inland Western	2.81%	2.74%
10	233	Madhya Pradesh	Malwa	68%	61%	10	241	Gujarat	South Eastern	1.45%	2.54%

Source: Authors' estimates based on NSS various rounds.

region. However, not a single region of Madhya Pradesh features among the top 10 of the between-region shares table, while Uttar Pradesh ranks the highest in terms of between-region shares of agriculture across the country. The overlaps between the two rankings (highlighted) indicate regions that not only have a high share of agriculture within the region, but are also among the top contributors to agriculture in terms of employment in the sector at a national level. These regions are Chhattisgarh, inland central Maharashtra, and northern and southern Bihar. There is a consistent dip in the shares of the top 10 as well as the bottom 10 regions in sync with the trajectories of developed countries which have experienced a slow but steady diversification of the regional economy away from agriculture.

We find that there is a substantial overlap in the bottom 10 (Table 4.3), both for within-region and between-region shares of employment in agriculture. These are mostly the union territories of Delhi, Chandigarh, Pondicherry, and Andaman and Nicobar Islands. Coastal Maharashtra and Goa also have lesser shares in agriculture, followed by the mountainous Jammu and Kashmir. It is to be noted that the bottom 10 list features north Punjab, which has the distinction of being known as the granary of India, along with Kerala, one of the highest-ranked regions in the human development index (HDI).

Manufacturing Share at Regional Level

For manufacturing, the regional picture is different from the state-level picture, with five regions having the highest share of the total employment in the region in manufacturing, overtaking Goa in the top 10 ranking of regions. Southern and inland Tamil Nadu had high shares in 2011–12 at 29 per cent and 24 per cent respectively. South-eastern Gujarat showed a rise in its share from 14 per cent in 2004–5 to 25 per cent in 2011–12, both at regional and sectoral levels. South Bengal plains in West Bengal ranked high on both lists in 2011–12, with manufacturing accounting for 28 per cent of regional employment and the region accounting for 7.54 per cent of national employment in manufacturing. The upper Gangetic plain and eastern Uttar Pradesh contribute to 6.67 per cent and 4.7 per cent of national employment in manufacturing respectively. It may be noted

Table 4.3 Bottom 10 Regions—Agriculture

Within-Region Shares – AGRI				per cent Share		Between-Region Shares -AGRI				per cent Share	
Rank 2011	No.	State	Region	2004–5	2011–12	Rank 2011	No.	State	Region Name	2004–5	2011–12
75	71	Delhi	Delhi	0%	0%	75	41	Chandigarh	Chandigarh	0.00%	0.00%
74	41	Chandigarh	Chandigarh	1%	1%	74	71	Delhi	Delhi	0.01%	0.00%
73	301	Goa	Goa	22%	4%	73	301	Goa	Goa	0.04%	0.01%
72	271	Maharashtra	Coastal	20%	10%	72	351	Andaman and Nicobar Islands	Andaman and Nicobar Islands	0.01%	0.01%
71	341	Pondicherry	Pondicherry	30%	13%	71	341	Pondicherry	Pondicherry	0.04%	0.03%
70	11	Jammu and Kashmir	Mountainous	35%	17%	70	141	Manipur	Plains	0.08%	0.08%
69	322	Kerala	South	29%	19%	69	11	Jammu and Kashmir	Mountainous	0.10%	0.08%
68	351	Andaman and Nicobar Islands	Andaman and Nicobar Islands	27%	20%	68	142	Manipur	Hills	0.12%	0.09%
67	31	Punjab	Northern	26%	23%	67	111	Sikkim	Sikkim	0.06%	0.09%
66	321	Kerala	Northern	37%	23%	66	131	Nagaland	Nagaland	0.09%	0.10%

Source: Authors' calculations basis NSSO surveys 61st and 68th round.

that the high population of Uttar Pradesh needs to be considered while interpreting these results. Also, in all regions of Uttar Pradesh the share of manufacturing has fallen during the period under consideration.

The north-eastern states are clearly and consistently at the bottom of the pile in terms of the share of employment in manufacturing. While this can be a function of the low population base in each of the north-eastern states, the low shares within regions indicate that manufacturing accounts for only 2 to 5 per cent of the regional employment in Arunachal, Mizoram, Nagaland, Manipur, Sikkim, Meghalaya, and Assam (Table 4.4). Tripura is the only one missing from this list, since in 2011–12 its share in manufacturing increased to 8 per cent. The reduction in the share of manufacturing in eastern Maharashtra from 12 per cent to 5 per cent in this period warrants further examination. We also find that while coastal Karnataka and both coastal and inland western Maharashtra feature in the top 10 lists, the bottom 10 lists (Table 4.5) include inland eastern Karnataka and eastern Maharashtra. This underscores the issue of regional differences even within states and the need to go beyond state-level generalizations which may not apply to all regions within a state. We may also find that eastern Maharashtra bears more similarity with inland eastern Karnataka than with other portions of its own state such as coastal Maharashtra.

Construction Share at Regional Level

Jammu and Kashmir and Rajasthan dominate the top 10 regions where construction enjoys the highest share in regional employment. All regions of Jammu and Kashmir (mountainous, outer hills, and the Jhelum valley) had construction contributing to over 20 per cent of the region's employment in 2011–12. Southern Rajasthan (37 per cent) and south-eastern Rajasthan (23 per cent) both have a sizable share of employment in construction. Interestingly, there is a marked increase in the shares of construction in most regions, especially in the case of Chhattisgarh, a primarily agrarian region, which shows a 6-fold increase from 3 per cent to 20 per cent from 2004–5 to 2011–12. In the case of between-region shares, coastal Maharashtra has the highest share of construction (5.71 per cent), a few notches above the usual suspects eastern Uttar Pradesh

Table 4.4 Top 10 Regions—Manufacturing

Within-Regions – MFG				per cent Share		Between-Regions – MFG				per cent Share	
Rank 2011	No	State	Region	2004–5	2011–12	Rank 2011	No	State	Region	2004–5	2011–12
1	334	Tamil Nadu	Inland	25%	29%	1	193	West Bengal	South Bengal Plains	5.61%	7.54%
2	193	West Bengal	South Bengal Plains	21%	28%	2	91	Uttar Pradesh	Northern Upper Ganga Plains	6.82%	6.67%
3	241	Gujarat	South Eastern	14%	25%	3	93	Uttar Pradesh	Eastern	4.83%	4.70%
4	333	Tamil Nadu	Southern	24%	24%	4	271	Maharashtra	Coastal	4.54%	4.68%
5	271	Maharashtra	Coastal	25%	24%	5	241	Gujarat	South Eastern	1.34%	4.32%
6	301	Goa	Goa	14%	23%	6	334	Tamil Nadu	Inland	3.65%	4.21%
7	242	Gujarat	Northern Plains	18%	22%	7	331	Tamil Nadu	Coastal Northern	3.60%	3.40%
8	71	Delhi	Delhi	25%	22%	8	282	Andhra Pradesh	Coastal Southern	3.96%	3.16%
9	245	Gujarat	Saurasthra	18%	22%	9	333	Tamil Nadu	Southern	3.19%	2.95%
10	291	Karnataka	Coastal and Ghats	17%	22%	10	272	Maharashtra	Inland Western	2.54%	2.83%

Source: Authors' estimates based on NSS various rounds.

Table 4.5 Bottom 10 Regions—Manufacturing

Within-Regions: MFG				per cent Share		Between-Regions: MFG				per cent Share	
Rank 2011	No	State	Region	2004–5	2011–12	Rank 2011	No	State	Region	2004–5	2011–12
85	121	Arunachal Pradesh	Arunachal Pradesh	1%	1%	85	121	Arunachal Pradesh	Arunachal Pradesh	0.01%	0.01%
84	151	Mizoram	Mizoram	2%	3%	84	351	Andaman and Nicobar Islands	Andaman and Nicobar Islands	0.02%	0.02%
83	235	Madhya Pradesh	South Western	5%	4%	83	151	Mizoram	Mizoram	0.01%	0.02%
82	131	Nagaland	Nagaland	4%	4%	82	142	Manipur	Manipur	0.01%	0.02%
81	292	Karnataka	Inland Eastern	5%	4%	81	131	Nagaland	Nagaland	0.02%	0.03%
80	142	Manipur	Manipur	2%	5%	80	111	Sikkim	Sikkim	0.02%	0.03%
79	183	Assam	Cachar Plains	1%	5%	79	41	Chandigarh	Chandigarh	0.12%	0.10%
78	171	Meghalaya	Meghalaya	5%	5%	78	171	Meghalaya	Meghalaya	0.12%	0.10%
77	101	Bihar	Northern	5%	5%	77	183	Assam	Assam	0.00%	0.11%
76	276	Maharashtra	Eastern	12%	5%	76	12	Jammu and Kashmir	Outer Hills	0.02%	0.11%

Source: Authors' calculations basis NSSO surveys 61st and 68th round.

and central/south Bengal plains, which typically emerge on top of the between-region shares lists by virtue of being the most populated. It is valuable to note that in the case of construction there is no overlap at all in the top 10 within-region and between-region shares (Table 4.6). It implies that regions having a high sector share within the region may not account for a high share in construction at the national level. It may also be noted that the regions of coastal Maharashtra, central Bengal plains, inland north-west Andhra, inland southern Karnataka, coastal northern Tamil Nadu, and Delhi, which have the highest between-region shares, are the ones that house the cities of Mumbai, Kolkata, Hyderabad, Bangalore, Chennai, and Delhi.

The Cachar regions of Assam and inland eastern Karnataka witnessed the lowest contribution of construction to regional employment at 1 per cent and 2 per cent respectively in 2011–12. Others from the bottom list include the eastern, southern, and Saurashtra regions of Gujarat and the inland northern and central regions of Maharashtra, with values ranging between 4 and 5 per cent. Nagaland is the only region which features on both the lists. The bottom 10 between-region list (Table 4.7) is dominated by north-eastern states and union territories, which are also low-population locations. It may be noted that the outer hills region of Jammu has among the bottom 10 between-region shares while also having one of the top 10 within-region shares. This implies that while construction accounts for nearly 20 per cent of its regional economy, it is a very small proportion (0.16 per cent) of the overall employment in construction in the country.

Services Share at Regional Level

The services sector is a composite of several subsectors such as trade, logistics, and so on, and we refer to our analysis at the 14-digit level to study trends. Delhi and Chandigarh have high shares in trade. Public administration forms the highest share of employment in union territories and the Northeast. In border states, government jobs account for more than 10 per cent of the total employment.

If we keep the union territories aside, Goa and Kerala (northern and southern) have the highest shares in services at 65 per cent and 48 per cent

Table 4.6 Top 10 Regions—Construction

Within-Regions – CON				per cent Share		Between-Regions – CON				per cent Share	
Rank 2011	No.	State	Region	2004–5	2011–12	Rank 2011	No.	State	Region	2004–5	2011–12
1	83	Rajasthan	Southern	22%	37%	1	271	Maharashtra	Coastal	1.80%	5.55%
2	12	Jammu and Kashmir	Outer Hills	16%	35%	2	193	West Bengal	South Bengal Plains	3.32%	4.95%
3	161	Tripura	Tripura	11%	33%	3	91	Uttar Pradesh	Northern Upper Ganga Plains	5.87%	4.95%
4	11	Jammu and Kashmir	Mountainous	11%	23%	4	282	Andhra Pradesh	Coastal Southern	2.74%	4.76%
5	84	Rajasthan	South-Eastern	4%	23%	5	93	Uttar Pradesh	Eastern	5.40%	3.98%
6	231	Madhya Pradesh	Vindhyas	3%	21%	6	293	Karnataka	Inland Southern	2.00%	3.27%
7	321	Kerala	Northern	11%	21%	7	331	Tamil Nadu	Coastal Northern	2.76%	3.21%
8	94	Uttar Pradesh	Southern	14%	21%	8	101	Bihar	Northern	1.42%	2.95%
9	201	Jharkhand	Ranchi Plateau	11%	20%	9	71	Delhi	Delhi	1.09%	2.89%
10	13	Jammu and Kashmir	Jhelum Valley	10%	20%	10	322	Kerala	Southern	3.60%	2.74%

Source: Authors' calculations basis NSSO surveys 61st and 68th round.

Table 4.7 Bottom 10 Regions—Construction

Within-Regions: CON				per cent Shares		Between-Regions: CON				per cent Shares	
Rank 2011	No.	State	Region	2004–5	2011–12	Rank 2011	No.	State	Region	2004–5	2011–12
85	183	Assam	Cachar Plains	0%	1%	85	351	Andaman and Nicobar Islands	Andaman and Nicobar Islands	0.06%	0.06%
84	292	Karnataka	Inland Eastern	3%	2%	84	111	Sikkim	Sikkim	0.08%	0.06%
83	131	Nagaland	Nagaland	2%	3%	83	142	Manipur	Hills	0.01%	0.07%
82	241	Gujarat	South Eastern	5%	4%	82	121	Arunachal Pradesh	Arunachal Pradesh	0.07%	0.08%
81	71	Delhi	Delhi	6%	4%	81	131	Nagaland	Nagaland	0.03%	0.11%
80	243	Gujarat	Dry Areas	5%	4%	80	151	Mizoram	Mizoram	0.03%	0.12%
79	245	Gujarat	Saurashtra	2%	5%	79	12	Jammu and Kashmir	Outer Hills	0.14%	0.16%
78	283	Andhra Pradesh	Inland North Western	4%	5%	78	141	Manipur	Plains	0.11%	0.16%
77	274	Maharashtra	Inland Central	5%	5%	77	341	Pondicherry	Pondicherry	0.14%	0.19%
76	273	Maharashtra	Inland North	4%	5%	76	41	Chandigarh	Chandigarh	0.07%	0.24%

Source: Authors' calculations basis NSSO surveys 61st and 68th round.

respectively. The only overlaps between the two lists are Delhi, southern Kerala, and coastal Maharashtra (Table 4.8). Coastal Maharashtra has the highest share between regions (5.55 per cent) due to its leadership in financial services, real estate, and health, as well as in hotels, transport, and communications. The education sector has the maximum contribution from West Bengal through the south/central Bengal plains.

The Northeast and the union territories dominate the bottom 10 between-region list for services (Table 4.9). Overall, the lowest within-region shares in the services sector are seen in Chhattisgarh, south Odisha, parts of Madhya Pradesh and Rajasthan, eastern Maharashtra, and so on. We hypothesize that some of these seemingly dissimilar regions group together in ways that set them apart from other regions in their own state. This makes a case for us to study whether southern Odisha and eastern Maharashtra may be more similar to each other than to coastal Odisha and inland Maharashtra respectively.

Setting the Stage

This chapter presents the trends and patterns in regional development over 2004–5 and 2011–12 with specific emphasis on sectoral shares. We move from an all India level to investigate patterns at both the state and the NSS region levels. We find sizeable variations across states and across the two periods studied. We deepen the analysis further at a regional level by identifying the top and the bottom 10 contributors to the four sectors of agriculture, manufacturing, construction, and services, both within regions and between regions.

This region-wise analysis provides a deeper understanding of the regional sectoral concentration as indicated by previous studies (Papola and Jena 2011; Thomas 2012). For instance, while the share of agriculture has reduced almost uniformly across regions, the share of construction has increased overall but to highly varying degrees across regions, with particular concentrations in parts of Rajasthan and Jammu and Kashmir. This ties in with some conclusions in the existing literature (Chandrasekhar and Sharma 2014) which finds a major inequality in the distribution of construction.

Table 4.8 Top 10 Regions—Services

Within-Region: SVS				per cent Share		Between-Regions: SVS				per cent Share	
Rank 2011	No.	State	Region	2004–5	2011–12	Rank 2011	No.	State	Region	2004–5	2011–12
1	41	Chandigarh	Chandigarh	75%	77%	1	271	Maharashtra Coastal	Coastal	4.64%	5.55%
2	71	Delhi	Delhi	68%	74%	2	193	West Bengal	South Bengal Plains	5.49%	4.95%
3	301	Goa	Goa	54%	65%	3	91	Uttar Pradesh	Northern Upper Ganga Plains	5.43%	4.95%
4	271	Maharashtra Coastal	Coastal	50%	59%	4	282	Andhra Pradesh	Coastal Southern	3.27%	4.76%
5	351	Andaman and Nicobar Islands	Andaman and Nicobar Islands	51%	54%	5	93	Uttar Pradesh	Eastern	4.18%	3.98%
6	341	Pondicherry	Pondicherry	39%	52%	6	293	Karnataka	Inland Southern	2.62%	3.27%
7	322	Kerala	Southern	41%	48%	7	331	Tamil Nadu	Coastal Northern	3.15%	3.21%
8	11	Jammu and Kashmir	Mountainous	41%	45%	8	101	Bihar	Northern	2.18%	2.95%
9	321	Kerala	Northern	38%	42%	9	71	Delhi	Delhi	2.81%	2.89%
10	331	Tamil Nadu	Coastal Northern	33%	41%	10	322	Kerala	Southern	2.94%	2.74%

Source: Author's calculations basis NSSO surveys 61st and 68th round.

Table 4.9 Bottom 10 Regions—Services

Within-Regions –SVS				per cent Share		Between-Regions – SVS				per cent Share	
Rank 2011	No.	State	State	2004–5	2011–12	Rank 2011	No.	State	State	2004–5	2011–12
85	83	Rajasthan	Southern	16%	13%	85	351	Andaman and Nicobar Islands	Andaman and Nicobar Islands	0.06%	0.06%
84	221	Chattisgarh	Northern	13%	14%	84	111	Sikkim	Sikkim	0.07%	0.06%
83	231	Madhya Pradesh	Vindhyas	13%	15%	83	142	Manipur	Plains	0.04%	0.07%
82	235	Madhya Pradesh	South Western	17%	15%	82	121	Arunachal Pradesh	Arunachal Pradesh	0.07%	0.08%
81	94	Uttar Pradesh	Southern	16%	17%	81	131	Nagaland	Nagaland	0.11%	0.11%
80	276	Maharashtra	Eastern	16%	17%	80	151	Mizoram	Mizoram	0.08%	0.12%
79	212	Odisha	Southern	14%	17%	79	12	Jammu and Kashmir	Outer Hills	0.04%	0.16%
78	84	Rajasthan	South Eastern	17%	17%	78	141	Manipur	Hills	0.17%	0.16%
77	274	Maharashtra	Maharashtra	17%	19%	77	341	Pondicherry	Pondicherry	0.13%	0.19%
76	21	Himachal Pradesh	Himachal Pradesh	20%	20%	76	41	Chandigarh	Chandigarh	0.25%	0.24%

Source: Author's calculations basis NSSO surveys 61st and 68th round.

What does this mean in terms of regional sectoral composition? We have looked at each of the four core sectors and have realized that some regions have a high concentration of agriculture while others have services as the primary economic driver, as revealed by the between- and within-region shares analysis. However, each region in itself is a composite of all sectors, the degree of concentration or diversification of which can be measured. The stage is now set to examine the important question of whether the Indian regional economy is characterized by specialization in one or two sectors or by a diverse palette, and how this plays out at the state, region, and city level.

5
Economic Diversity at the Region Level

Diversity is an important facet of agglomeration and has been defined as 'the presence in an area of a great number of different types of industries' (Rodgers 1957). It can also be described as 'the extent to which the economic activity of a region is distributed among a number of categories' (Parr 1965); or in terms of 'balanced employment across industry classes' (Attaran 1986). The sectoral mix of output or employment is a lens through which 'economies are viewed, labeled and classified'(Wagner and Deller 1998), and it defines the public imagination of specific regions. The existence of diverse industries in a region is said to bring together diverse knowledge sources which interact with each other, resulting in a proliferation of new ideas (Chinitz 1961). This boosts innovation and can lead to the development and testing of new technologies.

Why Is Diversity Relevant?

Such benefits of economic diversity accrue to all firms in the agglomeration irrespective of the industry. Jacobs (1969) contrasts Manchester and its decline as a specialized textile cluster with a highly diversified Birmingham which continued to grow. This is supported by Bairoch (1998) who contends that the '"diversity of ... activities quite naturally encourages the attempts to apply and adopt in one sector, technology solutions adopted in another sector'". Attaran (1986) further opines that sectoral diversity contributes to sustainability, so that in times when one sector may not be performing well, others sectors have the wherewithal to keep the economy afloat. Diversification is, therefore, valuable from a sustainability standpoint as it spreads the risk from economic fluctuations across several sectors.

Regional Economic Diversity. Poornima Dore and Krishnan Narayanan, Oxford University Press. © Oxford University Press India 2022. DOI: 10.1093/oso/9780190130596.003.0005

This chapter aims to construct a measure of sectoral diversification at the state level in the form of a diversity index (DV) and examine the differences in the state-level index values across two periods: 2004–5 and 2011–12. We deepen this analysis by constructing the index at the NSS region level and contend that it is diversification and not specialization that dominates the composition of regional economy in India. We also claim that in the last decade there has been a marked shift towards greater sectoral diversification across states in India.

We further examine the association of sectoral diversity with two specific macro-economic aspects, namely scale economies and skill intensity. These two facets are expected to go hand in hand with high levels of diversification and deserve a detailed examination.

Scale Economies

Enterprises obtain certain advantages due to size, output, or scale of operation, with the cost per unit generally decreasing with as scale increases, since fixed costs are spread out over more units. If scale economies did not exist, industries would be dispersed in order to minimize the transport cost. Hence, variables denoting size such as population, area, density, and so on, are used to reflect scale and are expected to be closely related to sectoral diversity, drawing from the literature that larger economic units such as large cities, regions, or states are expected to encourage a wider range of activities. This brings down costs and pushes up the average total productivity (Ciccone and Hall 1996; Combes 2000). The underlying argument is that larger economic units encourage heterogeneity of economic activities and increase the range of products available for consumers as well as producers. This is done via two routes: one is market size, which enables access to a wider array of goods and services for the firm and the consumer; and the second is technological spillovers which expand the production possibility frontier and raise the level of output (Abdel-Rahman 1988). We will test the veracity of these claims in the course of our analysis.

Skill Intensity

A diversified economy is expected to be much more amenable to opportunities that match the region's technology and labour force. To capture new activities, any economy needs to be flexible to mix and match possible technologies, inputs, and skill sets, with specific emphasis on knowledge-oriented human capital. A number of studies at the industry level have documented within-sector shifts in the composition of employment towards jobs requiring higher skill levels as the operations become more technologically complex (Quigley 1998; Rosenthal and Strange 2001). This would hold particularly in the case of formal jobs, more commonly termed as 'regular' employment. This could also imply a shift away from labour-intensive jobs, depicted by changes in the workforce participation rate, especially if it is a case of jobless growth. We take all of these factors together to denote the skill intensity of the workforce. In fact, in service predominant economies such as India, the Organization for Economic Corporation and Development (OECD) opines that skill intensity is expected to be a better measure of technical intensity than R&D intensity (OECD 2011). It is, therefore, essential to empirically test whether sectoral diversity is indeed closely associated with the skill intensity of the workforce.

The existing literature clearly outlines the importance of sectoral diversity in the context of regional economic outcomes. While there have been a few studies that have underscored the importance of diversity in the Indian context (Lall and Chakravorty 2005; Mukim and Nunnenkamp 2012; Ghani et al. 2014), this volume, to the best of our knowledge, would be the first instance of an empirical study in India that involves construction as a separate sector and a comparison of the diversity index at the state and regional levels across two points in time, estimating its relationship with scale economies and skill intensity.

Approach and Measurements

We construct a measure for diversity, namely the diversity index, to represent the extent of sectoral diversity in the economy. We consider a set of variables indicative of size-related characteristics to denote scale economies, and a set of variables indicative of labour-market characteristics representative of skill intensity, as elaborated presently in this section.

Our estimation model follows (Combes 2000) and takes the following reduced-form equation for each region:

$$DV_r = f\left(S, L, \varepsilon\right) \tag{1}$$

Where DV is the level of sectoral diversity as measured by the diversity index, S represents scale economies, L stands for skill intensity, and E for other factors, each being measured for region r.

We first analyse data for 2011–12, since it is the most recent year for which data is available, to test our hypotheses. We calculate the correlation of each parameter with the diversity index of the region in order to assess whether the parameters contributing to scale economies (namely area, population, and population density) and skill intensity (namely higher levels of skills, workforce participation, and regular employment) are associated with the greater sectoral diversity in the state or not.

We further strengthen our regression by drawing comparisons between the diversity index values of 2011–12 with those of 2004–5, carrying out cross sectional analyses using ordinary least squares (OLS) for 2004–5 and 2011–12 as well as a pooled regression at the state level. This is followed by calculating estimates for all of the above at the NSS region level to assess if these parameters continue to stay significant at the regional level. Therefore, we apply the OLS model both at the state and the NSS region levels.

We now present the detailed approach on variable construction.

Measuring Diversity: We construct a diversity index using occupational shares as the basis, in accordance with certain empirical studies (Lall and Chakravorty 2005), by converting the percentage employment shares by industry into ratios. We calculate the Hirschman Herfindahl Index 'Hr', which gives an index of concentration.

$$H_r = \Sigma_j \left[\frac{E_{jr}}{E_r}\right]^2 \tag{2}$$

Such that H_r is the sum of squares of employment shares of all industries j in region r.

The inverse of this, also known as the Simpson Index, can be interpreted as representing diversity. Therefore, the diversity index (DV) is given by:

$$DV_r = 1 - H_r \tag{3}$$

DV takes values in the range of 0 to 1. A score nearing 1 indicates a very high level of industrial diversity, while a score closer to 0 indicates that the regional economy is driven only by one or two key industries. In other words, a higher value of DV represents greater sectoral diversity in the concerned state. For state-level calculations, r is replaced by the subscript s to denote the unit of the state. For NSS region–level calculations, r denotes the NSS region.

Scale Economies: Scale economies are said to arise from the enlargement of the total size of the location under consideration. This size can be denoted by population, income, output, wealth, and so on. Several studies have used regional size to study the benefits accruing external to the industry in an area and have taken local population as a measure of the same (Sveikauskas 1975; Tabuchi 1986; Ciccone and Hall 1996). Greater the number of persons in a region, greater is the demand for goods and services, as also the ability to produce. This results in a larger market for varied goods and services and is expected to go hand in hand with inter-industry linkages, and hence diversity. Another straightforward measure of size is the geographic area measured in square kilometre. Population density is yet another measure which factors in both population and area. This follows the logic that concentrated populations provide a greater opportunity for colocation of sectors such as telecommunication, financial services, and so on. We expect that diversity index values would be higher in states with a more concentrated market demand, especially since the existing literature points towards size and diversity being positively associated.

Measuring Skill Intensity: This book adopts a direct approach to capture skill intensity, with more recently available data in the Indian context, as outlined in Chapter 3. Consider three aspects of the labour market that are relevant—workforce participation rate, proportion of highly skilled workers, and share of regular employment. For the purpose of our analysis, we consider the share of regular wage employment as a proportion of the total, as it represents formal sector employment which is expected to fuel a higher level of skill intensity. We also consider the skill levels as outlined in NCO 2004 and use the percentage share of level IV skills. We expect that high levels of diversity would be associated with higher skill levels, greater incidence of regular employment, and possibly a decline in the workforce participation rate as the economy moves away from labour-intensive sectors and means of production.

We further introduce a region-specific dimension of 'proximity to the coast'. We expect that coastal regions experience greater sectoral diversity. We argue that proximity to ports and external markets may result in coastal areas experiencing more rapid diversification as service providers, assemblers, or even manufacturers of goods and services. We introduce a coastal dummy 'Cd' to test for this. The set of variables considered are listed in Table 5.1.

Analysis of Economic Diversity

In this section, we seek to understand diversity, given the variation between states and in regions with respect to the sectoral mix. We divide this analysis into three segments: first, we present the values of the diversity index, its ranking across states, and its concentration towards higher values from a comparative perspective; second, we test the veracity of the claims on diversity and size-related variables being used interchangeably; and third, we test whether diversity appears to have an association with skill intensity based on the most recent data estimates. We focus on the state level as well as the regional picture.

Have Diversity Levels Increased Over Time and Space?

Indian states and regions are characterized by high levels of diversity in their economic structure. In addition, over the last decade the move towards higher diversity has intensified.

To substantiate this, we analyse the diversity index values that have been calculated for each state over the two periods under study, following the methodology outlined in the previous section. Table 5.2 provides the

Table 5.1 Variables and Data Sources

Nature of Indicator	Variables	Variable Name	Measurement	Data Source
Sectoral diversity	Diversity index	DV	$DV_r = 1 - H_r$ denoting the sectoral mix scale of 0 to 1	Constructed based on sectoral shares for 14 categories based on NIC codes from the 61st and 68th round NSSO surveys
Scale economies	Population	POPN	No of persons in the state/ region	Census of India 2001 and 2011
	Geographical Area	AREA	Geographical area of the state/ region as measured in km. square.	Census of India 2001 and 2011
	Population Density	POPDEN	Total population of the state/region divided by geographical area	Census of India 2001 and 2011
Skill Intensity	Share of high end skills	SKILLIV	Proportion of total workforce having level IV skills corresponding to occupations 0 to 2 as per the NCO codes	61st and 68th Round NSSO surveys
	Share of Regular Employment	REGEMP	Proportion of total workforce engaged in regular employment	
	Workforce Participation Rate	WPR	Proportion of population engaged in work as per UPS	
Proximity to the Coast	Coastal Dummy	Cd	Takes the value of 1 for states having a coastal boundary and 0 for states with no coastal boundary	Assigned by the author
Time	Year dummy	Yd (applicable only for the pooled analysis)	Takes the value of 1 for the year 2011–12, and 0 for the base year 2004–5)	N.A.

Table 5.2 Descriptive Statistics—Diversity Index

Statistics	2004–5	2011–12
Mean	0.6597	0.7288
SD	0.137	0.106
CV	20.70	14.57
Range	0.39 – 0.86	0.45 – 0.89
Difference	0.4638	0.4345
DV Ratio	2.17	1.95

Source: Authors' calculations basis NSSO surveys 61st and 68th round

comparative descriptive statistics of DV values. If we focus on the 2011–12 figures, we find that on a scale of 0 to 1, the mean DV is 0.73, which is on the higher side. DV values on the whole range from 0.45 to 0.89. Standard deviation (SD) is low at 0.106, indicating that the variations of DV values about the mean are not very substantial.

If we compare this with the 2004–5 values, we find that the mean has shifted up from 0.66 to 0.73. At the same time, the standard deviation and the coefficient of variation have reduced from 0.13 to 0.10 and from 20.17 to 14.5 respectively. In other words, while the overall level of the DV has gone up significantly, the variations between states have reduced. This is corroborated by the reduction in the difference between the highest and the lowest values, as also by the ratio between the two. This represents a shift, on the whole, towards a higher level of diversity across the board.

It is useful to examine whether state-level data corroborates this pattern. We classify the states along their scores on the basis of the diversity index. Given the substantial regional variations, we categorize them into four broad ranges of the diversity index. Values below the average DV of 2004–5 can be considered as reflecting low DV. We, therefore, classify DV values equal to or less than 0.64 as 'Low DV', between 0.65 and 0.74 as 'Low Middle DV', between 0.75 and 0.84 as 'High Middle DV', and above 0.85 as 'High DV' (Table 5.3 and Maps 5.1 and 5.2).

Table 5.3 outlines the frequency distribution of DV values across the four classifications from High to Low DV for 2011–12 and superimposes this against the values for 2004–5. We find that the distribution across class intervals has changed. The number of High DV states has increased

Table 5.3 Diversity Index—Classification of States

DV Classification	Range	Frequency 2004–5	Frequency 2011–12
High DV	0.85=<	3	6
High Middle (HM) DV	0.75-0.84	7	8
Low Middle (LM) DV	0.65-0.74	5	10
Low DV	<=0.64	17	8

Source: Authors' calculations basis NSSO surveys 61st and 68th round.

from 3 to 6; High Middle DV has increased from 7 to 8; Low Middle DV from 5 to 10; while Low DV states are down by half, from 17 to 8. This clearly indicates that the number of states in the Low and Low Middle DV range have reduced, marking a move towards higher diversity levels.

A state-wise comparison of both periods as presented in Table 5.4 ranks the states in order of diversity levels along with colour codes for each diversity slab. High DV state are highlighted in dark grey, High Middle DV in medium grey, Low Middle DV in light grey and Low DV in very light grey.

States with lower DV levels have moved into higher DV levels between the two periods, with the number of states in the low DV level down by half. Manipur and Uttarakhand stand out as two states which have moved from Low DV in 2004–5 to High Middle DV in 2011–12. With more defense troops moving into Manipur and Uttarakhand coming into its own as a state with tax incentives to attract industry, it is possible that both these states have witnessed an increase in the share of public administration and related sectors.

A closer look reveals that low diversity (0.45–0.65) is experienced the most in central India and in the Northeast. These regions have not been substantially penetrated by industry, and it is only in the last couple of years that Madhya Pradesh and Chhattisgarh have emerged as industrial investment destinations as well. In the low-middle category (0.651–0.75), we find a mix of states across the south, east, north, and west, such as Maharashtra, Gujarat, Karnataka, and Andhra Pradesh. The high-middle category (0.751–0.85) has some of the more prosperous states of the north, such as Punjab and Haryana, along with the industrialized states of Tamil Nadu and West Bengal. The high category (0.851–0.90) largely

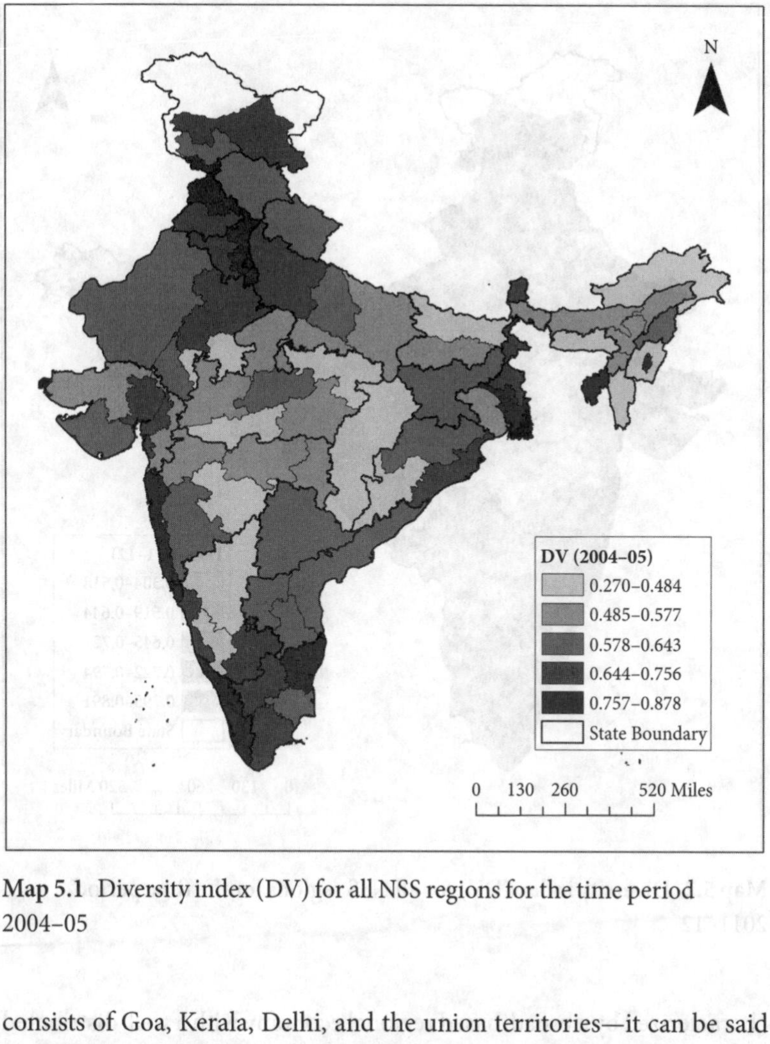

Map 5.1 Diversity index (DV) for all NSS regions for the time period 2004–05

consists of Goa, Kerala, Delhi, and the union territories—it can be said that these states are representative of much more compact geographies, most of which have a coastal boundary.

We deepen this analysis by constructing the diversity index (DV) for all NSS regions for both periods. A focused look at the top 25 regions by DV value gives an indication of how DV values and their distribution have changed over the two periods. The number of regions in the High DV slab has doubled from 5 to 10 between 2004–5 and 2011–12. We find that the degree of sectoral diversification in India has increased, with 31 out of 85 regions having a DV value greater than 0.75. These regions are

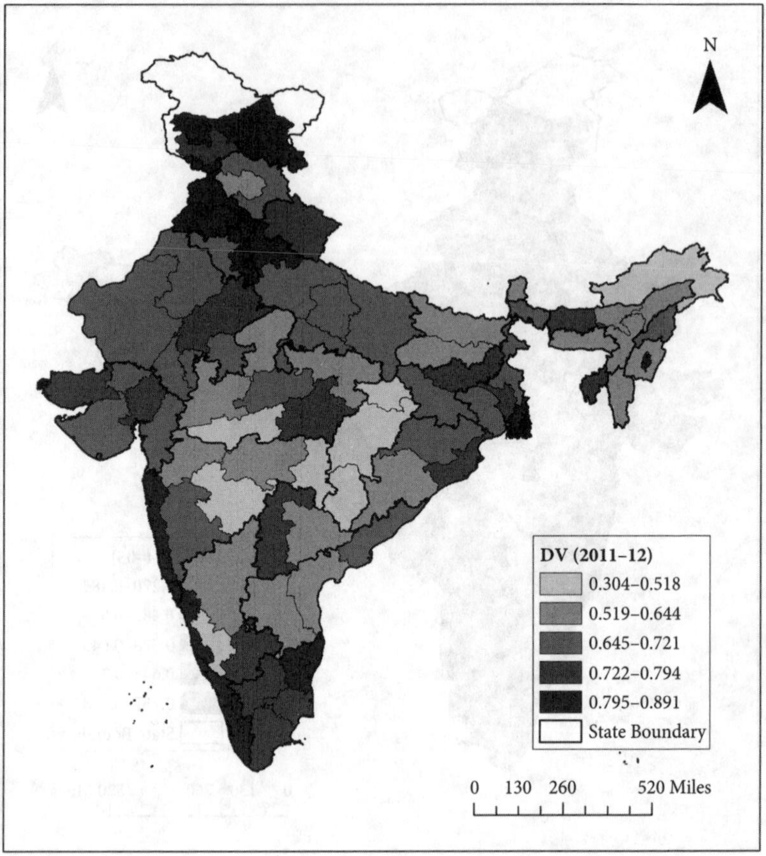

Map 5.2 Diversity index (DV) for all NSS regions for the time period 2011–12

characterized by a broad-based regional economy with a well-distributed share of three or four industrial sectors.

As evident from Table 5.5, the top 10 regions by DV are all in the west and the north, covering the western coast, certain union territories, and parts of Jammu and Kashmir. Pondicherry is the only exception in this case. The bottom 10 regions by DV are in eastern and central India, covering parts of Maharashtra, Chhattisgarh, Madhya Pradesh, Bihar, and the Northeast.

Table 5.4 State-Wise Variations in Diversity: 2004–5 to 2011–12

State	2004–5 DV	Rank	State	2011–12 DV	Rank
Chandigarh	0.8611	1	Goa	0.8912	1
Goa	0.8572	2	Pondicherry	0.8714	2
Andaman	0.8542	3	Andaman	0.8672	3
Delhi	0.8412	4	Kerala	0.8602	4
Pondicherry	0.8293	5	Chandigarh	0.8522	5
Kerala	0.8288	6	Delhi	0.8502	6
Punjab	0.8027	7	Punjab	0.8409	7
Tripura	0.8014	8	Jammu and Kashmir	0.8319	8
Jammu and Kashmir	0.7705	9	Tamil Nadu	0.8015	9
Haryana	0.7676	10	Haryana	0.7938	10
Tamil Nadu	0.7314	11	Tripura	0.7785	11
West Bengal	0.7307	12	West Bengal	0.7746	12
Sikkim	0.6742	13	Manipur	0.7685	13
Maharashtra	0.6648	14	Uttaranchal	0.7549	14
Gujarat	0.6539	15	Maharashtra	0.7386	15
Uttar Pradesh	0.6444	16	Jharkhand	0.7381	16
Rajasthan	0.6389	17	Uttar Pradesh	0.7227	17
Andhra Pradesh	0.6254	18	Gujarat	0.7178	18
Manipur	0.6230	19	Rajasthan	0.7163	19
Jharkhand	0.6184	20	Karnataka	0.7137	20
Nagaland	0.6134	21	Andhra Pradesh	0.6893	21
Himachal Pradesh	0.6125	22	Orissa	0.6826	22
Orissa	0.6013	23	Assam	0.6717	23
Uttaranchal	0.6008	24	Nagaland	0.6634	24
Karnataka	0.5784	25	Meghalaya	0.6436	25
Assam	0.5550	26	Himachal Pradesh	0.6434	26
Madhya Pradesh	0.5166	27	Mizoram	0.6414	27
Mizoram	0.4836	28	Madhya Pradesh	0.6340	28
Bihar	0.4701	29	Sikkim	0.6006	29
Meghalaya	0.4499	30	Bihar	0.5917	30
Arunachal Pradesh	0.4120	31	Arunachal Pradesh	0.5177	31
Chattisgarh	0.3972	32	Chattisgarh	0.4567	32

Source: Authors' calculations basis NSSO surveys 61st and 68th rounds

Table 5.5 Region-Wise Variations in Diversity: 2004–5 to 2011–12

Region Name (2004–5)	DV	Rank	Region Name (2011–12)	DV	Rank
Andaman and Nicobar Islands	0.8776	1	Goa	0.8912	1
Goa	0.8681	2	Pondicherry	0.8714	2
Chandigarh	0.8611	3	Coastal Maharashtra	0.8695	3
Southern Kerala	0.8589	4	Southern Kerala	0.8677	4
Coastal Maharashtra	0.8542	5	Andaman and Nicobar Islands	0.8672	5
Pondicherry	0.8455	6	Mountainous Jammu	0.8588	6
Northern Punjab (Majha-Doaba)	0.843	7	Northern Punjab (Majha-Doaba)	0.8587	7
Delhi	0.8412	8	Chandigarh	0.8522	8
South Bengal Plains	0.8348	9	Delhi	0.8502	9
Mountainous Jammu	0.818	10	Ladakh, Jammu and Kashmir	0.85	10
Northern Kerala	0.8107	11	Northern Kerala	0.8454	11
Eastern Haryana	0.8019	12	Coastal Northern Tamil Nadu	0.8418	12
Tripura	0.8018	13	Jhelum Valley, Jammu and Kashmir	0.8374	13
Manipur Plains	0.8004	14	South Bengal Plains	0.8366	14
Coastal Northern Tamil Nadu	0.7759	15	Eastern Haryana	0.8328	15
Jhelum Valley, Jammu and Kashmir	0.7564	16	Coastal and Ghats, Karnataka	0.8244	16
Coastal and Ghats, Karnataka	0.7498	17	Southern Punjab (Malwa)	0.823	17
Southern Tamil Nadu	0.7408	18	Manipur Plains	0.8215	18
Dry areas, Gujarat	0.7324	19	Northern Upper Ganga Plains, Uttar Pradesh	0.8211	19
Northern Plains, Gujarat	0.732	20	Inland Southern Karnataka	0.7945	20
Northern Upper Ganga Plains, Uttar Pradesh	0.7232	21	Inland Tamil Nadu	0.7857	21

Table 5.5 *Continued*

Region Name (2004–5)	DV	Rank	Region Name (2011–12)	DV	Rank
Inland Tamil Nadu	0.7159	22	Southern Tamil Nadu	0.7826	22
Southern Punjab (Malwa)	0.6875	23	Inland North Western Maharashtra	0.7785	23
Inland Southern Karnataka	0.6873	24	Tripura	0.7785	24
North-Eastern Rajasthan	0.6795	25	Western Assam Plains	0.7753	25

Source: Authors' calculations basis NSSO surveys 61st and 68th rounds

Are Size and Diversity Positively Associated?

In keeping with the existing literature, scale economies—as denoted by size-related variables—are reliable proxies for sectoral diversity.

We follow this classification of states along DV values and tabulate the average value for each variable representing scale economies for states in each slab. We find that population and geographic area do not follow any consistent pattern. Ideally, one would expect higher average values of population and geographic area to be associated with higher levels of diversity. But as we move down the columns of Table 5.6, we do not perceive any consistent trends. In the case of population density, we find marked increases only at very high diversity levels. From a correlation standpoint, however, our results reveal a negative correlation between size and diversity. The correlation value of -0.015, as also the state-wise population figures in order of diversity, does not provide a steady pattern. The Spearman Correlation Coefficient for diversity and population is 0.01, underscoring the fact that there is a very low positive rank correlation between population and diversity. Geographic size and diversity do not appear to be correlated (+0.045).

A related observation is that extreme values of diversity (starting from high to low) seem to go with lesser geographic size. Areas with a large geographical coverage, such as Uttar Pradesh, Maharashtra, and so on, seem to experience moderate levels of diversity, indicating that index values

Table 5.6 Scale Economies (State) by Diversity Slabs 2011–12

Categories	Intervals	Freq.	DV	POP	AREA	POPDEN
Low DV	<=0.64	8	0.59	23,521,319	90,954	242
Low Middle DV	0.65-0.74	11	0.710	62,636,391	188,440	338
High Middle DV	0.75-0.84	7	0.799	28,158,258	77,740	472
High DV	0.85=<	6	0.865	7,989,149	8,817	4074

Source: Authors' calculations basis NSSO survey 68th round, Population Census 2011

possibly even out across large regions. The rank correlation (ρ = 0.05) here is again close to zero. It indicates that sectoral diversity may not necessarily be a function of geographic size. It also seems to justify the use of the diversity index as a separate measure, as opposed to using the demographic or geographic size as a parameter by itself.

We now consider population density (POPDEN), which is a ratio of two factors: population/area = persons per sq. km. While population and area alone may capture size, density brings in a concentration element to the concept of size. The correlation matrix shows a moderate positive relationship between population density and diversity (+0.36). From our categorization of states by the diversity index, we find that only at very high levels of diversity does population density assume higher values as diversity increases (Table 5.7). For states in the 'high density' bracket, the population density increases by almost 10 times. This could also be particularly attributed to a few extremely high-density locations such as New Delhi and Chandigarh that might skew the results. The ρ values through the rank correlation of DV with POPDEN (+0.53) further reflect a strong positive correlation, conveying that states with very high scores on the diversity index have a greater density of population. We find that similar patterns hold at the NSS region level as well

What about the case of the city? Is it possible to argue that while our analysis may hold at the state and the regional levels, the city is a very specific case, and that the DV index and size may be seen as closely associated in more concentrated locations? Therefore, we take a step further and construct diversity indexes for the 27 million-plus cities identified as per the 68th round of the NSS based on the 2001 census population.

Table 5.7 Scale Economies (Region) by Diversity Slabs 2011–12

Categories	Range	No	DV	POPN	AREA	POPDEN
Low DV	<=0.64	28	0.57	12,668,566	44,537	275
Low Middle DV	0.65–0.74	26	0.69	16,960,409	45,238	403
High Middle DV	0.75–0.84	21	0.80	15,386,023	30,220	601
High DV	0.85=<	10	0.86	8,378,435	15,180	2,640

Source: Authors' calculations basis NSSO surveys 68th round, Population Census 2011

We find that among the million-plus cities in Table 5.8, the rank correlation between size and diversity is quite low at 0.27. The positive value suggests that the larger the city, the higher is the extent of industrial diversity. The low value can be attributed to the fact that larger agglomerations which rank high on size would, in reality, form the core metropolitan area. It is to be noted that the suburbs or satellite regions such as Kalyan-Dombivali, Thane, and Pimpri-Chinchwad are among the top four million-plus cities in terms of industrial diversity. They rank higher than Greater Mumbai or the Delhi Metropolitan region. Cities such as Greater Bombay, Bangalore, and so on, represent the urban core, which is known to have greater concentration.

The rise of the suburbs of Kalyan-Dombivali and Thane is evident from the table and finds an echo in the literature which shows that edge cities, or suburbs, have been found to display considerable independence from the nearby central cities and tend to have a more diverse industrial composition than the central cities (Phelps and Ozawa 2003), the central city being Greater Bombay in this case. The principle of borrowed size can be said to operate here, as populations of smaller settlements have access to better amenities of the larger settlements, such as shopping and entertainment facilities. Businesses in small settlements benefit specifically from having access to the wider, more flexible labour markets as well as to the warehousing and business services present in the nearby large urban areas. Similarly, Pimpri-Chinchwad can be considered a million-plus city, which is smaller and therefore borrows from the larger adjacent central city of Pune. This could be a possible explanation as to why the correlation between size and the diversity index is fairly low even in million-plus cities.

Table 5.8 Million-plus Cities Ranked by Diversity 2011–12

City		Region	State	DV
Kalyan-Dombivali	271	Coastal	Maharashtra	0.89
Thane	271	Coastal	Maharashtra	0.88
Hyderabad	283	Inland North Western	Andhra Pradesh	0.88
Pimpri-Chinchwad	272	Inland Western	Maharashtra	0.87
Nagpur	275	Inland Eastern	Maharashtra	0.87
Pune	272	Inland Western	Maharashtra	0.87
Chennai	331	Coastal Northern	Tamil Nadu	0.86
Patna	102	Central	Bihar	0.86
Greater Mumbai	271	Coastal	Maharashtra	0.85
Delhi Municipal	71	Delhi	Delhi	0.85
Meerut	91	Northern Upper Ganga Plains	Uttar Pradesh	0.85
Faridabad	62	Western	Haryana	0.83
Lucknow	92	Central	Uttar Pradesh	0.82
Jaipur	82	North-Eastern	Rajasthan	0.82
Bangalore	293	Inland Southern	Karnataka	0.82
Vadodara	241	South Eastern	Gujarat	0.82
Howrah	193	South Bengal Plains	West Bengal	0.80
Kolkata	194	Central Bengal Plains	West Bengal	0.79
Ludhiana	32	Southern (Malwa)	Punjab	0.77
Ahmedabad	242	Northern Plains	Gujarat	0.77
Agra	95	Southern Upper Ganga Plains	Uttar Pradesh	0.74
Nashik	273	Inland Northern	Maharashtra	0.73
Varanasi	93	Eastern	Uttar Pradesh	0.68
Kanpur	92	Central	Uttar Pradesh	0.67
Bhopal	232	Central	Madhya Pradesh	0.56
Surat	241	South Eastern	Gujarat	0.55
Indore	233	Malwa	Madhya Pradesh	0.32

Source: Authors' calculations basis NSSO surveys 68th round.

We, therefore, conclude that the standard size-related parameters of population and geographic area do not go hand in hand with diversification as there is little or no correlation between them in the Indian context. While the density of population may be considered as representing market size, its linkage to diversity is, at best, nuanced and hence may not be considered as a proxy either. Our analysis shows that this holds not only at the state level but also at the NSS region level. We go a step further to the city level since the million-plus cities framing is available for 2011–12 and prove that this correlation does not hold even at the city level.

Are Skill Intensity and Diversity Positively Associated?

High levels of diversity are associated with high levels of skill intensity. We tabulate the average values of variables denoting skill intensity across the diversity slabs. The distribution of skill levels across the diversity slabs provides a striking and clear trend of a shift in skill composition at higher values of the diversity index. As we move down the columns in Table 5.9, from lower to higher levels of diversity at the state level, we find a pronounced increase in the share of high-level skills from 8 per cent to 26 per cent. There is also a marked increase in the share of regular employment (REGEMP) at higher levels of diversity, with the highest slab registering an average of almost 50 per cent employment as being regular in nature. Workforce participation rate (WPR), an important labour market indicator, does not show a positive relationship with diversity; in other words, it is not necessary that in regions with greater diversity, a greater proportion of persons will be engaged in the workforce. This result needs to be examined in greater detail in the regression analysis.

Since the diversity index values are high and the differences between the values are miniscule, we employ Spearman's Rank Correlation

Table 5.9 Skill Intensity (State) by Diversity Slabs **2011–12**

Diversity Slab	Range	Frequency	DV	WPR	REGEMP	SKILL IV
Low DV	< =0.64	8	0.59	41%	16%	8%
Low Middle (LM) DV	0.65-0.74	10	0.71	36%	19%	10%
High Middle (HM) DV	0.75-0.84	8	0.79	33%	23%	13%
High DV	0.85=<	6	0.87	35%	50%	26%

Source: Authors' calculations basis NSSO surveys 68th round

Table 5.10 Skill Intensity (Region) by Diversity Slabs 2011–12

Diversity Slab	Range	No.	DV	WPR	REGEMP	SKILL IV
Low DV	<= 0.64	28	0.57	40%	13%	8%
Low Middle (LM) DV	0.65-0.74	26	0.69	36%	16%	8%
High Middle (HM) DV	0.75-0.84	21	0.80	36%	23%	13%
High DV	0.85=<	10	0.86	35%	47%	22%

Coefficient. As expected, there is a strong positive rank correlation (ρ=0.64) between diversity and level IV skills. This further substantiates the correlation matrix results, which relate high skills to diversity (0.65). The rank correlation exercise gives us a weak negative value for WPR (-0.16) and a strong positive value for regular employment (0.65). These results are in sync with the correlation matrix (Table 5.14), which gives a low negative relationship for diversity with WPR, but a strong positive relationship with the subset of regular employment (0.68). We find similar patterns at the NSS region level with the SKILL IV values ranging from 8 to 22 per cent as we move from low to high levels of diversity.

A large number of regions (28) continue to be in the low DV range, indicative of the fact that there are several regions which are yet to experience growth in multiple sectors. Of the 85 regions, 54 have a skill share of 8 per cent. This implies that although the range may be wider between states, region-level differences are more pronounced.

The next step is to examine the categories of work considered under each type of skill and how they stack up against the diversity slabs. In Table 5.11, each column represents one of the eight occupation types defined by the National Classification of Occupations (NCO), superimposed against the four levels of skills following the OECD classification: low technical intensity, low-medium, high-medium, and high technical intensity. Based on the NCO classifications, it is found that a very high percentage of the workforce handles purely elementary jobs (28.4 per cent). These are low-skilled jobs (skill level I) which include agricultural labourers, construction workers, and so on. Almost 30 per cent of the workforce is engaged in skilled agriculture and fishery work (level II). There is also production-related work which is further subdivided into the categories

Table 5.11 Occupational Classification by Diversity Slabs 2011–12

Technical Intensity Level	**Low**	**Low**	**Low-med**	**Low-med**	**High-med**	**High-med**	**High**	**High**	
State	Elementary Workers	Clerks	Skilled Agricultural and Fisheries Workers	Craft and Related Trades Workers	Plant and Machine Operators and Assemblers	Service Workers Shop Sales workers	Legislators Senior Officials and Managers	Professionals Technicians and Associates	DV
Himachal Pradesh	6.94	1.93	56.14	15.61	2.96	4.92	5.7	5.8	Low
Bihar	40.7	0.38	29.94	9.48	1.7	7.04	6.1	4.63	Low
Sikkim	5.12	1.41	61.74	6.62	3.45	6.35	6.86	8.46	Low
Arunachal Pradesh	8.41	1.86	66.27	3.59	2.18	6.48	1.31	8.54	Low
Mizoram	6.15	2.6	57.32	3.5	2.41	11.53	5.07	11.43	Low
Meghalaya	14.01	1.47	47.07	4.96	3.14	3.58	16.1	9.66	Low
Chattisgarh	37.33	0.82	44.32	4.08	1.49	5.65	2.37	3.82	Low
Madhya Pradesh	27.83	1.39	40.54	10.55	2.68	5.69	6.51	4.8	Low
Uttaranchal	15.8	2.2	40.88	7.7	3.33	6.06	17.75	6.29	LM
Rajasthan	24.3	1.36	43.88	9.13	3.75	7.64	3.35	6.6	LM
Uttar Pradesh	25.55	1.11	38.68	13.74	3.71	7.74	3.93	5.54	LM
Nagaland	1.48	5.11	53.56	4.5	3.08	16.08	2.9	13.29	LM

Table 5.11 *Continued*

Technical Intensity Level	Low	Low	Low-med	Low-med	High-med	High-med	High	High	
Assam	20.95	1.47	43.05	7.2	2.27	11.29	1.5	9.31	LM
Jharkhand	30.53	2.08	40.33	5.13	2.34	3.7	8.87	7.03	LM
Odisha	19.94	0.97	37.53	18.66	2.66	8.42	6.74	5.07	LM
Gujarat	26.27	2.12	29.38	10.19	10.59	8.71	7.37	5.37	LM
Maharashtra	27.13	3.65	26.78	9.72	5.92	7.36	10.37	9.07	LM
Andhra Pradesh	36.08	1.67	25.39	12.71	5.89	7.47	4.73	6.05	LM
Karnataka	26.85	2.56	28.79	9.7	4.84	4.71	14.53	8.02	LM
Jammu and Kashmir	29.02	2.82	22.78	13.07	4.66	14.73	3.61	9.16	HM
Punjab	25.08	2.51	18.25	18.6	7.69	8.98	10.46	8.43	HM
Haryana	24.51	1.69	30.54	10.37	5.99	5.54	10.41	10.76	HM
Manipur	11.93	2.36	40.86	12.7	4.3	17.61	0.24	9.87	HM
Tripura	40.32	1.98	23.44	4.55	1.76	5.23	0.19	20.22	HM
West Bengal	35.42	2.4	14.15	20.37	4.21	10.22	5.81	7.36	HM
Tamil Nadu	30.71	2.62	12.98	21.7	8.32	8.28	7.78	7.54	HM
Chandigarh	12.88	5.94	0.35	12.24	3.84	16.54	26.31	21.91	High
Delhi	13.01	8.59	0.17	14.49	10.98	11.55	23.91	17.07	High
Goa	18.66	11.75	2.91	4.24	8.68	12.17	25.47	16.12	High
Kerala	21.29	2.72	13.87	21.19	8.07	12.98	9.1	10.78	High

Source: Authors' calculations basis NSSO surveys 68th round.

of craftsmen (12.87 per cent), operators (4.99 per cent), and so on, which forms almost 16 per cent of the workforce (level II). Professionals and technical skilled workers account for 14 per cent of employment (level III and IV).

We find that elementary and agricultural jobs are more predominant in the low DV states, whereas high-medium and high technical intensity jobs are more aligned with the higher DV states. One exception, however, is that the share of elementary workers is high in certain high DV states such as Tamil Nadu, Kerala, Tripura, and West Bengal. This could be due to the incidence of unorganized sector jobs in some of these states.

Figure 5.1 depicts this at a regional level in a summarized form. The x-axis has the regions by DV slabs and the y-axis has skill levels I, II, III, and IV (average values) for each slab. This graphical representation helps us understand the shift better since it provides a bifurcation across skill levels. We find that the share of high-end professional skills (skill level IV) increases as we go from the low to high DV regions.

In fact, one can say that level III and IV skill shares are higher in states with higher DV. Skill level II forms the largest part of employment. The

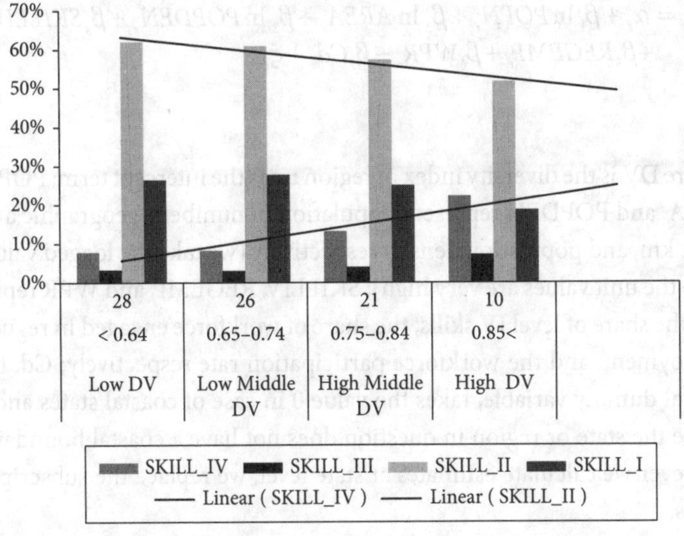

Figure 5.1 Skill Levels (Region) by Diversity Slabs 2011–12

Source: Authors' calculations basis NSSO surveys 68th round.

share of skill level II comes down with increase in diversity. Interestingly, the share of elementary jobs (skill level I) is low in case of states with very high DV. Their share is highest in the 'High Middle DV' regions, possibly indicative that the share of elementary jobs increases with diversity up to a point, beyond which the nature of jobs evolves to increase the share of skill levels III and IV instead.

This data is presented in the form of a preliminary analysis on regional trends and shares across occupational classifications. We propose to analyse this further to examine whether greater industrial diversity results in a more skilled workforce.

Determinants of Economic Diversity

Having established that states and regions in India are moving towards higher levels of sectoral diversity, and with significant differences in the variables under consideration, it is important to study the impact of scale economies and skill intensity on the economic structure of states and regions.

The expanded equation of 5.1 takes the form:

$$DV_r = \alpha_r + \beta_1 \ln POPN_r + \beta_2 \ln AREA_r + \beta_3 \ln POPDEN_r + \beta_4 SKILLIV_r + \beta_5 REGEMP_r + \beta_6 WPR_r + \beta_7 Cd_r + \xi_r \tag{4}$$

Where DV is the diversity index of region r;*a* is the intercept term; POPN, AREA, and POPDEN represent population in numbers, geographic area in sq. km, and population density respectively (we take the logged values since the unit values are very high); SKILLIV, REGEMP, and WPR represent the share of level IV skills, the share of workforce engaged in regular employment, and the workforce participation rate respectively; Cd, the coastal dummy variable, takes the value 0 in case of coastal states and 1 where the state or region in question does not have a coastal boundary; wherever we calculate estimates at state level, we replace the subscript r with s.

We study the determinants of diversity by first carrying out a cross sectional analysis for 2004–5 (Model 1a) and 2011–12 (Model 1b) at the state level to study the relationship of diversity with the attributes of size and skills. We also carry out a pooled regression (Model 2) at the state level, covering both periods 2004–5 and 2011–12. We then take the analysis to another level of granularity by doing a cross sectional analysis at the region level for 2004–5 (Model 3a) and 2011–12 (Model 3b), with an exclusive focus on variables that are significant at the state level to test if the same analysis holds at the region level. We extend this further through a pooled regression (Model 4) at the region level, covering both periods for the subset of significant variables.

The four models are represented by the following equations:

$$DV_s = \alpha_s + \beta_1 \ln POPN_S + \beta_2 \ln AREA_S + \beta_3 \ln POPDEN_S + \beta_4 SKILLIV_S + \beta_5 REGEMP_S + \beta_6 WPR_S + \beta_7 Cd_s + \xi_s$$

Model 1 (4a)

$$DV_s = \alpha_s + \beta_1 \ln POPN_S + \beta_2 \ln AREA_S + \beta_3 \ln POPDEN_S + \beta_4 SKILLIV_S + \beta_5 REGEMP_S + \beta_6 WPR_S + \beta_7 Cd_S + \xi_s + Yd$$

Model 2 (4b)

$$DV_r = \alpha_r + \beta_1 \ln POPN_r + \beta_2 \ln AREA_r + \beta_3 \ln POPDEN_r + \beta_4 SKILLIV_r + \beta_5 REGEMP_r + \beta_6 WPR_r + \beta_7 Cd_r + \xi_r$$

Model 3 (4c)

$$DV_r = \alpha_r + \beta_1 \ln POPN_r + \beta_2 \ln AREA_r + \beta_3 \ln POPDEN_r + \beta_4 SKILLIV_r + \beta_5 REGEMP_r + \beta_6 WPR_r + \beta_7 Cd_r + \xi_r + Yd$$

Model 4 (4d)

Table 5.12 depicts the mean, the standard deviation, and the minimum and maximum values for variables for the year 2011–12. It explains that the mean value of the diversity index for Indian states is 0.72 with a standard deviation of 0.10. The states experience a high variation in terms of variables depicting scale economies. Population per sq. km ranges from 17 to 11,297, the extreme values representing Arunachal Pradesh and Delhi respectively. The share of highly skilled workers and regular employment shows very high variations. Table 5.13 reflects the same at the regional level. Here, the mean DV stands at 0.70, but the standard

Table 5.12 State Level—Summary Statistics 2011–12

Characteristic	Variable	Variable Name	Unit	Observations	Mean	Std. Dev.	Min	Max
DIVERSITY	Diversity Index	DV	%	32	0.73	0.11	0.46	0.89
SCALE ECONOMIES	Geographic Area	AREA	Sq. Km.	31	104773	105361	114	342239
SCALE ECONOMIES	Population Density	POPDEN	Persons/ Sq. Km	32	1043	2482	17	11297
SKILL INTENSITY	Highly Skilled Workers	SKILLIV	%	32	0.13	0.083	0.04	0.35
SKILL INTENSITY	Regular Employment	REGEMP	%	32	0.25	0.15	0.06	0.63
SKILL INTENSITY	Workforce Participation	WPR	%	32	0.36	0.06	0.26	0.52

Source: Authors' calculations basis NSSO surveys 68th round.

Table 5.13 Region Level—Summary Statistics 2011–12

Characteristic	Variable	Variable Name	Unit	Observations	Mean	SD	Min	Max
DIVERSITY	Diversity Index	DV	%	85	0.70	0.12	0.30	0.89
SCALE ECONOMIES	Geographic Area	AREA	Sq. Km.	85	37760	25107	114	145045
SCALE ECONOMIES	Population Density	POPDEN	Persons/ Sq. Km	85	673	1560	5	11282
SKILL INTENSITY	Highly Skilled Workers	WPR	%	85	0.37	0.06	0.26	0.52
SKILL INTENSITY	Regular Employment	REGEMP	%	85	0.20	0.13	0.05	0.63
SKILL INTENSITY	Workforce Participation	SKILL IV	%	85	0.11	0.07	0.02	0.35

Source: Authors' calculations basis NSSO surveys 68th round

deviation is slightly higher at 0.12. Skill differences are slightly more pronounced, ranging from 2 to 35 per cent, while population density has a lower minimum value of 5 persons per sq. ft, for Ladakh as a sub region of Jammu and Kashmir.

Tables 5.14 and 5.15 show the correlation matrix between the variables used in the study, both at the state and the regional levels. As seen from

Table 5.14 Correlation Matrix (State)

	DV	POPN	AREA	POPDEN	WPR	SKILLIV	REGEMP
DV	1						
POPN	-0.0333	1					
AREA	-0.2511	0.5352	1				
POPDEN	0.3805	-0.1107	-0.2703	1			
WPR	-0.451	-0.2515	0.1296	-0.2116	1		
SKILLIV	0.6619	-0.2407	-0.4311	0.6983	-0.1686	1	
REGEMP	0.6922	-0.2834	-0.427	0.7064	-0.1498	0.8593	1

Table 5.15 Correlation Matrix (Region)

	DV	POPN	AREA	POPDEN	WPR	REGEMP	SKILLSIV
DV	1						
POPN	0.0451	1					
AREA	-0.2962	0.4038	1				
POPDEN	0.2885	0.0625	-0.2909	1			
WPR	-0.3517	-0.267	0.1144	-0.1615	1		
REGEMP	0.6744	-0.1508	-0.3676	0.5304	-0.0279	1	
SKILL_IV	0.5406	-0.0627	-0.3228	0.5272	-0.0906	0.7507	1

Source: Authors' calculations basis NSSO surveys 68th round.

the tables, diversity has a strong positive correlation with high skill levels and regular employment. This implies that states with a diversified economic base tend to have a more skilled workforce earning regular wages. Interestingly these are also positively correlated with population density, indicating that states with denser populations might experience higher levels of skills. Geographic area seems to either be unrelated or have a very low correlation with diversity.

We find a high correlation between regular employment and the share of professional skills. This could be because persons with professional skills are more likely to get regular employment, which then helps in the setting up of more durable industries across sectors, enabling better matching of labour to different types of jobs and requirements. Due to the high correlation of REGEMP and SKILL IV, we drop the variable REGEMP in our regression analysis, since it appears that its attributes might be captured in the SKILL IV variable itself.

We now discuss the results of the four models, applied to analyse sectoral diversity and its determinants.

Table 5.16 depicts the results of OLS applied at state level for cross sectional and pooled data (Models 1 and 2). As can be observed, the coefficient of determination (Adjusted R-squared) is moderate and the F value is statistically significant; therefore, the results can be interpreted meaningfully. Since variables such as population, area, and population density are part of the equation, the data is tested for multi-collinearity using the variance inflation factor (VIF). We also apply the Breusch-Pagan/Cook-Weisberg test for heteroscedasticity and find evidence of the same. Therefore, we report our results with robust standard errors and find that in the cross sectional analysis provided in models 1a and 1b, skill intensity is significant at 5 per cent, the coastal dummy is also significant at 5 per cent, and both have a positive coefficient. On the other hand, none of the scale economy variables are significant in their relationship with diversity. Workforce participation rate is significant at 5 per cent, but has a negative coefficient.

Model 2 provides the results of the state-level pooled regression model for 2004–5 and 2011–12. The coefficient of determination is high at 0.67 and the F value is significant. Skills IV and WPR are significant at 5 per cent here, along with the coastal dummy. This model can be interpreted more meaningfully, with the mean VIF value at 7.

We take a step further to assess whether this relationship between diversity and skill intensity holds at the NSS region level as well. Having established that size is not a significant determinant of diversity, for the remaining two models we focus our attention on the variables that turn significant at the state level. These are: share of professional skills (SKILL IV), workforce participation rate (WPR), and the presence of a coast (CD). Table 5.17 presents the cross sectional analysis for 2004–5 (Model 3a) and 2011–12 (Model 3b) at the region level with specific focus on these variables. We find that in this model the VIF values come down

Table 5.16. State Level Determinants of Sectoral Diversity

State Level - Variables	Variable Name	Model 1a 2004–5		Model 1b 2011–12		Model 2 Pooled	
		Coef.	t-value	Coef.	t-value	Coef.	t-value
Population (logged)	LogPOP	-0.01	-1.55	-0.188	-0.93	-0.005	-0.93
Area (logged)	LogAREA	0.009	0.78	0.172	0.83	-0.012	-1.69
Population Density (logged)	LogPOPDEN	-0.004	-0.41	0.198	0.93	0.004	0.35
Workforce participation rate	WPR	-1.28	(4.02)***	-0.599	(2.19)**	-0.926	(4.00)***
Share of high-end skills	SKILL IV	1.54	3.13***	0.588	2.92***	0.695	4.04***
Coastal dummy	CD	0.115	5.37***	0.094	3.8***	0.105	6.43***
Constant term	Cons	1.045	4.31***	0.87	3.94***	1.091	6.77***
Year Dummy	YD					-0.075	-1.19
F value		F(6, 25)	26.21	F(6, 25)	9.84	F(7, 56)	26.75
Prob > F			0.000		0.000		0.000
R-squared			0.7776		0.6469		0.7076
Adj R-squared			0.7243		0.5562		0.6711
VIF test			2.33		61		7
Breusch-Pagan Test for Heteroscedasticity							
Chi Square			0.73		2.55		2.88
Probability (Chi Square)			0.393		0.11		0.0897

Table 5.17 Region Level Determinants of Sectoral Diversity

Region Level - Variables	Variable Name	Model 3A 2004–5		Model 3b 2011–12		Model 4 Pooled	
		Coef.	t-value	Coef.	t-value	Coef.	t-value
Share of high end skills	SKILL IV	1.738	7.27***	0.743	6.55***	1.019	9***
Workforce participation rate	WPR	-0.508	(2.9)***	-0.712	(3.98)***	-0.639	(5.09)***
Coastal dummy	CD	0.066	2.86***	0.094	5.11***	0.084	5.42***
Constant term	Cons	0.675	9.33***	0.856	13.28***	0.779	15.43***
Year dummy	YD					0.022	1.51
F Value		F(3, 71)	34.26	F(3, 81)	26.62	F(4, 155)	42.53
Prob > F			0.000		0.000		0.000
R-squared			0.6		0.4886		0.5353
Adj R-squared			0.5832		0.4697		0.5233
VIF Test			1.07		1.09		1.09
Breusch-Pagan Test for Heteroscedasticity							
Chi Square			0.94		4.32		2.24
Probability (Chi Square)			0.3313		0.0376		0.1349

significantly to average at 1.09. More importantly, all independent variables continue to be significant at 5 per cent level, with both SKILL IV and CD having positive coefficients but with WPR having a negative coefficient. Model 4 is an extension of the earlier models and involves a pooled regression for 2004–5 and 2011–12 at the regional level, with specific focus on SKILL IV, WPR, and CD. This method upholds our hypothesis as well since all skill variables are significant at the NSS region level. The fact that the time dummy is insignificant both at the state and the regional levels goes to show that the relationship between diversity and skill intensity holds across both the periods considered.

Based on the four models analysed, we arrive at the following findings:

Scale Economies: In our models, the variables representing size, namely population, geographic area, and population density do not turn significant. The coefficient of population is in fact negative. Geographical area has a negative coefficient in the cross sectional model and turns positive in the pooled analysis. The coefficient of population density is positive, emphasizing that densely populated regions are more likely to have a diversified economic structure, but the results are statistically insignificant, therefore the effect of population density on sectoral diversity cannot be interpreted. This indicates that sheer size represented in absolute terms or through density may not govern the colocation of diverse industries or the differences in diversity across regions, which may be a function of several other factors related to access and markets. This result contradicts the findings of Ciccone and Hall (1996), who conclude that population density explains more than 50 per cent of state productivity differences. At the same time, our findings are in line with Ghani, Kerr, and Tewari (2014) who also do not see a direct association with size and find that the growth of diverse industries is more in rural areas, that too in districts with a low population density. This indicates that while size may be associated with sectoral diversity in a nuanced way, a causation cannot be concluded.

Skill Intensity: In all four models, results of the skill intensity–related variables are statistically significant. This implies that the ability of a region to have a diverse economic base is strongly rooted in its skill intensity. This reaffirms the view of some scholars (Rajan 2006) that in India's case particularly, skill levels of the workforce have been responsible for the differential growth of various regions. The coefficient of higher-level skills is positive and statistically significant, and the coefficient value is also high. This implies that states with a higher share of skilled manpower experience greater diversity in their economic structure, as skilled labour force is able to take up different kinds of activities and match the needs of emerging industries, enabling them to collocate. This is similar to the findings of Berman, Bound, and Machin (1998) who suggest that a 'pervasive' skill-biased technological change was indicated by shifts away from unskilled labour in 12 OECD countries during the 1980s. We drop regular employment due to its high correlation with SKILL IV. A negative and statistically significant coefficient has been obtained for workforce participation rate in all the models. This is an important result as it indicates that regions with high sectoral diversity are characterized by lower workforce participation rates. In other words, expanding the presence of multiple industries need not necessarily create more employment. The demand for higher-end skills with greater productivity and regular employment seems to go hand in hand with a reduction in employment generation, underscoring the jobless growth experienced by the nation in the last several years.

Coastal Dummy: The coastal dummy has a positive coefficient and is statistically significant in all of our models. Hence, we can conclude that access to a coast has a strong impact on sectoral composition and influences diversity. With connectivity to ports, both for inputs and for access to export markets, coastal states have strong incentives to diversify their economic base. This builds on the findings of Lall and Chakravorty (2007) that coastal regions experience cumulative causation and attract more foreign direct investment as well.

Thus, we establish beyond a doubt that size is clearly not a significant influencer of diversity in our analysis and it is the skill level which turns out to be significant time after time, whichever cut of analysis one may consider.

A Varied Palette

We confirm our hypothesis that it is diversification and not concentration that characterizes the regional economy across states in India. We construct a diversity index which measures the level of sectoral diversity and classify the states into four categories based on the diversity index values. We find a large proportion of states at the higher end of the spectrum, as of 2011–12. A comparison with 2004–5 reveals that through this time several states have, indeed, shifted from lower to higher levels of diversity. We calculate the diversity index for all NSS regions across both periods, which reaffirms the move away from specialization and towards diversification at the level of regional economy.

On analysing the determinants of diversity with respect to scale economies, we assert that size- and diversity-related variables cannot be used interchangeably and make a case for applying discretion in the usage of these metrics in the case of Indian as well as for agglomeration analysis in general. Measures such as population, area, population density, and related variables may be used to analyse the size of a region or the market potential, as adopted by several scholars (Tabuchi 1986; Combes 2000), but those seeking to study the sectoral mix in India or the degree of urbanization economies cannot assume that larger regions or markets will have a more diversified economic structure. Studies focusing on diversity or specialization will need to use measures that actually reflect the sectoral mix. We confirm the findings of other authors (Ghani, Kerr, and Tewari 2014) that there are clear examples where diversity is not purely a function of size-related variables.

Skill levels on the other hand turn out to be more important in explaining inter-state and inter-regional differences in the diversification of economic activities. Low levels of infrastructure and labour-intensive manufacturing has meant that the only way to stay competitive is to focus on high-skill industries (Rajan 2006). This is underscored by the fact that workforce participation is inversely associated with diversity, since a significant portion of the workforce in India today is engaged in elementary jobs. Hence, while the development of fresh sectors requires high-end skills, it may not end up creating labour-intensive jobs or employ the bulk of the workforce. Our results, therefore, reveal that the economic structure of a region is influenced by several factors and cannot be limited to the traditional concepts of size and economies of scale. For a proper matching of labour and technology to be possible, the availability of appropriate workforce in such locations is critical. We also find that coastal regions are clearly more diversified, reaffirming the findings of Lall and Chakravorty (2005) on the bias of fresh investments in favour of coastal regions.

Thus, we conclude that size and sectoral diversity do not necessarily move together. While size could be a necessary condition for sectoral diversity in some situations, it is most certainly not a sufficient condition for sectoral diversity. The share of scientifically and technically skilled manpower turns out to be very important, which affects the ability of a region to attract industry and demonstrate agglomeration economies, especially in coastal areas. This ties in with the assessment presented by Drèze and Sen (2013) according to which states (and regions) that have invested heavily in building the capabilities of their human capital are likely to experience better outcomes. In order to have a greater share of the workforce engaged in professional skills, one needs a strong base of education that prepares people to enter the workforce, and investments in health that will enable people to stay in the workforce longer and improve productivity. Hence, there is a case for greater investments in developing skills and in other aspects related to building human capabilities to improve the quality of the workforce, if such diversified economic regions are expected to grow and multiply.

6
Regional Value Added and Its Determinants

In this chapter, we move a step further and provide, for the first time in India, estimates of output of specific regions along with an understanding of critical underlying factors over 2004–5 to 2011–12 across all regions. We use the proportion of regional workers to total state workers and adjust for productivity differentials between regions to arrive at an estimate of the regional value added (RVA). Our aim is to understand inter-regional differences in value added (VA) in the Indian context and explain how these differences could be correlated with aspects of agglomeration, such as urbanization and sectoral diversity, along with issues such as skill levels and access to finance.

Size of the Regional Economy

The problem of defining a region becomes crucial whenever attempts are made to obtain estimates of regional income and output. Such estimates are often essential because policy objectives are commonly set in terms of achieving a stipulated per capita income or production level for a region. Studies pertaining to certain other developing countries such as Brazil and Indonesia provide some level of regional granularity by using metropolitan-level data (da Mata et al. 2007) or post office codes (Deichmann et al. 2008). We draw from these works and extend our analysis to India in two aspects: one, we consider the region as a unit to calculate and compare value added for the first time at the regional level; and two, we cover both the organized and the unorganized sectors in understanding regional differences in value added.

Regional Economic Diversity. Poornima Dore and Krishnan Narayanan, Oxford University Press. © Oxford University Press India 2022. DOI: 10.1093/oso/9780190130596.003.0006

We contend that the ranking of states in India in their contribution to VA would be relatively unchanged over this time. However, while VA per se has increased in every state, leaving the relative ranks unaffected, the magnitude of the increase in absolute terms differs widely across states. We further try to analyse the contribution to RVA at a more granular level of NSS regions. At a regional level, we expect to find significant variations in value added in both absolute terms and relative terms. We carry out a ranking of the top 20 regions by RVA and expect the rankings to change substantially at the regional level, as opposed to the fairly static relative picture at the state level. This would indicate that the contribution to RVA (at the region level) is much more dynamic over time than what is revealed by the analysis of state-level data.

In other words, we propose that state-level trends mask the highly dynamic and varied regional growth patterns, both within the state and also between regions as standalone units. This underscores the need for the next task, which is to study the determinants of these variations in greater detail at the regional level, with specific reference to three factors: agglomeration, skills, and access to finance.

First, spatial concentration of production and population is a critical driver of growth due to the presence of increasing returns to scale (Krugman 1991). Empirical evidence on the existence of these agglomeration economies has been somewhat mixed. Moomaw (1981), Segal (1976), and Sveikauskas (1975) observe that productivity is generally higher in larger economic units, particularly cities. The share of urbanization is, therefore, an important indicator of the degree of agglomeration economies. Mills and Hamilton (1997) argue that the demand in any one industry (with a few exceptions), can be volatile over time and be subject to random uncorrelated, seasonal, or cyclical fluctuations. As a result, it is helpful for a region to have diverse sectors driving the economy, so that when one sector does not perform well, others sectors may have the ability to keep the economy buoyant (Attaran 1986). The presence of multiple industries in a region is also said to generate a higher level of employment and growth. Hence, the level of sectoral diversity is also indicative of the size of the productive market as well as sharing and matching opportunities (Duranton and Puga 2004). The presence of large cities would, as a corollary, have an impact on the overall output of a region as well, since they act as regional hubs and markets for enhanced economic activity.

Second is the dichotomy of a large segment of unemployed population coexisting with the reality that several sectors deplore the lack of skilled labour. Growth in any one sector has a tendency to spill over to other sectors through the mechanism of forward and backward linkages (Romer 1986). This is best utilized when there is an availability of human capital to best leverage the labour-matching opportunities and technological advances that economic development brings with it (Duranton and Puga 2004). It is argued that, in the Indian context, high skill levels raise the average productivity and, hence, contribute to growth (Rajan 2006).

Third, access to finance largely determines the spatial location and growth of enterprises, which are critical for high levels of value added in any region. Shortage of finance is one of the most critical problems faced by unorganized manufacturing enterprises, service sector enterprises, start-ups, small entrepreneurs, and R&D intensive efforts.[1] The availability of finance at a regional level gives insights about both the presence of institutional structures and the ability of individuals to access the same. Access to the formal banking system is expected to significantly improve the economic and social outcomes of a region through enhanced savings, entrepreneurship, and investments, in addition to building resilience to shocks. Where the institutional finance footprint is weak, the dependence on moneylenders and, subsequently, the interest rates are also high. Thus, the ability of enterprises and households to engage in productive growth is constrained by the limitations of financial access.

We have already established the importance of region as a unit of analysis in the literature and in the previous chapters where we observed a substantial variation across NSS regions even within a state. This chapter attempts to identify and analyse the determinants of inter-regional differences in levels of output over a specific period of time in the Indian context.

Model Formulation

We construct a measure for RVA, since there are no official estimates for the same. For a discussion at the state level, the NSDP data is readily

[1] At an all India level as per the NSS 62nd round data, this figure is said to stand at 42 per cent (with the highest being Tripura at 93 per cent).

available. We draw on Mitra and Mehta (2011) and their approach of using the UN Habitat guidelines to construct a variable denoting RVA for NSS regions. This is a unique contribution of our study, since output at the NSS region level has not been computed so far or used for regional analysis in India. We take the net state domestic product per capita (NSDPPC) and apply population weights to arrive at the state domestic product. This method assumes that the unit-level share of output is proportionate to the employment share, factoring in productivity differentials. The methodology of construction is explained in detail in Chapter 3.

$$\begin{aligned} &\textit{Regional Domestic Product or Regional Value Added } (VA) \\ &= \textit{State Domestic Product} * \frac{\textit{Regional Employment}}{\textit{State Employment}} * \frac{\textit{Regional WPR}}{\textit{State WPR}} \end{aligned}$$

We apply this method and tabulate the RVA for all NSS regions for both 2004–5 and 2011–12. We further divide the RVA by population to arrive at the regional value added per capita (RVAPC) as well. We seek to understand how value added has changed across regions, and also estimate the determinants of value added.

Following Combes (2000) and Bhat and Siddharthan (2012), we apply a production function approach (Cobb and Douglas 1928) to calculate output in terms of value added:

$$Q = F(L, K, \varepsilon) \quad (1)$$

$$R\,VA_r = F(L_r, K_r, Z_r) \quad (2)$$

Where L is labour related factors, K is capital related factors, and Z is other agglomeration variables, each being measured for region r.

We carry out a cross sectional analysis for 2004–5 and 2011–12 with variables as outlined in Table 6.1. We also pool the data for the two periods and carry out a pooled cross-sectional analysis.

We consider sectoral diversity and urbanization as two important dimensions of agglomeration for the purpose of our study. We consider the diversity index as calculated and discussed in detail in Chapter 5. Rapidly urbanizing regions are expected to have a greater contribution to value

Table 6.1 Variables and Data Sources

Nature of indicator	Variables	Variable name	Measurement	Data source
Value added	Regional value added	RVA	Constructed by applying relevant regional weights to state level output	Handbook of Statistics on Indian economy 2004–5 and 2011–12, RBI; 61st and 68th Round NSSO Surveys
	Regional value added per capita	RVAPC	RVA/ Regional Population	
Agglomeration	Diversity index	DV	$DV_r = 1 - H_r$ denoting the sectoral mix scale of 0 to 1	Constructed based on sectoral shares for 14 categories based on NIC codes from the 61st and 68th Round NSSO Surveys
	Diversity index squared	DVSQ	Squared value of DV	
	Urbanization share	URB	Proportion of population living in urban areas as a measure of urbanization	61st and 68th Round NSSO Surveys
Sectoral shares	Share of agriculture	AGRI	Proportion of total workers engaged in agriculture	Classification based on NIC codes of industrial classification as followed by the 61st and 68th Round NSSO surveys. The 14 categories at 2digit level are further collapsed into the four core sectors
	Share of manufacturing	MFG	Proportion of total workers engaged in manufacturing	
	Share of construction	CON	Proportion of total workers engaged in construction	
	Share of services	SVS	Proportion of total workers engaged in service sector	
	Share of tertiary sector	TERT	Proportion of total workers engaged in construction and service sector	

(*continued*)

Table 6.1 *Continued*

Nature of indicator	Variables	Variable name	Measurement	Data source
Skills	Share of high-end skills	SKILLIV	Proportion of workforce with level IV skills corresponding to 0 to 2 as per the NCO codes	61st and 68th Round NSSO Surveys
Access to finance	Bank branch offices	LnOFF	Number of bank branch offices	Basic Statistical Returns of Scheduled Commercial Banks in India, 2005 and 2010, RBI.
	Credit per branch	LnCRE	Volume of credit outstanding/ number of branch offices	
Million plus dummy	Dummy for million plus cities	MNd	Takes the value of 1 if the region contains a million plus city, else 0	List of cities treated as individual stratum in 68th Round NSSO Survey
Year dummy	Year dummy	Yd	Takes the value of 1 for the year 2011–12, and 0 for 2004–5	N.A.
RVA dummy	Dummy for regions with top 10 RVA values	TOP10d	Takes the value of 1 if the region ranks between 1–10 in terms of RVA and 0 if the region ranks above 10	Authors calculations of RVA
RVAPC dummy	Dummy for regions with top 10 RVAPC values	TOP10PCd	Takes a value of 1 if the region ranks between 1–10 in terms of RVAPC and 0 if the region ranks above 10	Authors calculations of RVAPC

Source: Authors' Calculations

added, and the urban share is calculated as the proportion of urban population to the total population in the state, based on the NSSO classification. We further include sectoral shares as control variables to assess whether the variations in sectoral shares explain some of the differences in value added. We filter the employment data from the NSS rounds by NIC codes and construct sectoral shares, as explained in Chapter 4.

For our analysis, we have looked at access to human capital in terms of 'skilling', as this is more directly related to the occupational structure and economic output. In order to assess the regional skill levels, we draw from the NCO at a single-digit level to look at the differences between states across industry subsectors. We study access to finance in terms of both outreach and volume to assess its impact on RVA. There appears to be a significant disparity in the availability of banking services across the country, with a positive correlation between per capita income and banking penetration, and an increasing disparity in banking outreach (Basu and Srivastava 2004). We measure access to finance in terms of the availability of bank branch offices and the volume of credit per branch, which provides a measure of the penetration and institutional access. The presence of bank branches and the volume of credit reflect the ability of individuals as well as businesses and other institutions to access credit and engages in a robust savings behaviour, thus enabling savings and capital formation.

We also include a dummy for million-plus cities, which takes the value of 1 or 0 depending on the presence or absence of a million-plus city in a given region. This helps us examine whether the existence of a million-plus city in a region accounts for its contribution to value added. Wherever pooled data is utilized, we include a year dummy. We add variants to the model by also introducing dummies for the top 10 RVA regions and the top 10 RVAPC regions to assess whether the top 10 regions behave differently.

Preliminary Findings

We divide our analysis into three segments, where we first address our hypothesis related to state-level variations in value added. Secondly, we construct and examine the RVA variable at a regional level, along with

RVAPC, and then study their association with the determinants related to capital, labour, and agglomeration.

Does the Ranking of States Change?

We contend that the ranking of states in contribution to value added would be relatively unchanged. While the value added per se has increased in every state, the magnitude of the increase differs widely across states.

We categorize the state level VA for both 2004–5 and 2011–12 in Table 6.2. We classify the states as high, medium, moderate, and low based on the VA levels of 2011–12. We plot the change in VA over the two periods, as well as the growth over this interval. We rank the states in the order of highest to lowest VA. As per Table 6.3, the difference between the highest and lowest VA figures has doubled. The mean VA has increased by 1.8 times. The standard deviation has almost doubled. The coefficient of variation indicates divergence through a slight increase. However, the ratio of the state with the highest VA to that with the lowest VA has declined, which indicates that the increase in output of the lowest VA state has been more than the increase of the output of the highest VA state. This is understandable since the base value of the lowest state is likely to be less in any case.

We find that the quantum of change and the growth rate vary across regions substantially. As per Table 6.4, most states seem to have retained their positions in terms of contribution, as the relative ranking of states has not changed much. The only exceptions where the ranks have changed by two positions or more are seen in case of Delhi (highlighted

Table 6.2 Value Added (State) Levels and Frequency

VA Level	Range of VA INR Cr.	Number of States (2011–12)	Number of States (2004–5)
High	>=200,000	8	3
Medium	100,000-199,999	7	6
Moderate	10,000-99,999	10	13
Low	<=9,999	7	10

Source: Authors' Calculations

Table 6.3 Value Added (State) Summary Statistics

RVA (INR in CINR)	2004–5	2011–12
Mean	77,949	139,811
Standard Deviation	87514	164313
Covariance	112.27	117.52
Difference (Highest-Lowest)	368,390	734,192
VA Ratio	226.62	213.87

Source: NSDP at constant prices as reported in the Handbook of Statistics on the Indian Economy (RBI).

in light grey), which has fallen from the 8th to the 11th position, and Pondicherry, which has moved from the 25th to the 27th position. While ranks are more or less stable, the disparity between VA across states has gone up, as shown by the difference between the highest and the lowest VA values. This finding is reinforced by Panagariya et al. (2014).

Does the Ranking of Regions Change?

At the regional level, we expect to find substantial variation in value added in absolute as well as relative terms.

We calculate the RVA following the methodology outlined in the previous section. We contend that within respective states the experience across state-regions is also varied, and so it is important to understand these inter-regional differences. Based on the mean, standard deviation (SD), and the coefficient of variation, we examine the hypothesis of increasing inequality in value added. If we take the mean RVA in 2011–12 and divide the entire sample at this midpoint, we take the set of regions below the mean as 'low RVA' and those above the mean as 'high RVA'. We find that the increase in VA between low RVA and high RVA regions is highly unequal (Table 6.5).

Increases in RVA therefore seem to be concentrated, with high RVA regions cornering higher shares of the increase. The SD also varies, with the SD of high RVA regions in 2011–12 being twice that of the low RVA regions. We carry out a ranking of the top 20 regions by VA and, as expected, find substantial variations at the regional level in Table 6.6. Bold

Table 6.4 State-wise Ranking* by Value Added (INR CINR)

Rank 2011–12	Rank 2004–5	State/ Union Territory	VA in INR Cr. 2004–5	VA in INR Cr. 2011–12	VA Change	Growth	VA Level
1	1	Maharashtra	370,023	737,641	367,619	0.99	High
2	2	Uttarakhand	231,029	370,150	139,121	0.60	High
3	4	Tamil Nadu	193,645	369,291	175,646	0.91	High
4	3	Andhra Pradesh	201,303	358,801	157,498	0.78	High
5	6	Gujarat	172,265	342,088	169,823	0.99	High
6	5	West Bengal	190,029	307,453	117,424	0.62	High
7	7	Karnataka	148,729	252,377	103,648	0.70	High
8	11	Delhi	94,717	201,653	106,936	1.13	High
9	8	Rajasthan	112,636	197,537	84,901	0.75	Medium
10	9	Kerala	104,776	186,998	82,222	0.78	Medium
11	10	Madhya Pradesh	99,940	177,786	77,846	0.78	Medium
12	12	Haryana	86,222	161,635	75,413	0.87	Medium
13	13	Punjab	86,108	137,275	51,167	0.59	Medium
14	14	Bihar	70,167	130,281	60,114	0.86	Medium
15	15	Orissa	67,987	101,907	33,920	0.50	Medium
16	16	Jharkhand	53,056	81,327	28,271	0.53	Moderate
17	17	Assam	47,181	70,544	23,363	0.50	Moderate
18	18	Chhattisgarh	41,387	68,796	27,410	0.66	Moderate
19	20	Uttar Pradesh	22,288	50,180	27,893	1.25	Moderate
20	19	Jammu & Kashmir	23,292	34,492	11,199	0.48	Moderate
21	21	Himachal Pradesh	21,189	33,762	12,572	0.59	Moderate
22	22	Goa	10,999	20,257	9,258	0.84	Moderate
23	24	Chandigarh	7,610	14,400	6,790	0.89	Moderate
24	23	Tripura	8,170	14,397	6,228	0.76	Moderate
25	27	Pondicherry	5,033	10,244	5,210	1.04	Moderate
26	25	Meghalaya	5,846	9,748	3,902	0.67	Low
27	26	Nagaland	5,421	8,718	3,297	0.61	Low
28	28	Manipur	4,603	6,763	2,160	0.47	Low
29	29	Arunachal Pradesh	3,188	5,152	1,964	0.62	Low
30	30	Mizoram	2,400	4,594	2,194	0.91	Low
31	32	Sikkim	1,511	4,263	2,752	1.82	Low
32	31	Andaman & Nicobar Islands	1,633	3,449	1,816	1.11	Low

Note: *Reference year for ranking is 2011–12.

Source: Ranking based on NSDP data published in the Handbook of Statistics on Indian economy.

Table 6.5 Summary Statistics across Low and High RVA Regions

RVA	2004–5	2011–12	Change	CV 2004–5	CV 2011–12
Low RVA	15,288	22,338	7,050	103	73
High RVA	45,408	92,537	47,129	45	34

Source: Authors' calculations basis NSSO surveys 61st and 68th rounds

Table 6.6 Region-wise Ranking by Regional Value Added (RVA)

Rank 2011–12	Rank 2004–5	No.	Region	State	2004–5	2011–12	Change	Growth
1	2	272	**Inland Western**	Maharashtra	84,673	152,128	67,455	0.8
2	New	241	**South Eastern**	Gujarat	36,642	146,435	109,793	3
3	10	271	**Coastal**	Maharashtra	61,932	144,858	82,926	1.34
4	5	71	**Delhi**	Delhi	74,411	142,297	67,886	0.91
5	11	294	**Inland Northern**	Karnataka	59,218	132,606	73,388	1.24
Average of top 5 Regions					63,375	143,665	80,290	1.46
Rank 2011–12	**Rank 2004–5**	**No.**	**Region**	**State**	**2004–5**	**2011–12**	**Change**	**Growth**
6	6	91	*Northern Upper Ganga Plains*	Uttar Pradesh	72,248	127,169	54,920	0.76
7	15	334	**Inland**	Tamil Nadu	48,277	120,948	72,670	1.51
8	9	274	**Inland Central**	Maharashtra	65,923	119,063	53,139	0.81
9	16	293	**Inland Southern**	Karnataka	47,605	116,828	69,222	1.45
10	1	93	*Eastern*	Uttar Pradesh	88,157	116,284	28,127	0.32
11	14	331	**Coastal Northern**	Tamil Nadu	53,911	107,189	53,278	0.99
12	8	322	*Southern*	Kerala	67,056	105,199	38,142	0.57
13	12	275	*Inland Eastern*	Maharashtra	57,019	103,170	46,151	0.81
14	13	61	*Eastern*	Haryana	54,902	97,824	42,922	0.78
15	New	233	**Malwa**	Madhya Pradesh	25,969	96,158	70,188	2.7
16	23	333	**Southern**	Tamil Nadu	39,590	92,159	52,569	1.33
17	New	245	**Saurashtra**	Gujarat	32,445	79,527	47,082	1.45
18	24	273	**Inland Northern**	Maharashtra	38,690	76,496	37,806	0.98
19	New	235	**South Western**	Andhra Pradesh	12,038	73,823	61,784	5.13
20	New	101	**Northern**	Bihar	32,007	73,163	41,157	1.29

Note: *Details of RVA for all NSS regions for 2004–5 and 2011–12 provided in Appendix 10 and 11 respectively.
Source: Authors' Calculations

text represents an increase in ranking, while italics represents a decline. Five regions which were in the top 20 in 2004–5 have dropped out of the list in 2011–12. The new additions are the regions of Gujarat (Vadodara, Panchmahal, Dahod Bharuch, Navsari, Valsad, Sundarnagar, Bhavnagar, Rajkot, Jamnagar, and Porbandar), Andhra Pradesh (Warangal, Khamam, Karimnagar, and Adilabad), Madhya Pradesh (Rajgarh, Shajapur, Indore, Ujjain, Ghar, Barwani, Dewas, Hoshangabad, Betul, and Khargone), and Bihar (Champaran, Sitamarhi, Araria, Katihar, Darbhanga, Muzzafarpur, Vaisali and adjoining areas). Maharashtra and Tamil Nadu stand out at the regional level as well, as five out of six regions in Maharashtra and three out of four regions in Tamil Nadu feature in the top 20 RVA list.

Variations in Regional Value Added

We further study the top 10 and the bottom 10 regions by RVA as well as RVAPC. We find that in the rankings by RVA, five regions (Delhi and parts of Maharashtra and Uttar Pradesh) continue to figure in the top 10 over both periods, and several new regions enter the list to assume the other ranks in Table 6.7 and Maps 6.1 and 6.2. This includes south-eastern Gujarat; inland, northern, and southern Karnataka; and inland and coastal northern Tamil Nadu. They appear to displace parts of Uttar Pradesh, West Bengal, Andhra Pradesh, and Kerala. The bottom 10 regions, more or less, remain the same and largely cover Jammu and Kashmir and the Northeast.

If we consider RVAPC, we find that a slightly different set of regions emerge in the top 10 and bottom 10 in Table 6.8 and Maps 6.3 and 6.4. Some regions such as Delhi, inland central Maharashtra, and south-eastern Gujarat continue to be common, which means that even after adjusting for population their contribution to VA continues to be high. Between 2004–5 and 2011–12, these regions, along with Chandigarh, Goa, and Pondicherry, were consistently among the top 10 regions by RVAPC. As far as the bottom 10 regions by RVAPC are concerned, regions of Uttar Pradesh and Bihar find a prominent position in this list. Interestingly, eastern UP was high on RVA value in absolute terms in period 1 but features among the bottom 10 in terms of RVAPC. This appears to be due to Uttar Pradesh being the most populous state; since

Table 6.7 Top 10 and Bottom 10 Regions by RVA

Top 10 Regions 2004–5 by RVA				Top 10 Regions 2011–12 by RVA			
Region	State	Region Name	RVA INR Cr.	Region	State	Region Name	RVA INR Cr.
93	Uttar Pradesh	Eastern	88157	272	Maharashtra	Inland West	152128
272	Maharashtra	Inland West	84673	241	Gujarat	South Eastern	146435
193	West Bengal	South Bengal Plains	83017	271	Maharashtra	Coastal	144858
281	Andhra Pradesh	Coastal Northern	78069	71	Delhi	Delhi	142297
71	Delhi	Delhi	74411	294	Karnataka	Inland Northern	132606
91	Uttar Pradesh	Northern Upper Ganga Plains	72248	334	Tamil Nadu	Inland	120948
282	Andhra Pradesh	Coastal Southern	70249	274	Maharashtra	Inland Central (Aurangabad)	119063
322	Kerala	Southern	67056	293	Karnataka	Inland Southern	116828
274	Maharashtra	Inland Central (Aurangabad)	65923	93	Uttar Pradesh	Eastern	116284
271	Maharashtra	Coastal	61932	331	Tamil Nadu	Coastal Northern	107189

(*continued*)

Table 6.7 *Continued*

Top 10 Regions 2004–5 by RVA				Top 10 Regions 2011–12 by RVA			
Bottom 10 Regions 2004–5 by RVA				Bottom 10 Regions 2011–12 by RVA			
Region	State	Region Name	RVA INR Cr.	Region	State	Region Name	RVA INR Cr.
11	Jammu and Kashmir	Mountainous Jammu	3871	12	Jammu and Kashmir	Outer Hills	7493
131	Nagaland	Nagaland	2319	221	Chhattisgarh	Northern	7474
121	Arunachal	Arunachal	2244	131	Nagaland	Nagaland	5153
142	Manipur	Manipur Hills	1851	111	Sikkim	Sikkim	3838
141	Manipur	Manipur Plains	1775	121	Arunachal	Arunachal	3639
151	Mizoram	Mizoram	1686	151	Mizoram	Mizoram	3370
12	Jammu and Kashmir	Outer Hills	1389	141	Manipur	Manipur Plains	2958
111	Sikkim	Sikkim	1301	351	Andaman and Nicobar Islands	Andaman and Nicobar	2256
183	Assam	Cachar Plains	1279	142	Manipur	Manipur Hills	2212
351	Andaman and Nicobar Islands	Andaman and Nicobar	1139	14	Jammu and Kashmir	Ladakh (New region)	556

Source: Authors' calculations basis NSSO surveys 61st and 68th rounds.

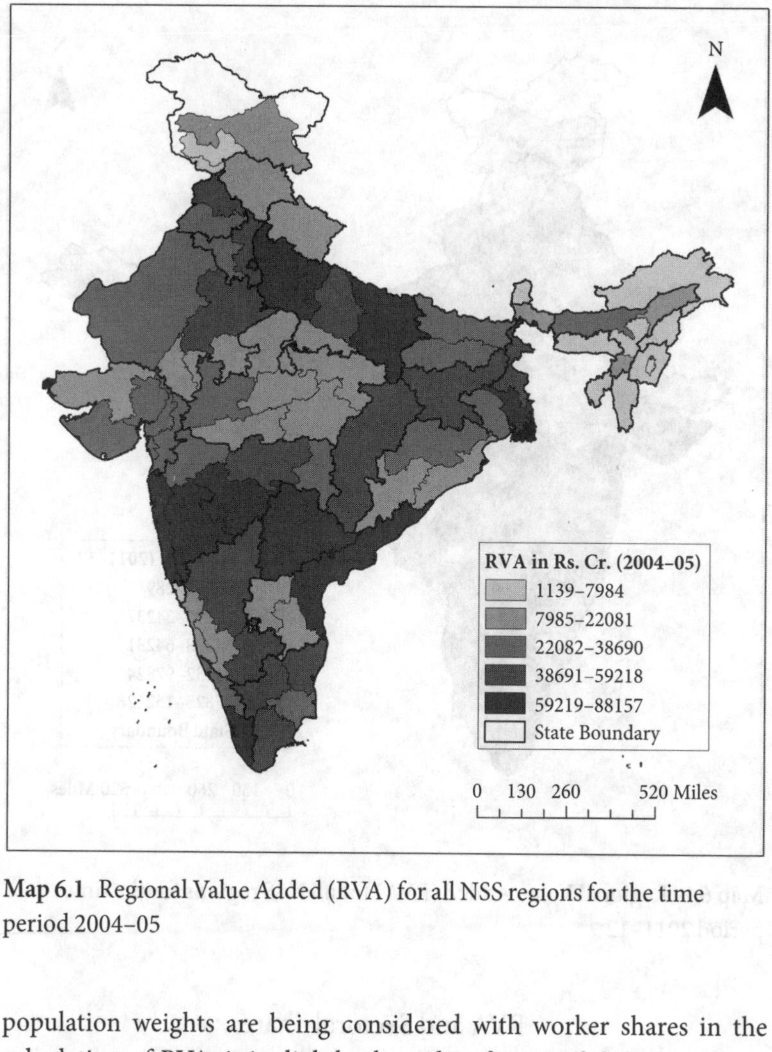

Map 6.1 Regional Value Added (RVA) for all NSS regions for the time period 2004–05

population weights are being considered with worker shares in the calculation of RVA, it is slightly skewed in favour of the more populous states. We also find parts of Assam and Manipur in the bottom 10 during both periods, along with coastal Odisha. This implies that while coastal Odisha might have a higher RVA in absolute terms among other regions of Odisha, it finds itself ranked lower in per capita terms, possibly due to the population pressure in the coastal region which is more fertile and better off. We also find that the regions of Madhya Pradesh seem to have moved up and are no longer part of the bottom 10 regions by RVAPC in 2011–12.

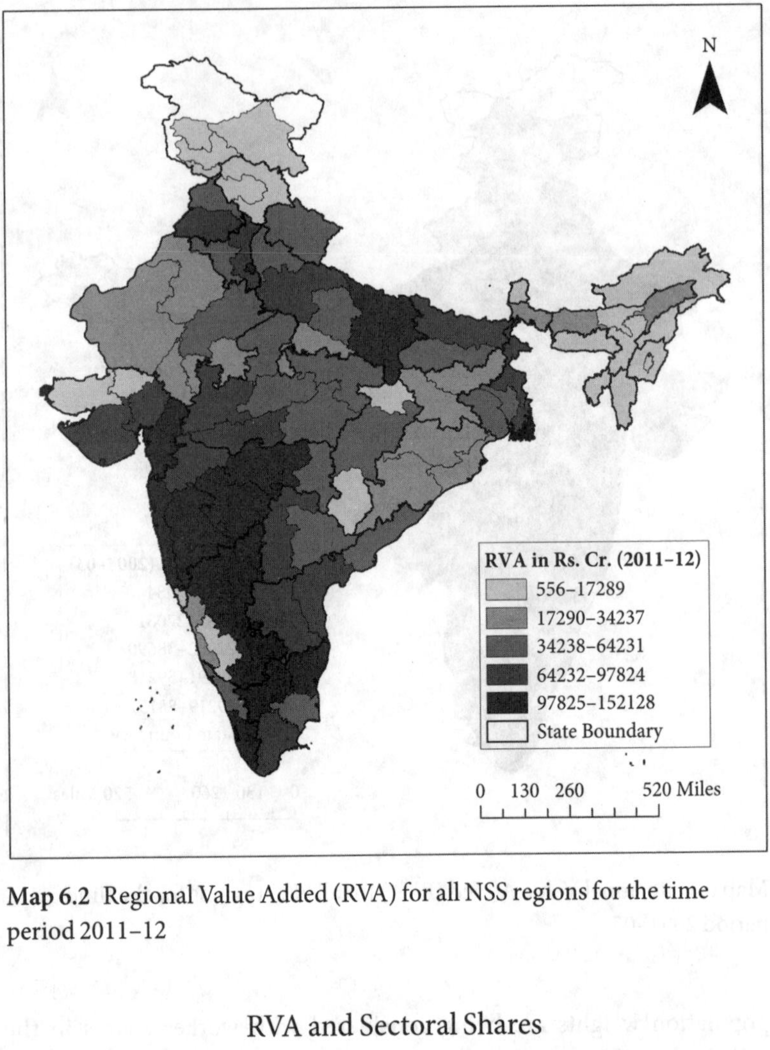

Map 6.2 Regional Value Added (RVA) for all NSS regions for the time period 2011–12

RVA and Sectoral Shares

We now consider employment in the four major sectors: agriculture (AGRI), manufacturing (MFG), construction (CON), and services (SVS), and examine their shares in terms of both RVA and RVAPC. We take the top 10 and bottom 10 regions identified in both periods and compare their employment shares. Figure 6.1 demonstrates the sectoral shares by RVA. In case of the top 10 RVA regions, we find that the average share of agriculture is less than 50 per cent for both periods. It reduces from 44 per cent in 2004–5 to 39 per cent in 2011–12. The average share

Table 6.8 Top 10 and Bottom 10 Regions by Regional Value Added per capita (RVAPC)

Top 10 Regions 2004–5 by RVAPC				Top 10 Regions 2011–12 by RVAPC			
Region	State	Name	RVAPC INR	Region	State	Name	RVAPC INR
301	Goa	Goa	76967	301	Goa	Goa	129397
41	Chandigarh	Chandigarh	74173	71	Delhi	Delhi	110779
71	Delhi	Delhi	63877	235	Madhya Pradesh	South Western	97421
341	Pondicherry	Pondicherry	48301	41	Chandigarh	Chandigarh	80800
276	Maharashtra	Eastern	45478	276	Maharashtra	Eastern	80756
274	Maharashtra	Inland Central	41905	341	Pondicherry	Pondicherry	80516
351	Andaman and Nicobar Islands	Andaman and Nicobar Islands	40921	334	Tamil Nadu	Inland	75252
61	Haryana	Eastern	39343	274	Maharashtra	Inland Central	74039
275	Maharashtra	Inland Eastern	38561	111	Sikkim	Sikkim	73703
241	Gujarat	South Eastern	38093	241	Gujarat	South Eastern	72012

(continued)

Table 6.8 *Continued*

Top 10 Regions 2004–5 by RVAPC				Top 10 Regions 2011–12 by RVAPC			
Region	State	Name	RVAPC INR	Region	State	Name	RVAPC INR
93	Uttar Pradesh	Eastern	14011	184	Assam	Central Brahmaputra Plains	20405
94	Uttar Pradesh	Southern	13981	141	Manipur	Manipur Plains	20105
183	Assam	Cachar Plains	13654	182	Assam	Western Assam Plains	20099
92	Uttar Pradesh	Central	13384	183	Assam	Cachar Plains	19948
232	Madhya Pradesh	Central	13097	211	Odisha	Coastal	19752
211	Odisha	Coastal	13039	91	Uttar Pradesh	Northern Upper Ganga Plains	17921
91	Uttar Pradesh	Northern Upper Ganga Plains	11595	95	Uttar Pradesh	Southern Upper Ganga Plains	17338
236	Madhya Pradesh	Northern	10983	93	Uttar Pradesh	Eastern	16688
102	Bihar	Central	8059	102	Bihar	Central	13695
101	Bihar	Northern	7809	101	Bihar	Northern	12838

Source: Authors' calculations basis NSSO surveys 61st and 68th rounds

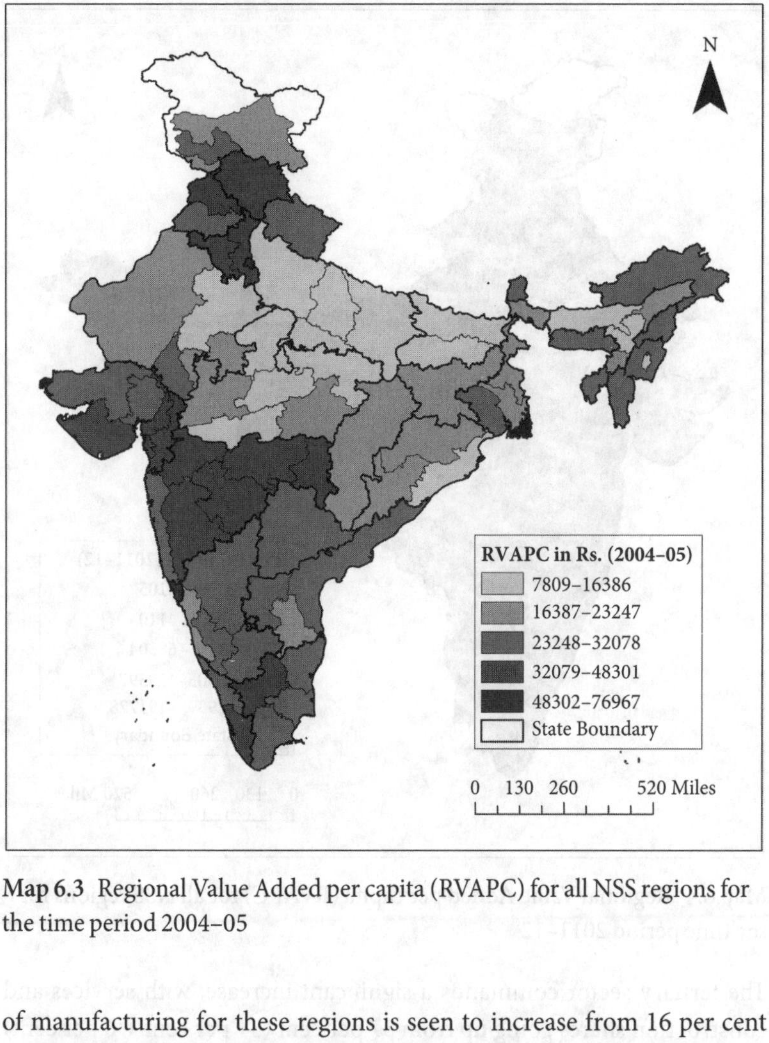

Map 6.3 Regional Value Added per capita (RVAPC) for all NSS regions for the time period 2004–05

of manufacturing for these regions is seen to increase from 16 per cent in 2004–5 to 18 per cent in 2011–12. Interestingly, employment is dominated by construction and services, which collectively accounts for 40 per cent in 2004–5 and increases to 43 per cent in 2011–12 as the single largest consolidated sector. For future reference, we refer to construction and services collectively as the tertiary sector (TERT).

The bottom 10 regions by RVA in the lower panel of Figure 6.1 have a comparatively higher share of workforce engaged in agriculture, which reduces from 57 per cent in 2004–5 to 49 per cent in 2011–12. The share of manufacturing remains more or less constant between 6–7 per cent.

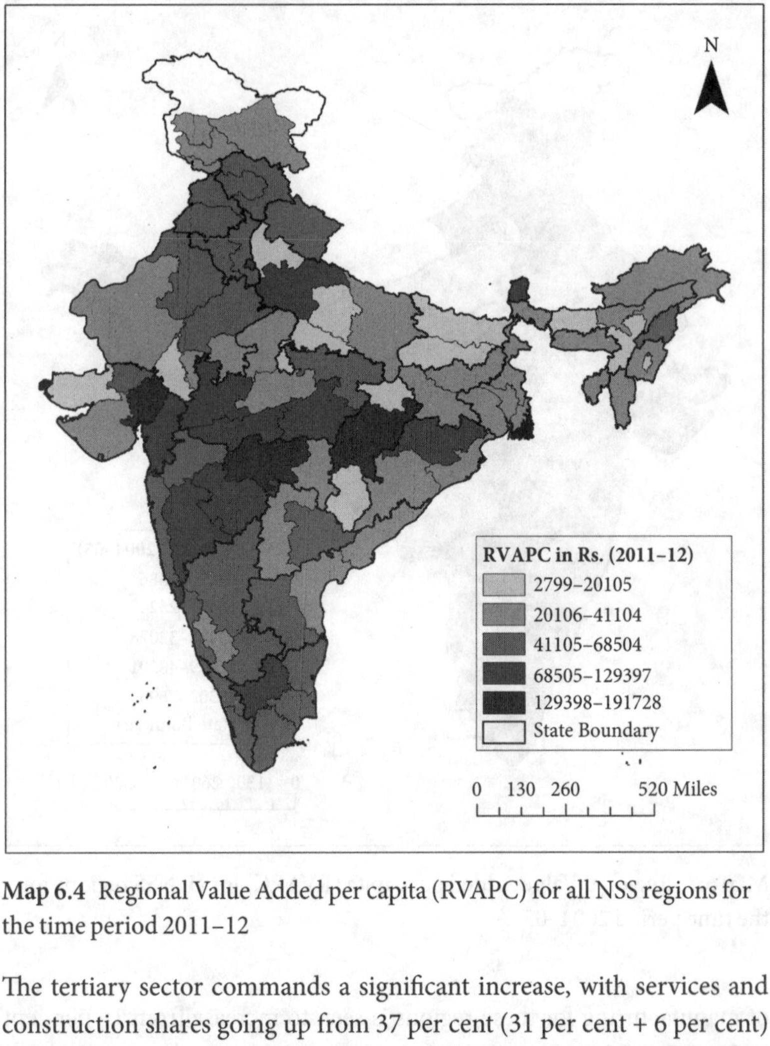

Map 6.4 Regional Value Added per capita (RVAPC) for all NSS regions for the time period 2011–12

The tertiary sector commands a significant increase, with services and construction shares going up from 37 per cent (31 per cent + 6 per cent) in 2004–5 to 44 per cent (32 per cent + 12 per cent) in 2011–12. There seems to be a shift in employment from agriculture to construction, possible due to construction works being taken up in rural areas and small towns. Jammu and Kashmir and states of the Northeast form a large part of the bottom RVA regions. As depicted in Chapter 4, these regions have seen a rise in the share of construction and, to some extent, services during the period under consideration.

We now consider the sectoral shares in the top 10 and bottom 10 regions by RVAPC (Figure 6.2). Here we find a more decisive pattern

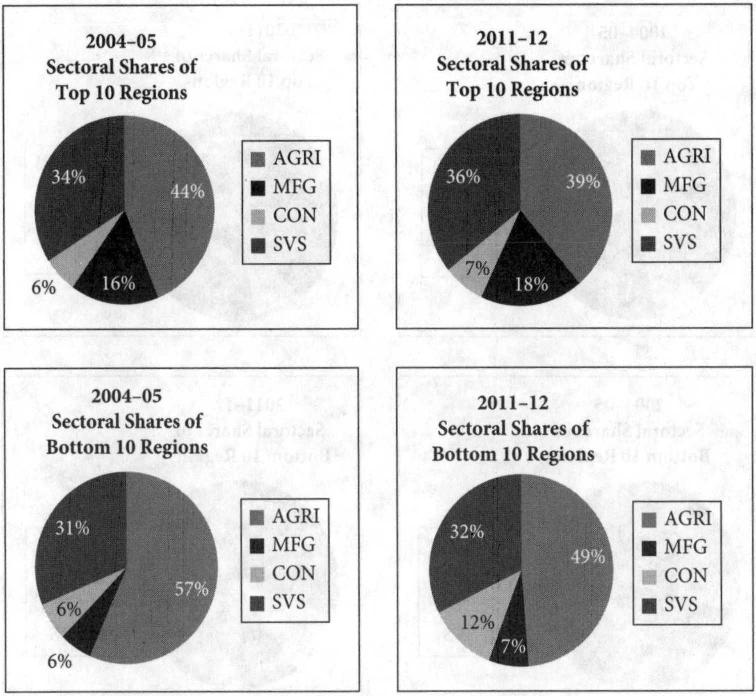

Figure 6.1 Sector Shares by RVA
Source: Authors' calculations basis NSSO surveys 61st and 68th rounds.

emerging. The share of agriculture in the top 10 regions is clearly lesser than 40 per cent in both periods. Manufacturing forms about 14–15 per cent of employment. The tertiary sector (construction + services) accounts for 47 per cent of employment in both periods and clearly dominates the economy. In case of the 10 regions with the lowest RVAPC, the share of agriculture is 50 per cent or more. In fact, the share of agriculture has come down from 61 per cent in 2004–5 to 50 per cent in 2011–12. The share of manufacturing is constant at about 10 per cent. The tertiary sector shows a clear increase from 29 per cent (23 per cent + 6 per cent) in 2004–5 to 40 per cent (30 per cent + 10 per cent) in 2011–12.

Thus, as the share of the tertiary sector increases, there appears to be an increase in output per capita. We examine this relationship in the next section, when we test for causality of both RVA and RVAPC.

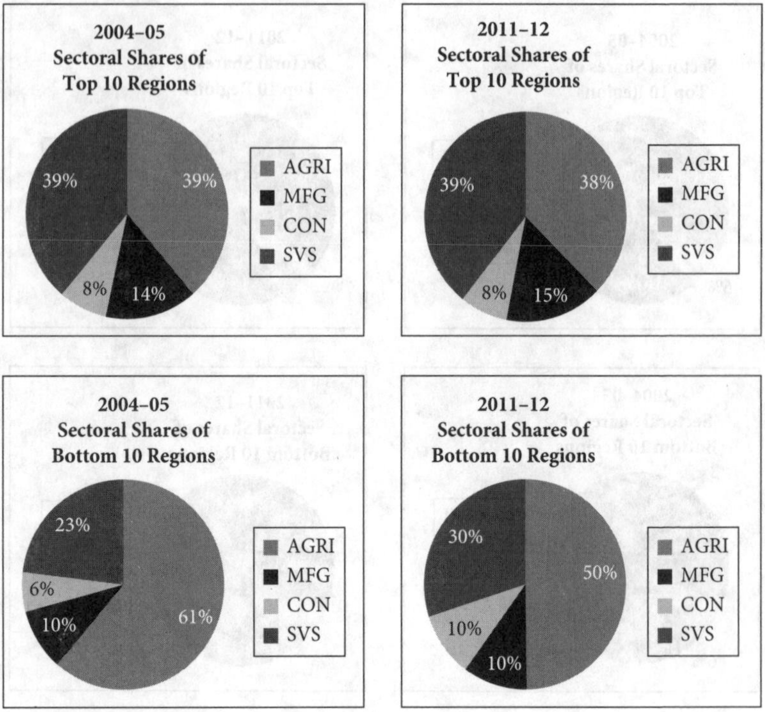

Figure 6.2 Sector Shares by RVAPC
Source: Authors' Calculations

RVA and Agglomeration

It is useful to further examine these patterns in the context of agglomeration. We look at the diversity index values for the top 10 and bottom 10 RVA regions, as well as their share of urban population (Table 6.9 and Maps 6.5–6.8). The diversity index, as explained before, is a composite index across 14 industry sectors which helps us understand the position of the region on the spectrum ranging from specialization to diversification of the economy. We find that the average DV levels have gone up from 0.63 in 2004–5 to 0.70 in 2011–12 on a scale of 0 to 1. These overall and region-wise shifts have been discussed in detail in Chapter 5. In this section, we consider the DV values for the top 10 regions by RVA, and find that the regions of Andaman and Nicobar Islands and Goa, which have the highest DV values in each of the two periods, do not find mention among the regions with the highest RVA. We will come back to this observation later. We also find that for the bottom 10 RVA regions,

Table 6.9 Agglomeration for Regions ranked by RVA

2004–5 Top 10 by RVA				2011–12 Top 10 by RVA			
Region	RVA	DV	URB	Region	RVA	DV	URB
93	88157	0.58	11%	272	152128	0.72	37%
272	84673	0.64	33%	241	146435	0.67	40%
193	83017	0.83	42%	271	144858	0.87	79%
281	78069	0.64	27%	71	142297	0.85	92%
71	74411	0.84	92%	294	132606	0.61	29%
91	72248	0.72	27%	334	120948	0.79	45%
282	70249	0.63	26%	274	119063	0.50	28%
322	67056	0.86	26%	293	116828	0.79	51%
274	65923	0.46	23%	93	116284	0.69	13%
271	61932	0.85	72%	331	107189	0.84	53%
Average	**74574**	**0.71**	**38%**	**Average**	**129864**	**0.73**	**47%**
National Average	**29746**	**0.63**	**26%**	**National Average**	**50530**	**0.70**	**29%**
2004–5 Bottom 10 by RVA				**2011–12 Bottom 10 by RVA**			
Region	RVA	DV	URB	Region	RVA	DV	URB
11	3871	0.82	28%	12	7493	0.74	10%
131	2319	0.61	31%	221	7474	0.30	12%
121	2244	0.41	12%	131	5153	0.66	35%
142	1851	0.27	3%	111	3838	0.60	18%
141	1775	0.80	36%	121	3639	0.52	19%
151	1686	0.48	40%	151	3370	0.64	49%
12	1389	0.63	13%	141	2958	0.82	40%
111	1301	0.67	12%	351	2256	0.87	36%
183	1279	0.58	10%	142	2212	0.64	2%
351	1139	0.88	36%	14	556	0.85	13%
Average	**1885**	**0.62**	**22%**	**Average**	**3895**	**0.66**	**23%**
National Average	**29746**	**0.63**	**26%**	**National Average**	**50530**	**0.70**	**29%**

Source: Authors' calculations basis NSSO surveys 61st and 68th rounds.

the average DV increases from 0.62 in 2004–5 to 0.66 in 2011–12. This ties in with our finding in the previous chapter that there is a gradual but definite shift towards higher levels of DV in the Indian case for the period considered.

We also find that while the average share of urban population has increased pan India from 26 per cent in 2004–5 to 29 per cent in 2011–12, regions with high RVA are seen to have significantly higher shares of urbanization. The average share of urbanization for the top 10 RVA regions has gone up from 38 per cent in 2004–5 to 47 per cent in 2011–12. The bottom 10 RVA regions have a very low share of urbanization, around 22–3 per cent. At the extreme high end we have Delhi (92 per cent) and coastal Maharashtra (79 per cent) in 2011–12, ranked 3rd and 4th highest on RVA, while at the extreme low end are Manipur hills, which has only 2 per cent of its population that is urban, and the outer hills of Jammu, with only 10 per cent urban population in 2011–12, ranked 2nd and 10th from the bottom on RVA respectively. This accentuates the stark nature of our inter-regional variations. In the next section we will explore whether the share of urbanization has a causal relationship with output at the regional level.

We now study agglomeration-related variables and their association with regions ranked by RVAPC (Table 6.10 and Maps 6.9–6.12). This helps to study whether there is any difference if we examine this association in per capita terms. Urbanization seems to go hand in hand with higher levels of RVAPC. However, we find a decline in the average DV values for the top 10 regions, from 0.72 in 2004–5 to 0.70 in 2011–12, while also experiencing an increase in the average DV values for the bottom 10 regions, from 0.59 in 2004–5 to 0.69 in 2011–12. This seems to indicate a certain level of plateauing of DV when RVA is measured in per capita terms. It is possible that there are limits to sectoral diversification and that, beyond a point, the regions with higher DV values may not be the ones contributing to a very high RVAPC. We further plot RVA as well as RVAPC as functions of DV (Figures 6.3 and 6.4) and do not find a very clear linear pattern emerging. This warrants further study, and hence in our next section we examine a non-liner relationship between DV and output levels.

RVA and Access to Finance, Skills, and Markets

To what extent do access to finance, a qualified workforce, and proximity to markets influence the ability of a region to have high levels

Table 6.10 Agglomeration for Regions ranked by RVAPC

2004–5 Top 10 by RVAPC				2011–12 Top 10 by RVAPC			
Region	RVAPC	DV	URB	Region	RVAPC	DV	URB
301	76967	0.87	0.39	301	129397	0.89	0.5
41	74173	0.86	0.89	71	110779	0.85	0.92
71	63877	0.84	0.92	235	97421	0.45	0.22
341	48301	0.85	0.64	41	80800	0.85	0.92
276	45478	0.55	0.2	276	80756	0.50	0.19
274	41905	0.46	0.23	341	80516	0.87	0.63
351	40921	0.88	0.36	334	75252	0.79	0.45
61	39343	0.80	0.3	274	74039	0.50	0.28
275	38561	0.56	0.37	111	73703	0.60	0.18
241	38093	0.51	0.14	241	72012	0.67	0.4
Average	50762	0.72	0.44	Average	87467	0.70	0.47
National Average	26998	0.63	0.26	National Average	44708	0.70	0.29
2004–5 Bottom 10 by RVAPC				**2011–12 Bottom 10 by RVAPC**			
Region	RVAPC	DV	URB	Region	RVAPC	DV	URB
93	14011	0.58	0.11	184	20405	0.54	0.06
94	13981	0.57	0.22	141	20105	0.82	0.4
183	13654	0.58	0.1	182	20099	0.78	0.13
92	13384	0.62	0.23	183	19948	0.63	0.12
232	13097	0.64	0.31	211	19752	0.74	0.17
211	13039	0.68	0.13	91	17921	0.82	0.32
91	11595	0.72	0.27	95	17338	0.69	0.25
236	10983	0.56	0.26	93	16688	0.69	0.13
102	8059	0.53	0.15	102	13695	0.60	0.17
101	7809	0.43	0.05	101	12838	0.59	0.06
Average	11961	0.59	0.18	Average	17879	0.69	0.18
National Average	26998	0.63	0.26	National Average	44708	0.70	0.29

Source: Authors' calculations basis NSSO surveys 61st and 68th rounds.

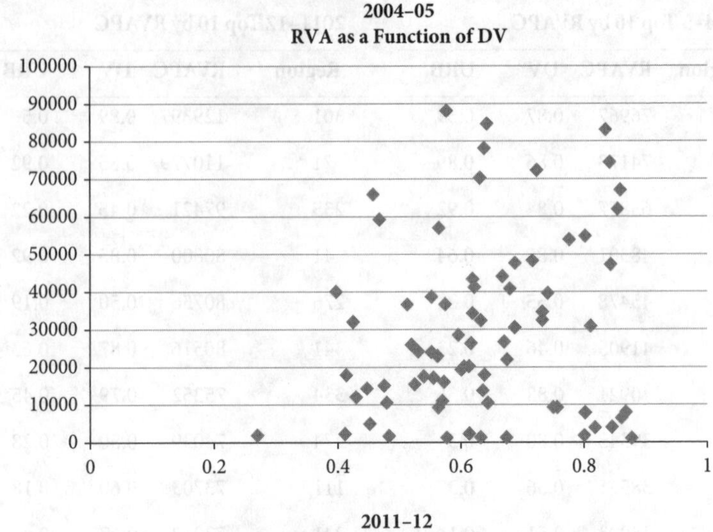

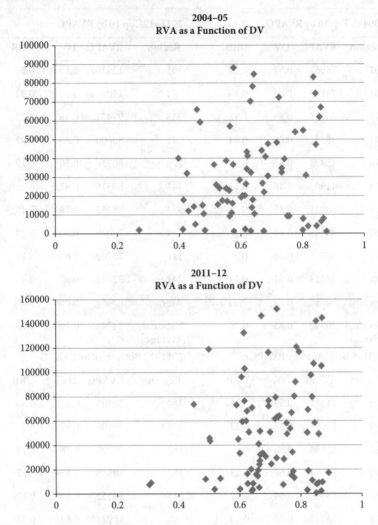

Figure 6.3 Relationship between RVA and DV

Source: Authors' Calculations

of output? To study this, we look at the access levels for the top 10 and bottom 10 regions by RVA and find a clear pattern emerging (Table 6.11). We find that in the top 10 regions the number of bank branches per region were 2,183 in 2004–5, as compared to the national average of 907. While the average branches per region increased from 907 in 2004–5 to almost 1,000 in 2011–12, we find that the average for the top 10 regions

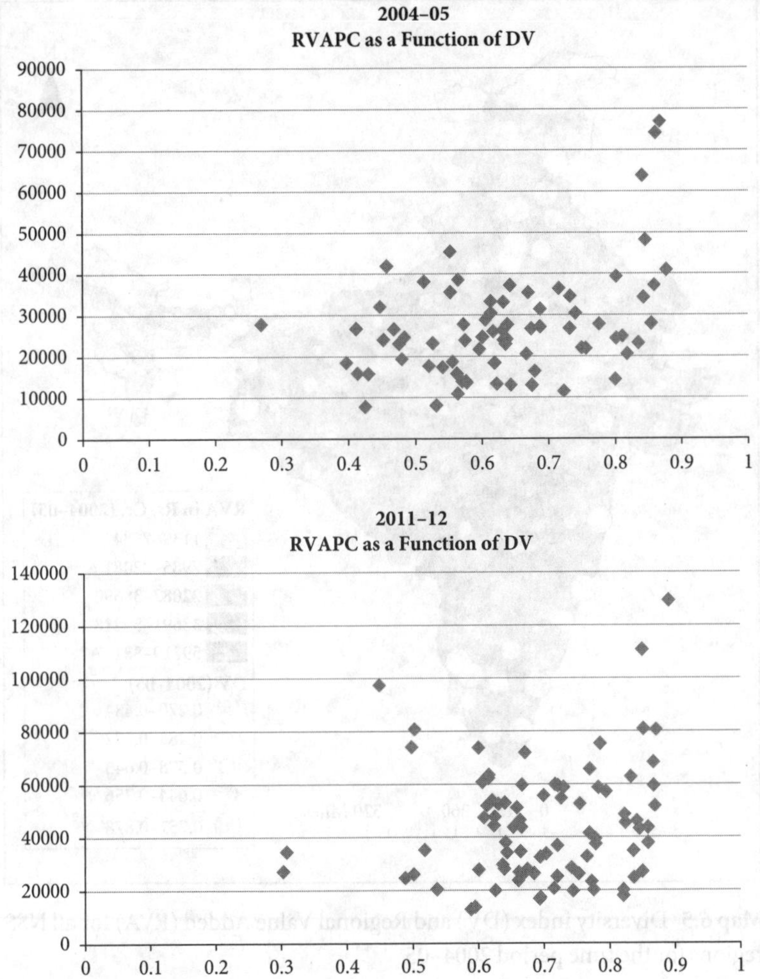

Figure 6.4 Relationship between RVAPC and DV
Source: Authors' Calculations

decreased marginally from 2,183 to 2,100. We see the same pattern for the bottom 10 regions, for which the number of bank branches per region declined from 95 in 2004–5 to 76 in 2011–12. This could be partially due to the closing down of unprofitable branches, but also due to the inclusion of different regions in the top 10 and bottom 10 ranks during the two periods. However, one point to be noted here is that the average number

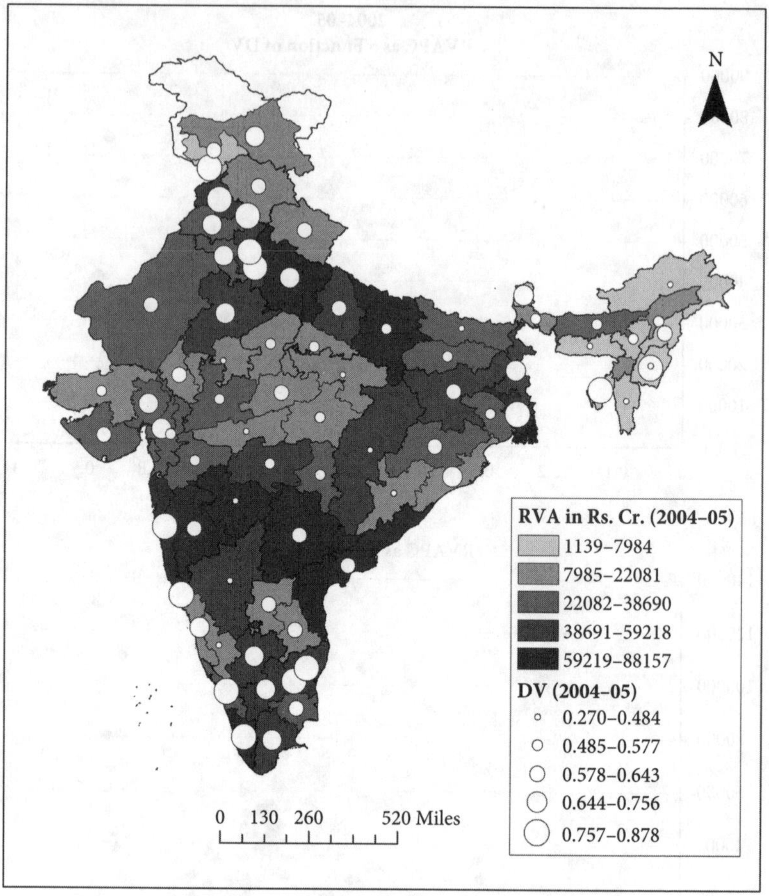

Map 6.5 Diversity index (DV) and Regional Value Added (RVA) for all NSS regions for the time period 2004–05

of bank branches for the top 10 regions is much higher than the national average, while the average for the bottom 10 is abysmally low.

Similarly, the top 10 regions have very high levels of credit per branch, which has doubled from INR 30.04 Cr in 2004–5 to INR 76.91 Cr in 2011–12. This mirrors the increase in the national average from INR 11.68 Cr of credit per branch in 2004–5 to INR 25.41 Cr in 2011–12. The bottom 10 regions are well below the national average but register an increase from INR 4.83 Cr in 2004–5 to INR 11.62 Cr in 2011–12. The RVA for the bottom 10 regions has also more than doubled from 1,885 Cr in

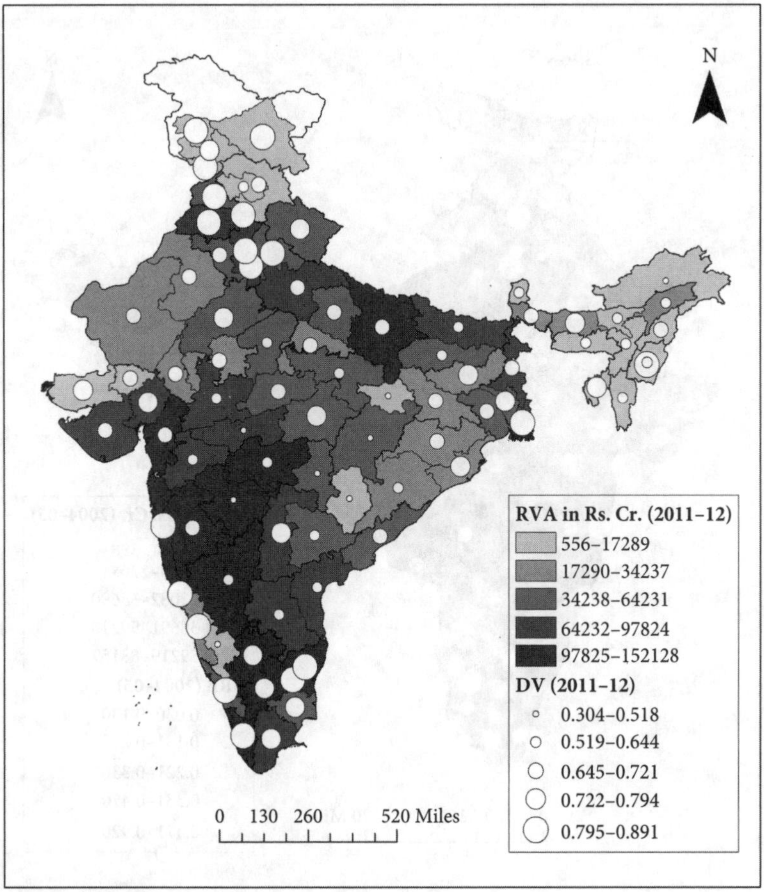

Map 6.6 Diversity index (DV) and Regional Value Added (RVA) for all NSS regions for the time period 2011–12

2004–5 to 3,895 Cr in 2011–12. Thus, RVA and credit per branch appear to be moving together.

The share of high-end skills in the workforce has increased in the top 10 regions from 11 per cent in 2004–5 to 18 per cent in 2011–12. This is well above the national average, which registers an increase from 8 per cent in 2004–5 to 11 per cent in 2011–12. At the same time, the bottom 10 regions show a marginal decline in the share of high-end skills from 9 per cent in 2004–5 to 8 per cent in 2011–12. This implies that the regions with the highest RVA appear to also be regions with access to a highly skilled

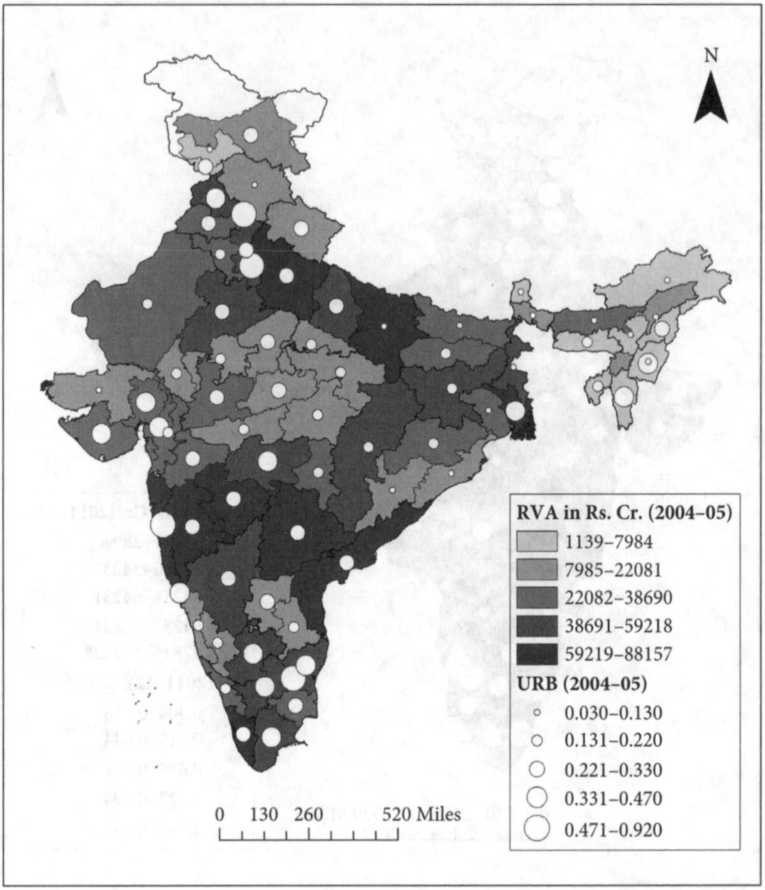

Map 6.7 Urbanization (URB) and Regional Value Added (RVA) for all NSS regions for the time period 2004–05

workforce. Higher shares of skilled workforce possibly contribute to significant gains in RVA.

In terms of access to markets, we look at regions which have high population densities with the likelihood of offering both product and service markets. We use proximity to million-plus cities as a proxy for this. While arguably the mere presence of a million-plus city does not guarantee the presence of a robust market, it is still worth evaluating, as the argument for investment in million-plus cities is that they are the growth drivers of the economy. We find that several high-RVA regions (highlighted in grey)

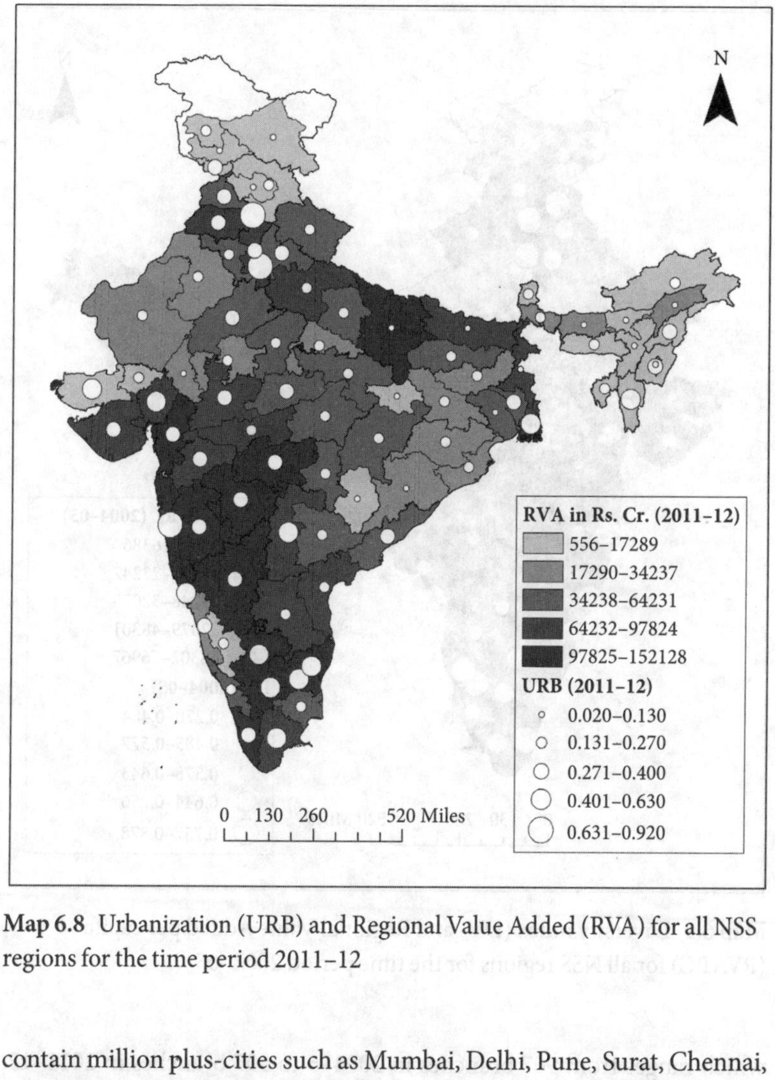

Map 6.8 Urbanization (URB) and Regional Value Added (RVA) for all NSS regions for the time period 2011–12

contain million plus-cities such as Mumbai, Delhi, Pune, Surat, Chennai, Bangalore, and so on. Interestingly, not a single one of the bottom 10 RVA regions contain any million-plus cities. These bottom 10 regions largely comprise of the states of the Northeast and Jammu and Kashmir, which clearly have market access and transport-cost related constraints.

If we consider access levels for the top 10 and bottom 10 regions by RVAPC, we find a slightly different pattern (Table 6.12). The top 10 regions have a bank branch outreach that ranges from 652 branches in 2004–5 to 778 branches in 2011–12. This is much lower than the national average

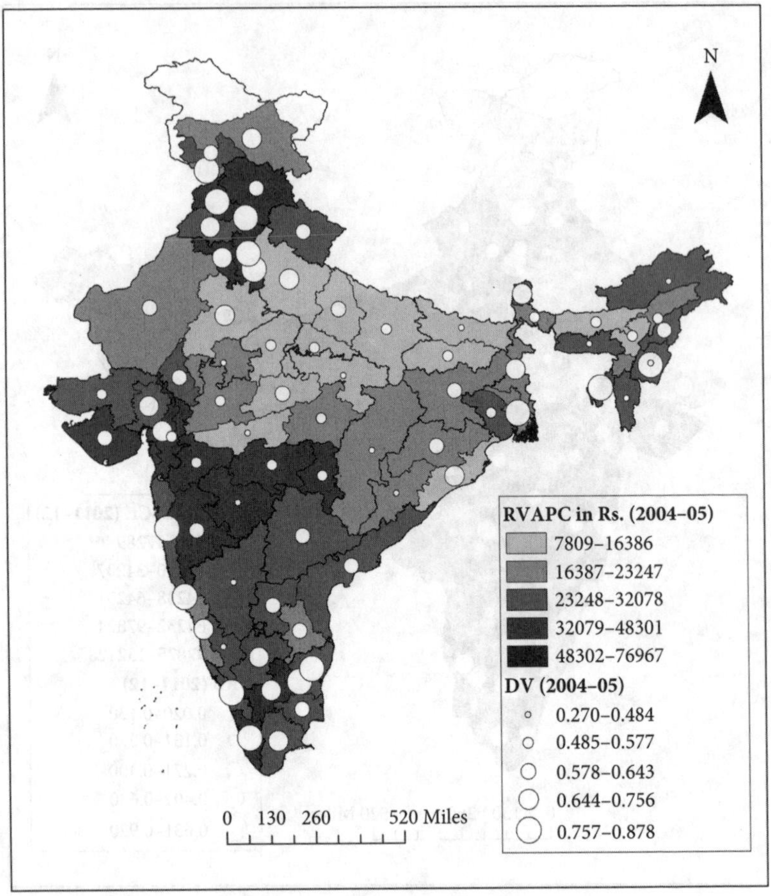

Map 6.9 Diversity index (DV) and Regional Value Added per capita (RVAPC) for all NSS regions for the time period 2004–05

which ranges from 907 branches in 2004–5 to 997 branches in 2011–12. The reverse is true for the bottom 10 RVAPC regions, having a higher bank branch outreach ranging from 1,364 branches in 2004–5 to almost 1,400 branches in 2011–12. Credit per branch follows the exact inverse pattern, with the top 10 RVAPC regions having high values, ranging from INR 19.7 Cr. per branch in 2004–5 to INR 46.43 Cr. per branch in 2011–12, almost double the national average. For the bottom 10 regions, the credit per branch ranges from INR 6.28 Cr. in 2004–5 to INR 12.69 Cr. in 2011–12. As evident from Table 6.12, this is about half the national average. This is

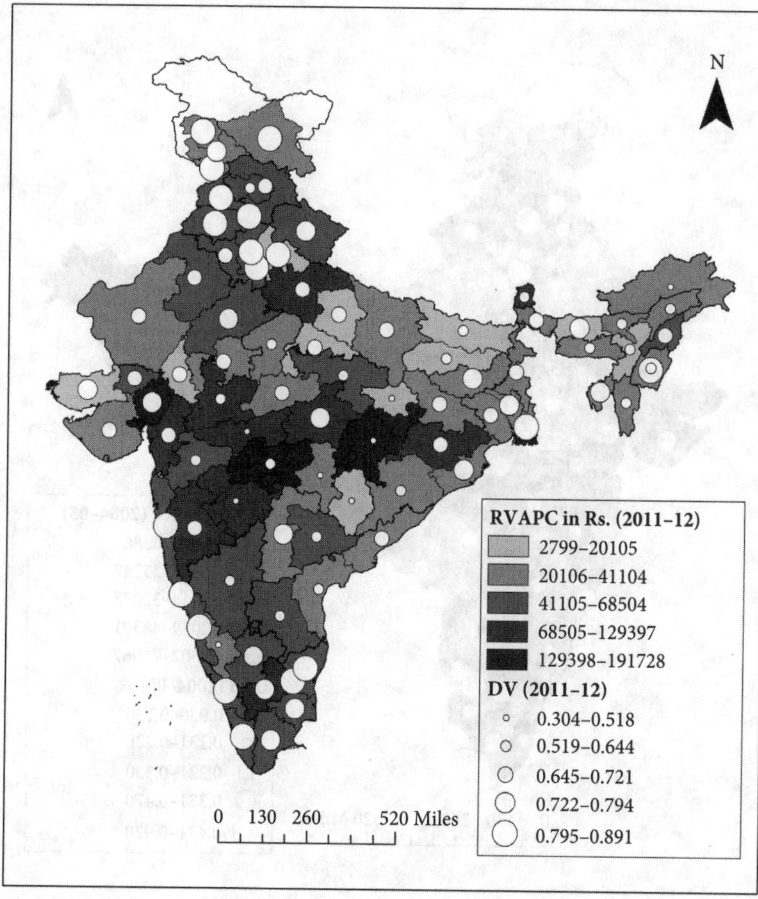

Map 6.10 Diversity index (DV) and Regional Value Added per capita (RVAPC) for all NSS regions for the time period 2011–12

possibly due to the fact that high RVAPC regions may be compact geographies, or regions with high output but low population. In such cases, the number of bank branches is likely to be lesser, while credit off-take could be high. In case of low RVAPC regions, many of them are highly populated, as in the case of the states of Uttar Pradesh and Bihar, and are likely to have high bank branch penetration. However, the presence of bank branches does not necessarily ensure high credit off-take. These regions have not had a very positive credit history and have a low industrial base. Also, there is limited potential for collateral, given the high population

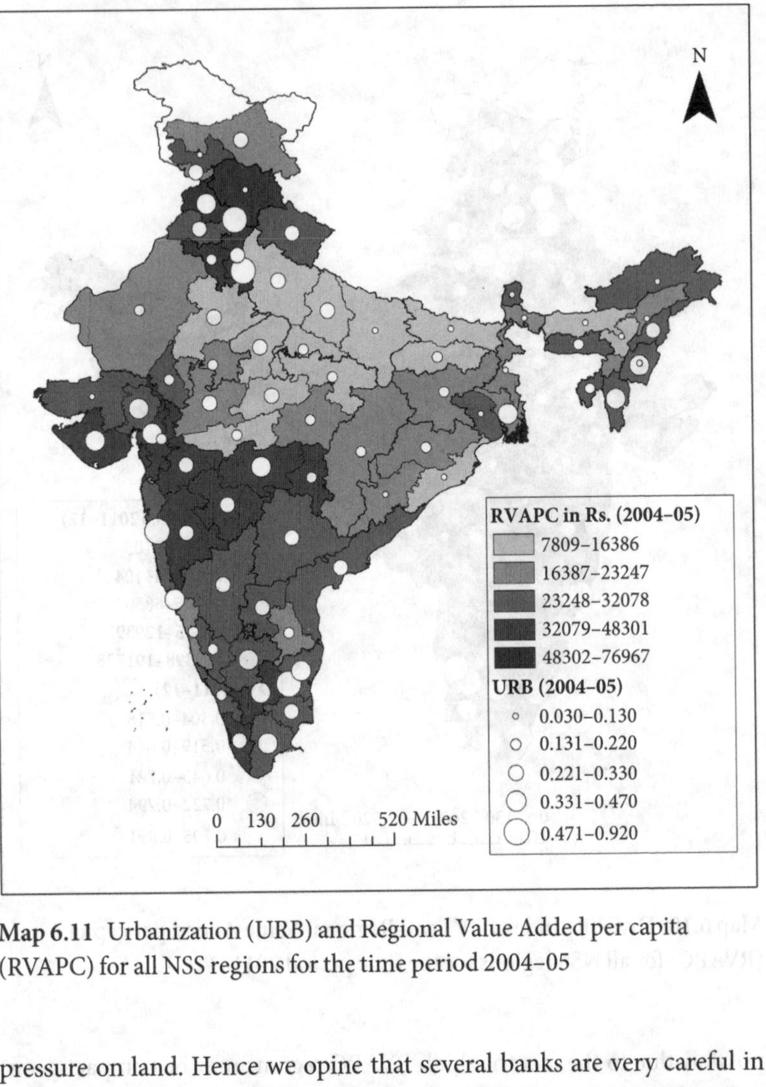

Map 6.11 Urbanization (URB) and Regional Value Added per capita (RVAPC) for all NSS regions for the time period 2004–05

pressure on land. Hence we opine that several banks are very careful in extending credit to customers in these regions. This is an aspect that warrants further investigation and is a potential area for further research.

The share of skilled workforce is high in case of the top 10 RVAPC regions, ranging from 13 per cent in 2004–5 to 18 per cent in 2011–12. This share is seen to increase even for the bottom 10 RVAPC regions, from 5 per cent in 2004–5 to 8 per cent in 2011–12, although this is less than the national average, which ranges from 8 per cent in 2004–5 to 11 per cent in 2011–12. There is a clear 10 per cent differential in the shares of skills between the top 10 and the bottom 10 RVAPC regions. On analysing

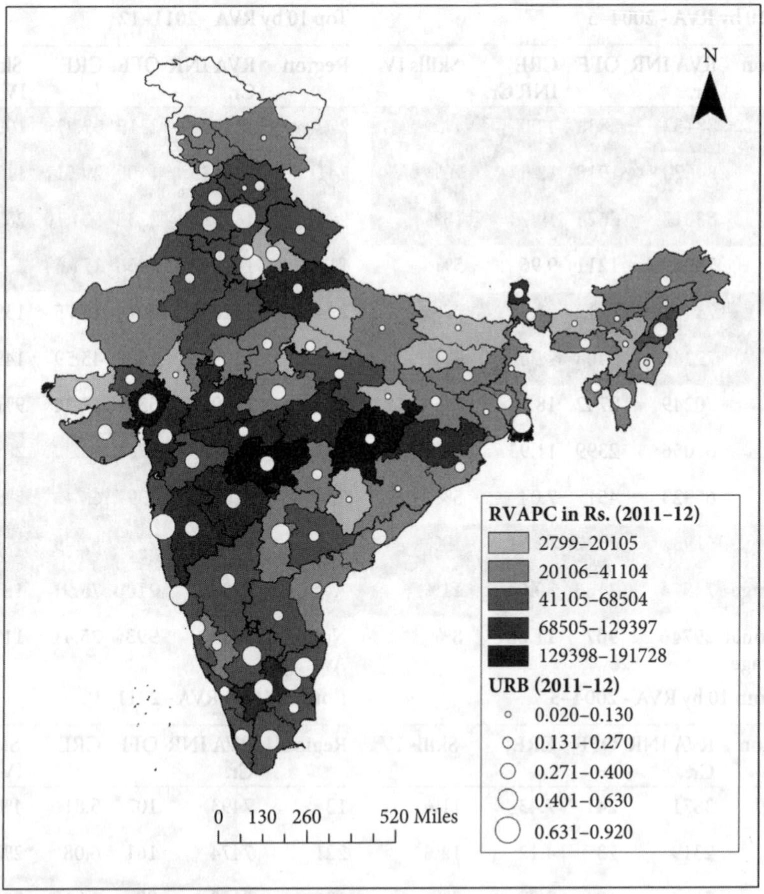

Map 6.12 Urbanization (URB) and Regional Value Added per capita (RVAPC) for all NSS regions for the time period 2011–12

the presence of million-plus cities, we find their presence in very few top 10 RVAPC regions such as Delhi, Surat, and so on (highlighted in grey). However, in contrast to the earlier case, several of the bottom 10 RVAPC regions have million-plus cities. This is particularly true for the more populous states such as UP, which house the cities of Lucknow, Varanasi, Meerut, Kanpur, and so on. It is therefore important to examine the nature of the relationship between output and proximity to million-plus cities, and whether it varies when we consider RVA and RVAPC respectively.

Thus, a detailed descriptive analysis throws up some interesting patterns when we study the relationship of sectoral shares, agglomeration,

Table 6.11 Access Levels by RVA

Top 10 by RVA - 2004–5				
Region	RVA INR Cr.	OFF	CRE INR Cr.	Skills IV
93	88157	2838	4.06	4%
272	84673	1918	12.57	10%
193	83017	2624	19.73	13%
281	78069	1211	9.96	5%
71	74411	1712	81.58	27%
91	72248	3408	7.26	7%
282	70249	2742	18.17	7%
322	67056	2399	11.93	12%
274	65923	451	7.04	5%
271	61932	2527	12.81	19%
Average	74574	2183	30.04	11%
National Average	29746	907	11.68	8%
Bottom 10 by RVA - 2004–5				
Region	RVA INR Cr.	OFF	CRE	Skills IV
11	3871	241	7.43	11%
131	2319	73	4.12	12%
121	2244	68	3.87	5%
142	1851	30	2.76	5%
141	1775	48	7.07	11%
151	1686	80	4.72	8%
12	1389	159	2.38	5%
111	1301	55	6.78	14%
183	1279	161	3.26	3%
351	1139	33	5.91	18%
Average	1885	95	4.83	9%
National Average	29746	907	11.68	8%

Top 10 by RVA - 2011–12				
Region	RVA INR Cr.	OFF	CRE	Skills IV
272	152128	2319	32.47	19%
241	146435	1509	29.51	11%
271	144858	2232	301.10	28%
71	142297	2456	171.64	33%
294	132606	2014	18.75	13%
334	120948	1523	43.59	14%
274	119063	539	17.34	9%
293	116828	2767	60.20	28%
93	116284	3397	6.74	5%
331	107189	2247	87.79	17%
Average	129864	2100	76.91	18%
National Average	50530	993	25.41	11%
Bottom 10 by RVA - 2011–12				
Region	RVA INR Cr.	OFF	CRE	Skills IV
12	7493	107	5.81	4%
221	7474	161	6.08	2%
131	5153	90	14.10	7%
111	3838	74	15.77	10%
121	3639	80	14.21	4%
151	3370	98	12.15	8%
141	2958	52	16.84	7%
351	2256	37	15.93	19%
142	2212	29	8.96	2%
14	556	27	6.36	12%
Average	3895	76	11.62	8%
National Average	50530	993	25.41	11%

Source: Authors' Calculations

Table 6.12 Access Levels by RVAPC

Top 10 by RVAPC (2004–5)					Top 10 by RVAPC (2011–12)				
Region	RVAPC	OFF	CRE	SKILL IV	Region	RVAPC	OFF	CRE	SKILL IV
301	76967	351	8.31	14%	301	129397	443	17.45	34%
41	74173	233	47.35	26%	71	110779	2456	171.64	33%
71	63877	1712	81.58	27%	235	97421	415	11.72	8%
341	48301	90	11.96	15%	41	80800	326	126.62	35%
276	45478	321	3.35	3%	276	80756	353	6.55	2%
274	41905	451	7.04	5%	341	80516	145	24.13	19%
351	40921	33	5.91	18%	334	75252	1523	43.59	14%
61	39343	1170	12.58	12%	274	74039	539	17.34	9%
275	38561	949	7.20	6%	111	73703	74	15.77	10%
241	38093	1211	12.43	7%	241	72012	1509	29.51	11%
Average	50762	652	19.77	13%	Average	87467	778	46.43	18%
National Average	26998	907	11.68	8%	National Average	44708	993	25.41	11%

Bottom 10 by RVAPC (2004–5)					Bottom 10 by RVAPC (2011–12)				
Region	RVAPC	OFF	CRE	Skills IV	Region	RVAPC	OFF	CRE	Skills IV
93	14011	2838	4.06	4%	184	20405	177	9.49	7%
94	13981	441	4.76	2%	141	20105	52	16.84	7%
183	13654	161	3.26	3%	182	20099	546	17.75	6%
92	13384	1541	8.02	5%	183	19948	173	9.19	12%
232	13097	356	12.98	4%	211	19752	1229	22.45	14%
211	13039	968	9.30	8%	91	17921	2779	17.80	9%
91	11595	3408	7.26	7%	95	17338	1489	12.19	7%
236	10983	333	6.62	6%	93	16688	3397	6.74	5%
102	8059	1464	3.90	5%	102	13695	1700	8.39	6%
101	7809	2128	2.60	3%	101	12838	2384	6.10	9%
Average	11961	1364	6.28	5%	Average	17879	1393	12.69	8%
National Average	26998	907	11.68	8%	National Average	44708	993	25.41	11%

Note: *Highlighted regions indicate presence of million-plus cities.

Source: Authors' calculations basis NSSO surveys 61st and 68th rounds and Basic Statistical Returns 2004 and 2009.

and access levels along with both RVA and RVAPC. It also helps us identify and build models in the next section to further examine the determinants of inter-regional differences in value added, both in absolute and per capita terms.

Determinants of RVA

Given the significant differences in output as well as variables under consideration across regions, it is important to examine certain critical factors that have an impact on output levels, both in terms of RVA and RVAPC. Since we did not find a clear linear relationship between output and sectoral diversity in our analysis in 'Preliminary Findings' of this chapter, we include DV and its square term DVSQ to test for non-linearity. We also find that the share of the tertiary sector (construction and services combined) is high in case of high output regions, and hence include the variable TERT to capture the share of employment in the tertiary sector. All other variables are described in 'Model Formulation' of this chapter.

To estimate the determinants of value added across regions and test for causality, we carry out a cross-sectional regression for 2004–5 and 2011–12 independently (Model 1a and 1b respectively) and then apply a pooled cross-sectional regression model across 2004–5 and 2011–12 (Model 2). While some scholars have expressed concerns regarding the pooling of cross-sectional data (Pesaran and Ron 1995; Robertson and Symons 1992), the proponents of pooling (Maddala 1991) have acknowledged the potential heterogeneity among cross-sectional units but assume that 'the efficiency gains from pooling outweigh the costs' (Baltagi and Griffin 1997). We then include a dummy variable for the regions with top 10 RVA values to gauge whether the top 10 regions in each period are different from the rest. This is done for the cross-sectional data (Models 3a and 3b) as well as for the pooled cross section (Model 4). We then carry out the entire set with RVAPC as the dependent variable to study the determinants of RVAPC. These form Models 5, 6, 7, and 8. As above, Models 7 and 8 include the dummy variables for regions with top 10 RVAPC. We take logged values of RVA, RVAPC, OFF, and DEP, since the unit values are very high.

Our expanded equations, therefore, take the form:

$$LnRVA_r = \alpha_r + \beta_1 DV_r + \beta_2 DVSQ_r + \beta_3 URB_r + \beta_4 SKILLIV_r + \beta_5 LnOFF + \beta_6 LnCRE_r + \beta_7 TERT_r + \beta_8 MNd_r + \varepsilon_r$$

Model 1
(4a)

$$LnRVA_r = \alpha_r + \beta_1 DV_r + \beta_2 DVSQ_r + \beta_3 URB_r + \beta_4 SKILLIV_r + \beta_5 LnOFF + \beta_6 LnCRE_r + \beta_7 TERT_r + \beta_8 MNd_r + \beta_9 Yd + \varepsilon_r$$

Model 2
(4b)

$$LnRVA_r = \alpha_r + \beta_1 DV_r + \beta_2 DVSQ_r + \beta_3 URB_r + \beta_4 SKILLIV_r + \beta_5 LnOFF + \beta_6 LnCRE_r + \beta_7 TERT_r + \beta_8 MNd_r + \beta_9 TOP10d_r + \varepsilon_r$$

Model 3
(4c)

$$LnRVA_r = \alpha_r + \beta_1 DV_r + \beta_2 DVSQ_r + \beta_3 URB_r + \beta_4 SKILLIV_r + \beta_5 LnOFF + \beta_6 LnCRE_r + \beta_7 TERT_r + \beta_8 MNd_r + \beta_9 TOP10d_r + \beta_{10} Yd + \varepsilon_r$$

Model 4
(4d)

$$LnRVAPC_r = \alpha_r + \beta_1 DV_r + \beta_2 DVSQ_r + \beta_3 URB_r + \beta_4 SKILLIV_r + \beta_5 LnOFF + \beta_6 LnCRE_r + \beta_7 TERT_r + \beta_8 MNd_r + \varepsilon_r$$

Model 5
(4e)

$$LnRVAPC_r = \alpha_r + \beta_1 DV_r + \beta_2 DVSQ_r + \beta_3 URB_r + \beta_4 SKILLIV_r + \beta_5 LnOFF + \beta_6 LnCRE_r + \beta_7 TERT_r + \beta_8 MNd_r + \beta_9 Yd + \varepsilon_r$$

Model 6
(4f)

$$LnRVAPC_r = \alpha_r + \beta_1 DV_r + \beta_2 DVSQ_r + \beta_3 URB_r + \beta_4 SKILLIV_r + \beta_5 LnOFF + \beta_6 LnCRE_r + \beta_7 TERT_r + \beta_8 MNd_r + \beta_9 TOP10PCd_r + \varepsilon_r$$

Model 7
(4g)

$$LnRVAPC_r = \alpha_r + \beta_1 DV_r + \beta_2 DVSQ_r + \beta_3 URB_r + \beta_4 SKILLIV_r + \beta_5 LnOFF + \beta_6 LnCRE_r + \beta_7 TERT_r + \beta_8 MNd_r + \beta_9 TOP10PCd_r + \beta_{10} Yd + \varepsilon_r$$

Model 8
(4h)

Given that certain variables exhibit strong correlation with each other, the data is tested for multi-collinearity using the variance inflation factor (VIF) before applying other techniques. The average VIF is high across models due to the inclusion of DV and DVSQ. We also apply the Breusch-Pagan test for heteroscedasticity and reject the null hypothesis wherever $p \geq 0.05$, implying that there is indeed heteroscedasticity in the data. For such cases, we run the regression again and report results with robust standard errors.

If we observe Table 6.13, we find that the first four columns cover Models 1a and 1b, while the last two columns cover the pooled Model 2. We have represented the coefficient values and t values indicating the degree of significance. The term DV and DVSQ both turn significant in Model 1b as well as Model 2. The share of urbanization (URB) is also significant for these models, while the million-plus dummy is not. The number of bank branches turns significant in both the cross-sectional as well as the pooled model. The share of the tertiary sector (TERT) is significant in 2004–5 and the pooled model, with a negative coefficient. The year dummy is significant in the case of Model 2.

Overall, the explanatory powers of Models 1a, 1b, and 2 are high with the adjusted R squared ranging from 0.81 to 0.85. The VIF test for multicollinearity has a high value due to the presence of DV and its squared term. We find heteroscedasticity only in Model 2, for which we report only robust standard errors. This result, with DV and DVSQ both turning significant and with DV having a positive coefficient and DVSQ having a negative coefficient, is reflective of a possible inverted-U association between RVA and DV. The share of urbanization also appears to have a significant impact on RVA, while this does not seem to be driven by million-plus cities, since the dummy does not turn significant.

In Table 6.14, we introduce a dummy variable where the top 10 regions by RVA take the value of 1 and all the rest are 0. This means that Model 3a and 3b will have 10 regions each for 2004–5 and 2011–12 with a value of 1, whereas Model 4 will have 20 regions with a value of 1, since it pools

Table 6.13 Determinants of Regional Value Added (RVA) Models 1 and 2

Independent Variables	Variable Name	Model 1a 2004–5		Model 1b 2011–12		Model 2 Pooled (Robust)	
		Coef.	t-value	Coef.	t-value	Coef.	t-value
Diversity index	DV	5.2867	1.28	5.6142	1.67**	5.5792	2.32***
Diversity index squared	DVSQ	−2.1626	−0.68	−4.8466	(2.03)***	−3.6773	(2.09)***
Urbanization share	URB	0.7462	1.13	1.0194	1.7**	0.9308	1.74**
Share of high-end skills	SKILLIV	2.3185	0.81	−0.8717	−0.82	−0.3267	−0.33
Bank branch offices (logged)	LnOFF	0.8662	12.78***	0.8888	16.1***	0.8679	24.45***
Credit per branch (logged)	LnCRE	−0.0192	−0.14	0.0751	0.58	0.0469	0.44
Share of tertiary sector	TERT	−1.5114	(2.93)***	−0.4159	−1.14	−0.8377	(2.55)***
Dummy for million plus cities	MNd	0.0063	0.04	0.0029	0.02	−0.0129	−0.13
Constant term	Cons	−0.1117	−0.06	2.0108	1.22	0.8342	0.7
Year dummy (2004–5 as base)	Yd					0.5428	5.3***
F value		F(8, 66)	41.02	F(8, 76)	83.86	F(9, 150)	97.55
Prob > F			0.0000		0.000		0.000
R-squared			0.8326		0.8704		0.8541
Adj R-squared			0.8123		0.8568		0.8453
VIF Test			25.76		19		19.46
Breusch-Pagan Test for Heteroscedasticity							
Chi Square			4.79		0.85		8.97
Probability (Chi Square)			0.0287		0.3557		0.0027

Source: Authors' Calculations
p value significance level: *.05, **.01, ***.001

Table 6.14 Determinants of Regional Value Added (RVA) Models 3 and 4

Independent Variables	Variable Name	Model 3a 2004–5		Model 3b 2011–12		Model 4 Pooled (Robust)	
		Coef.	t-value	Coef.	t-value	Coef.	t-value
Diversity index	DV	7.0671	1.73***	5.1306	1.57	5.9344	2.54***
Diversity index squared	DVSQ	−3.3582	−1.07	−4.5079	(1.95)**	−3.8950	(2.25)***
Urbanization share	URB	0.7138	1.11	1.0174	1.75**	0.9091	1.7**
Share of high-end skills	SKILLIV	2.3482	0.84	−1.4379	-1.36	−0.7479	−0.75
Bank branch offices (logged)	LnOFF	0.8065	11.36***	0.8727	16.19***	0.8347	22.01***
Credit per branch (logged)	LnCRE	−0.0378	−0.28	0.0226	0.18	0.0120	0.11
Share of tertiary sector	TERT	−1.6568	(3.28)***	−0.3043	-0.86	−0.8176	(2.54)***
Million plus-cities dummy	MNd	−0.0278	−0.18	−0.0281	-0.21	−0.0415	-0.43
Top 10 RVA dummy	TOP10d	0.4442	2.24***	0.4270	2.44***	0.4135	3.17***
Constant term	Cons	−0.4472	−0.24	2.7953	1.71**	1.1598	0.97
Year dummy (2004–5 as base)	Yd					0.5823	5.58***
F value		F(9, 65)	39.23	F(9, 75)	65.08	F(10, 149)	107.13
Prob > F			0.0000		0.000		0.000
R-squared			0.8445		0.8799		0.8637
Adj R-squared			0.823		0.8655		0.8545
VIF Test			23.8		17.52		17.7
Breusch-Pagan Test for Heteroscedasticity							
Chi Square			4.99		1.69		10.98
Probability (Chi Square)			0.0255		0.1935		0.0009

Source: Authors' Calculations

data from both periods. We find the dummy variable to be significant in Models 3a, 3b, and 4, implying therefore that the top 10 regions in each period do, in fact, behave differently compared to the rest, further reaffirming that a higher RVA leads to greater divergence. The number of bank branches continues to be significant across all three models. As in the case of Models 1a and 2, Models 3a and 4 also find the share of tertiary sector to be significant but with a negative coefficient. We also find that in Model 3a only DV is significant, while in Model 3b only DVSQ is significant. DV and DVSQ are both significant in the pooled Model 4, with DV having a positive coefficient and DVSQ having a negative coefficient. The year dummy is significant, implying that there are differences in RVA values that are attributable to the time interval. The VIF is high and ranges from 17.52 to 23.8. There is heterogeneity only in the case of Model 4, which leads us to report only robust standard errors. These models, like the previous set, have high explanatory power with an adjusted R squared ranging from 0.82 to 0.86.

For the next set of models, we take RVAPC as the dependent variable. In Table 6.15, Models 5a and 5b capture the determinants of RVAPC for cross-sectional periods of 2004–5 and 2011–12 respectively. Model 6 considers the pooled data for both periods. These models have a much lower explanatory power compared to the previous ones, possibly because several additional factors might influence the value added on a per capita basis. We would still like to study the causal relationship of individual variables with RVAPC. We find that DV and DVSQ are significant in Model 5b as well as Model 6. The share of high-end skills is significant in 2004–5 as well as the pooled model. Based on the descriptive statistics, it appears that while high-end skills have increased a lot in the second period, this is possibly more for the topmost regions and not across the board. The Breusch-Pagan test reveals that there is no heteroscedasticity in the data.

We further introduce a dummy variable in Table 6.16, with the top 10 RVAPC regions taking the value of 1 and the others 0. This again gives us 10 regions with value 1 in 2004–5 and 2011–12 for Models 7a and 7b respectively, and 20 regions for the pooled Model 8. In all these three models this dummy variable is significant, which means that regions with the highest RVAPC indeed behave differently as compared to the rest of the regions. For Model 7b and the pooled results in Model 8, DV and DVSQ continue to be significant. Interestingly the number of bank branches per region (OFF) does not turn out to be significant but has a

Table 6.15 Determinants of Regional Value Added per capita (RVAPC) Models 5 and 6

Independent Variables	Variable Name	Model 5a 2004–5		Model 5b 2011–12		Model 6 Pooled	
		Coef.	T-value	Coef.	t-value	Coef.	t-value
Diversity index	DV	1.5151	0.51	12.8004	2.46***	6.0836	2.02***
Diversity index squared	DVSQ	−0.4532	-0.2	−8.8449	(2.4)***	−4.0132	(1.79)**
Urbanization share	URB	0.7055	1.47	0.5682	0.61	0.7780	1.49
Share of high-end skills	SKILLIV	4.8118	2.31***	1.3707	0.83	2.0480	1.67**
Bank branch offices (logged)	LnOFF	-0.0592	-1.21	-0.0061	−0.07	−0.0320	−0.62
Credit per branch (logged)	LnCRE	0.0116	0.11	0.2645	1.32	0.1281	1.14
Share of tertiary sector	TERT	−0.5499	−1.47	−0.4624	−0.82	−0.3791	−1.09
Million plus-cities dummy	MNd	−0.1464	-1.26	−0.0818	−0.38	−0.1050	−0.83
Constant term	Cons	8.4661	6.19***	3.4409	1.35	6.5071	4.63***
Year dummy (2004–5 as base)	Yd					0.3274	2.67***
F value		F(8, 66)	5.32	F(8, 76)	2.82	F(9, 150)	7.35
Prob > F			0.0000		0.000		0.000
R-squared			0.3921		0.2288		0.306
Adj R-squared			0.3184		0.1476		0.2644
VIF test			25.76		19.42		19.46
Breusch-Pagan Test for Heteroscedasticity							
Chi Square			1.47		0.39		1.37
Probability (Chi Square)			0.2258		0.5341		0.2423

Source: Authors' Calculations

negative coefficient in all models with RVAPC as the dependent variable. This ties in with the finding in our descriptive analysis earlier, where regions with higher RVAPC were seen to have a lower banking footprint. Credit per branch on the other hand is significant in Models 7b and 8 and

Table 6.16 Determinants of Regional Value Added per capita (RVAPC) Models 7 and 8

Independent Variables	Variable Name	Model 7a 2004–5		Model 7b 2011–12		Model 8 Pooled (Robust)	
		Coef.	t-value	Coef.	t-value	Coef.	t-value
Diversity index	DV	2.5899	0.97	11.0847	2.57***	6.2528	2.44***
Diversity index squared	DVSQ	−1.3277	−0.65	−7.3008	(2.38)***	−4.1863	(2.19)***
Urbanization share	URB	0.2745	0.63	0.0740	0.1	0.1604	0.35
Share of high-end skills	SKILLIV	3.6311	1.95**	0.3777	0.27	1.2074	1.15
Bank branch offices (logged)	LnOFF	−0.0464	−1.07	-0.0284	-0.4	−0.0242	−0.55
Credit per branch (logged)	LnCRE	0.0580	0.64	0.3313	1.99***	0.1939	2.02***
Share of tertiary sector	TERT	−0.4872	−1.47	-0.3113	-0.67	−0.2651	-0.89
Million plus-cities dummy	MNd	−0.1526	−1.48	-0.3609	(1.95)**	−0.2136	(1.96)**
Top 10 RVAPC dummy	TOP10PCd	0.5615	4.39***	1.2693	5.99***	0.9482	7.6***
Constant term	Cons	7.9697	6.56***	3.8218	1.81**	6.2485	5.22***
Year dummy (2004–5 as base)	Yd					0.3046	2.92***
F value		F(9, 65)	8.17	F(9, 75)	7.64	F(10, 149)	14.9
Prob > F			0.0000		0.0000		0.0000
R-squared			0.5309		0.4784		0.5001
Adj R-squared			0.466		0.4158		0.4665
VIF Test			23.27		17.51		17.65
Breusch-Pagan Test for Heteroscedasticity							
Chi Square			3.04		3.98		0.29
Probability (Chi Square)			0.0814		0.0461		0.5901

Source: Authors' Calculations

corroborates our descriptive analysis that higher RVAPC regions do seem to have a higher credit off-take. The million-plus cities dummy is significant but with a negative sign, which seems to indicate that regions with a million-plus city might actually have a lower RVAPC.

To summarize, the overall results can be clubbed under the following heads:

Agglomeration: The variables DV and DVSQ are statistically significant across almost all of the models, particularly in 2011–12 and in the pooled cross sections for RVA in absolute as well as per capita terms. This is a very pertinent finding, since it not only repeatedly underscores the value of sectoral diversity in determining the levels of regional output over time but is also indicative of the fact that there might be a threshold limit beyond which diversity has a negative relationship with output. In other words, while diversification into more than one sector is very desirable and strongly associated with economic development of a region, there may be limits to which a region should diversify. In graphical terms, we therefore propose that the relationship between sectoral diversity and regional output takes the form of an inverted-U (Figure 6.5). We also attempt to identify the point of inflection using the following equation:

$$y = Ax + Bx^2$$
$$\frac{dy}{dx} = A + 2Bx \tag{5}$$

Where y denotes the dependent variable RVA and x is DV for corresponding values of y. At the maximum value of y, we solve for x:

$$\frac{dy}{dx} = 0$$
$$i.e.\ A + 2Bx = 0$$
$$x = \left(-\frac{A}{2B}\right)$$
$$x = \left(-\frac{6.7591}{2 * -(4.1374)}\right)$$
$$x = \left(\frac{6.7591}{2 * (4.1374)}\right)$$
$$x = \left(\frac{6.7591}{8.2748}\right)$$
$$x = 0.81$$

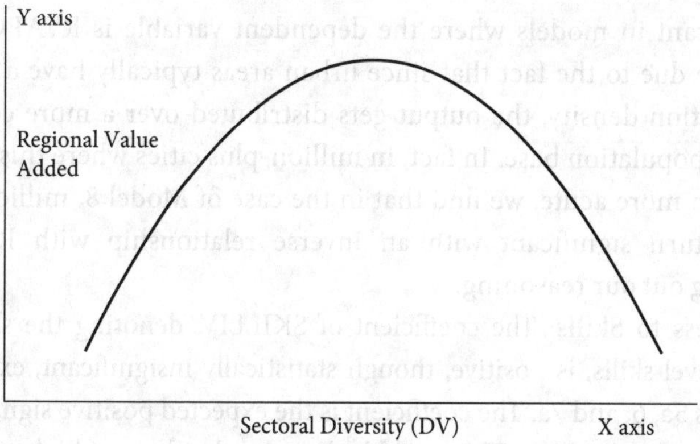

Figure 6.5 Generalized Relationship between RVA and DV
Source: Authors' Calculations

Therefore, we get our point of inflexion at 0.81. This implies that 0.81 is the diversity index value beyond which sectoral diversity and output are inversely related. This means that initially the economy is specialized in only one sector and has a DV value of 0. As the regional economy begins to diversify, output levels are seen to increase; this is expected to continue till the optimum level (peak) of diversification is reached. Beyond this, for higher values of the diversity index (beyond 0.81 in this case), we expect output levels to fall. Therefore, specialized diversification may be a good model to follow, and policy makers may be better advised to ensure that regions specialized in only one sector are encouraged to diversify and substantially diversified regions consolidate and strengthen their performance in sectors where they have competitive advantage. This also builds the case that while specialization by itself is risky for long-term economic sustainability, specialized diversification appears to be an avenue worthy of examination.

Urbanization and Million-plus Cities: The share of urbanization is also found to be very significant and has a positive coefficient, while the dummy variable for million-plus cities is insignificant. This gives an interesting insight and indicates that while urbanization definitely accounts for growth, this is not supported by million-plus cities alone. While this association is very significant in models where the dependent variable is RVA, the share of urbanization does not emerge significant in models where the dependent variable is RVAPC. This may be due to the fact that since urban areas typically have a higher population density, the output gets distributed over a more concentrated population base. In fact, in million-plus cities where this would be even more acute, we find that in the case of Model 8, million-plus cities turn significant with an inverse relationship with RVAPC, bearing out our reasoning.

Access to Skills: The coefficient of SKILLIV, denoting the share of high-level skills, is positive, though statistically insignificant, except in Models 5a, 6, and 7a. The coefficient is the expected positive sign, but its value is not very high. This could be because the share of high-end skill levels in the workforce have been low in general, and some part of their impact may be captured by the diversity variable, since skill levels are directly associated with the levels of diversity. Not all growth is propelled by high-end skills alone, given that a large proportion of employment in certain states continues to be significantly agrarian, although these shares are changing. This is reflected by the significance of the share of employment in the tertiary sector, which combines employment in construction and services. The coefficient is negative, possibly due to the nature of construction of the VA variable, which includes employment shares and the workforce participation rate. Given that service sector employment is in highly productive sectors, it is seen to go hand in hand with a reduction in workforce participation rate.

Access to Finance: The study confirms a very strong association of RVA with the number of bank branches in the region. The volume of credit per branch turns significant in Models 7 and 8. The signs of both variables are, as expected, positive. This underscores access to finance as a critical growth-driver and builds the case to expand bank branch networks or taking banking to people's doorsteps through a robust banking correspondent model. For increases in per capita output, it is important to have additional measures to boost the volume of credit, as the branch footprint by itself is not sufficient. It is evident from the data available that access to finance through the formal institutional network is essential for high regional output levels. Hence policy measures to boost financial inclusion are likely to impact the local economy directly.

A Nuanced Relationship

Our analysis of NSS regions across India over 2004–5 and 2011–12 reveals significant increases in VA during this period coupled with differences in the level of increase across locations. The results confirm our hypothesis that while the relative rankings across states remain fairly unchanged, the rankings across regions, especially the top 20, vary significantly.

We find that much of the RVA differences can be explained by agglomeration economies. Access to finance and skills also plays an important role, but the relationship is nuanced: for instance, while high RVA regions clearly have a very high share of level IV skills in the workforce, this association does not hold across all regions, possible since the proportion of skilled labour in the economy as such is not very high. Similarly, a high bank branch penetration is closely associated with high regional output in absolute terms, but in per capita terms the volume of credit becomes more important.

We further observe that while sectoral diversity is positively associated with higher levels of RVA, specialized diversification is emerging as an interesting phenomenon and has the potential to be examined as an important aspect of regional and industrial planning. This ties in with some of the findings in the international context which postulate that diversity might indeed be good for regional economic development (Kemeny and Storper 2014), and yet the relationship between the two may not be entirely straightforward. Farhauer and Kröll (2012) find that smaller cities in Germany that are specialized in a few sectors are positively associated with economic performance. Our results indicate that there are thresholds to the ability of diversification that contribute to high levels of value added. We, therefore, opine that the term 'specialized diversification' may be more representative of this phenomenon, since it is diversity and not specialization that is the defining characteristic. This means that regions which have already attained peak values on the diversity index can be encouraged to specialize in sectors where they have a competitive advantage. More importantly, regions which have low index values can be encouraged to diversify their economic base to enable them to move up the continuum.

We also find that higher levels of urbanization account for higher output levels, and this experience is not associated with the presence or absence of a million-plus city. It implies that high output levels are not restricted to million-plus cities alone; in fact, it is possible that smaller cities might be experiencing greater value added. Our results reaffirm the findings of Mitra (2011) and Denis et al. (2012) who argue that growth is more in the periphery and the smaller cities in India. This builds a case for greater focus and investment in the smaller cities as possible growth engines.

7
Inter-temporal Differences across Regions

Changes over Time

Given that there are sizeable variations across states and regions in India, it is important to understand the underlying factors that explain these changes across regions between 2004–5 and 2011–12. If we analyse the literature on patterns of economic development over time, there are two competing points of view. At one end of the spectrum is the convergence hypothesis – that over time, regions trace a path of convergence and tend to move towards equilibrium levels of income, wages, and output. There is a counter view that rich regions are likely to get richer relative to poorer regions, which will see the incidence of virtual cycles of poverty and prosperity that are relatively difficult to break.

It is important to understand these two arguments and look at the empirical evidence so far and situate our study of inter-temporal differentials in this context. Theories about growth and regional economic development have been claid out in several pioneering works ranging from backwash to spread effects and polarization to trickle-down effects (Young 1928; Myrdal 1957; Hirschman 1958; Williamson 1965). While there are studies that find evidence of convergence in India (Saradamoni 1969; Cashin and Sahay 1996), there are others that find evidence of divergence (Bajpai and Sachs 1996; Lall and Chakravorty 2007). The conclusions of these studies differ according to which group of states is examined, the unit of area being analysed, and the time being considered. There are very few studies which have looked at differences at the sub-state level or which focus exclusively on the past decade.

Regional Economic Diversity. Poornima Dore and Krishnan Narayanan, Oxford University Press. © Oxford University Press India 2022. DOI: 10.1093/oso/9780190130596.003.0007

This chapter compares major aspects of economic structure and access in Indian regions across 2004–5 and 2011–12. The study covers all states and union territories across the country and breaks up the larger states into smaller and more comparable sub-regional units of NSS regions. The analysis deals with what differentiates regions over the two time periods across different elements of economic structure and access: namely value added, consumption, diversity, sectoral shares, degree of urbanization, population with high-end skills, and financial penetration. Our approach takes the difference between initial endowments in the first time period as given and looks at the process of incremental change over two time periods. We first use a univariate statistical criterion to evaluate the significance of the difference between these economic structure and access indicators over time. The factors that differentiate the behaviour of regions are then analysed with the help of a multivariate discriminant analysis.

The next segment of the chapter is a brief outline of these two debates and the background in India. In the third section, we provide an examination of the factors that are palpably felt to be changing over time. The fourth section discusses the empirical results of our analysis, followed by the conclusion.

Divergence and Convergence

The divergence argument draws its genesis from Young (1928) who postulates that 'the economic growth process under the condition of increasing returns is progressive and propagates itself in a cumulative way'. Young draws from both Smith (1776) and Marshall (1890) to say that the link between division of labour and the size of the market can also be the reverse, that is, size of the market can be determined by the volume of production. By this, one can say that 'division of labour depends to a large extent on division of labour' Young (1928), thus resulting in a mutually reinforcing impact also called positive feedback loops. This has been further specified by Myrdal (1957) in his theory of cumulative causation. Different regions have different initial starting points and levels of development. The process of economic development can be viewed as one of increasing demand and increasing supply reinforcing each other.

There must be some factor that creates a stimulating effect. The additional necessary condition lies in the nature of reciprocal demand and supply functions, that is, the elasticity of the Marshallian offer curves when commodities exchanged are produced under conditions of increasing returns. Basically when the demand for each commodity is elastic (in the special case that a small increase in its supply is an increase in demand for other commodities), progress is bound to be cumulative and it may be supposed that every increase in individual commodity demand will invoke an increase in supply. Since elasticity of demand and supply will be different for different products, some industries and regions will grow faster than others, increasing the distance over time.

The convergence argument is centred primarily around the inverted-U hypothesis (Kuznets 1955; Williamson 1965) which states that if one takes a historical view of economic development, nations are seen to initially experience increased disparities, which narrow over time as nations move ahead on the development continuum. Those in higher brackets need to keep reinventing themselves to stay on top and maintain high growth rates—there is very little space to manoeuvre or engage in inter-industry shifts for high income populations.

In other words, the dynamism of a growing free economic society will solicit a move towards convergence. For instance, Kuznets argues that as the level of urbanisation increases, it reflects the ease with which migrants are able to access a better lifestyle in the economy. These are indications of whether the less advantaged are able to benefit in proportion to their economic struggle. Kaldor (1957) uses the Keynesian approach on induced investment to argue that while Young (1928) looked at demand and supply as flow variables (outside the market), it is also important to look at their role as stock variables (inside the market). It has been argued that since the manufacturing sector has increasing returns, this will have dynamic effects in the form of technological innovations which improve productivity as well. Labour transfer from the agricultural to the industrial sector results in the simultaneous improvement of productivity in both sectors, resulting in the movement to a higher orbit of output and productivity.

It is important to note that proponents of neither divergence nor convergence deny the possibility that both counteracting forces might exist simultaneously. Myrdal clearly speaks of spread effects, but does not emphasize them as he does not believe that the market by itself would move towards convergence, without specific policy intervention. Similarly, Kuznets also considers divergence, but sees it as a necessary point in the continuum towards the end state of convergence.

There have been a few studies examining the pattern of interstate disparities in development in India, covering different periods of time since Independence. The pre-independence period saw huge gaps between pockets of vibrancy and the hinterland. Awasthi (1991) in his analysis of Indian economic history explains that regions with limited access to facilities and opportunities had starkly different socio-economic conditions. Nair (2004) claims that during the 1950s and 60s, the state of inequality was unchanged. There are other studies that argue that this period has witnessed a narrowing down of disparity (Saradamoni 1969; Mathur 1983; Awasthi 1991). The sectoral shares, however, are seen to move in opposite directions, with the secondary sector following an inverted U-shaped path and the primary sector having the reverse. Gupta (1973) suggests that this period was marked with public sector investments forming 70 per cent of total investments and this, played an important role in reducing disparities. The next period from 1975 to the mid-1990s is characterized by a reversal in trend towards increasing disparities between states (Bajpai and Sachs 1996). It is interesting to note that this was also the period of deregulation, liberalization, greater role of the private sectors and emergence the services sector.

There is a view that reforms strengthen 'spread effects' and trigger more balanced regional development as they mark a move towards seamless flow of 'goods, services and factors of production' (Elizondo and Krugman 1992). This appears to hold in the Indian case at the state level over the 1960s to the 1990s across 20 states by Cashin and Sahay (1996) and by Dholakia (2009), both of which find evidence of reducing disparity between regions. In contrast, a number of scholars report results that confirm divergence during this period (Rao et al. 1999; Dasgupta et al. 2000; Kurian 2000). The NSDP per capita is seen to follow a pattern of cumulative causation, with rich states getting richer and a clear dichotomy emerging between forward and backward states. Lall and Chakravorty (2007) also find that new investments are spatially more concentrated in the post-reform period than in the pre-reform period. This implies that the push towards greater reliance on market forces and reduction of interventionist measures by the government, directs financial and human resources naturally toward forward regions and therefore supports the 'return of cumulative causation and divergence'.

Most of the existing studies examine regional disparity and focus on two aspects, namely state level data and annualized information on NSDP or per capita income and other indicators. Among the papers examined, the last time period considered is on or before 2003–4. While Dholakia (2009) mentions that there are additional variations at a regional level, he does not empirically describe the same. We address this by carrying out our analysis at a sub-state level with the NSS region as the unit of analysis and look at the latest available data of 2004–5 and 2011–12. In the previous chapter we examined the differences across states and regions and found clusters being formed and changing between the two time periods. In this chapter, we seek to build on it and examine the extent to which such regional disparities have increased in India between 2004–5 (t_1) and 2011–12 (t_2), and which factors explain the changes. We specify the periods as this forms the grouping criteria for the discriminant analysis carried out in subsequent sections of this chapter. In the absence of annualized data, estimating the degree of divergence or convergence is beyond the scope of this study. Having outlined the contours of the continuum since independence till date, and also established that the variations have increased, we focus on the specific time segment of 2004–5 to 2011–12, and identify what drives regional disparity in this time period at the NSS region level.

Discriminant Analysis

We examine region level data for all NSS regions for the period 2004–5 and 2011–12 and attempt to identify the important factors accounting for changes across the two time periods with the help of discriminant analysis. Discriminant analysis (DA) is a statistical technique used to study the differences between two or more groups of observations with respect to several variables simultaneously (Klecka 1980). The DA involves the determination of a linear equation like ordinary least squares regression that can also predict which group the case belongs to. The DA is used when the dependent variable is categorical with the predictor independent variables are at interval level such as age, income, attitudes, perceptions, and years of education. Dummy variables can also be used as predictors as in multiple regression. This differs from logistic regression on two counts. First, logistic regression is limited to a dichotomous dependent variable, whereas DA can have two or more categories of the dependent variable. Also logistic regression independent variables can be of any level of measurement, but DA independent variables are at either interval level or dummies.

Underlying Assumptions

The major underlying assumptions of DA are:

1. The observations are randomly sampled;
2. Each predictor variable is normally distributed;
3. Each of the allocations for the dependent categories in the initial classification are correctly classified;
4. There must be at least two groups or categories, with each case belonging to only one group so that the groups are mutually exclusive and collectively exhaustive (all cases can be placed in a group);
5. Each group or category must be well defined, clearly differentiated from any other groups and natural. Partitioning quantitative variables is only justifiable if there are easily identifiable gaps at the points of division; for instance, three groups taking three available levels of amounts of housing loan;
6. The groups or categories should be defined before collecting the data;
7. The attributes used to separate the groups should discriminate quite clearly between the groups so that group or category overlap is clearly non-existent or minimal; and
8. Group sizes of the dependent should not be grossly different and should be at least five times the number of independent variables.

In our analysis, we have two groups represented by the two time periods t_1 and t_2. All variables representing data for 2004–5, therefore, are a part of group 1 and those representing 2011–12 are a part of group 2. This is data that has already been collected by NSS for these given time periods and so the groups are clearly defined. The usage of the attribute of time to distinguish between the two groups, that too two periods separated by an eight-year gap, minimizes the chances of a data overlap. We have 75 NSS regions in t_1 and 85 NSS regions in $t_{2.}$ The group sizes of the dependent are therefore in a close range and are more than five times the number of independent variables. Our sample thus meets the requirements and key assumptions to carry out a robust discriminant analysis.

Classifying Cases

There are several purposes of DA:

1. To investigate differences between groups on the basis of the attributes of the cases, indicating which attributes contribute most to group separation. The descriptive technique successively identifies the linear combination of attributes known as canonical discriminant functions (equations) which contribute maximally to group separation.
2. Predictive DA addresses the question of how to assign new cases to groups. The DA function uses a person's scores on the predictor variables to predict the category to which the individual belongs.
3. To classify cases into groups. Statistical significance tests using chi square enable you to see how well the function separates the groups.
4. To test theory whether cases are classified as predicted.

The purpose of the function is to maximize the distance between the categories, that is, come up with an equation that has strong discriminatory power between groups. After using an existing set of data to calculate the discriminant function and classify cases, any new cases can then be classified. The number of discriminant functions is one less the number of groups. Hence there is only one function for the two group discriminant analysis that we carry out.

In this study, the significance of the regional differences between the two time periods is first evaluated by the univariate statistical criterion. The univariate test is non-parametric. It is basically used to test for the equality of group's means for every variable considered in the study. The testing criterion is 'Wilks' Lambda (W) and F-value (F). In the univariate analysis, Wilks' 'Lambda is given by:

W = Within-group sum of squares/total sum of squares,

W = 1 if the observed group means are equal, and

W 0 (tends to be close to zero) when within group variability < total variability.

A smaller W score is, therefore, preferable. Variables are assessed on the basis of the W scores and their significance determined by the F values. Once the variables undergo the univariate analysis, all the variables are introduced in a multivariate statistical procedure to identify the discriminants.

The best separation between the two groups is given by:

$$PD = \alpha_0 + \alpha_1 X_1 + \alpha_2 X_2 + \dots\dots + \alpha_n X_n \qquad (1)$$

Where PD = discriminate function, α = the discriminant coefficient or weight for that variable, X = respondent's score for that variable and n = the number of predictor variables.

This function is similar to a regression equation or function. The α's are unstandardized discriminant coefficients analogous to the b's in the regression equation. These α's maximize the distance between the means of the criterion (dependent) variable. The aim of the statistical analysis in DA is to combine (weight) the variable scores in some way so that a single new composite variable, the discriminant score, is produced. PD is the discriminant score for regions in period t_1 and t_2.

The purpose of the analysis is to maximize the distance between the categories, that is, come up with an equation that has strong discriminatory power between groups. Standardizing the variables ensures that scale differences between the variables are eliminated. Standardized discriminant coefficients can also be used like beta weight in regression. When all variables are standardized, absolute weights (that is, ignore the sign) can be used to rank variables in terms of their discriminating power, the largest weight being associated with the most powerful discriminating variable.

Table 7.1 List of Variables and Data Sources*

Variables	Variable Name	Measurement	Data Source
Regional Value Added per capita	RVAPC	Regional Value Added/ Total Population of the Region	Handbook of Statistics on Indian economy 2004–5 and 2011–12, RBI; 61st and 68th Round NSSO Surveys
Disposable income per capita	MPCE	Monthly per capita Expenditure	61st and 68th Round NSSO Surveys
Diversity Index	DV	$DV_r = 1 - H_r$ denoting the sectoral mix scale of 0 to 1	Constructed based on sectoral shares for 14 categories based on NIC codes from the 61st and 68th Round NSSO surveys
Share of Agriculture	AGRI	Proportion of total workers engaged in Agriculture	Classification based on NIC codes of industrial classification as followed by the 61st and 68th Round NSSO surveys. The 14 categories at 2 digit level are further collapsed into the four core sectors.
Share of Manufacturing	MFG	Proportion of total workers engaged in Manufacturing	
Share of Construction	CON	Proportion of total workers engaged in Construction	
Share of Services	SVS	Proportion of total workers engaged in service sector	
Bank Branch Offices	OFF	No. of bank branch offices	Basic Statistical Returns of Scheduled Commercial Banks in India, 2005 and 2010, RBI.
Credit per branch	CRE	Volume of credit outstanding (Rs. Cr.)/ branch offices	
Deposit per branch	DEP	Volume of deposits in Rs. Cr./ branch offices	
Workforce Participation Rate	WPR	Proportion of population engaged in work as per usual principal status	61st and 68th Round NSSO Surveys
Urbanisation share	URB	Proportion of total population living in urban areas	
Share of Regular Employment	REGEMP	Proportion of total population engaged in regular work	
Share of High-end skills	SKILLIV	Proportion of total workforce with level IV skills in occupations coded 0 to 2	61st and 68th Round NSSO Surveys based on NCO codes 2004.

*Detailed in Chapter 3, relevant variables reproduced here for ease of reference.

Source: Authors' Calculations

Variables with large weights are those which contribute mostly to differentiating the groups. Good predictors tend to have large weights (>0.3).

At the end of the DA process, it is hoped that each group will have a normal distribution of discriminant scores. The degree of overlap between the discriminant score distributions can then be used as a measure of the success of the technique. In a two-group situation predicted membership is calculated by first producing a score for PD for each case using the discriminate function. Then cases with PD values smaller than the cut-off value are classified as belonging to one group while those with values larger are classified into the other group. Predicted group membership and PD scores are saved as new variables. The group centroid is the mean value of the discriminant score for a given category of the dependent variable. There are as many centroids as there are groups or categories. The cut-off is the mean of the two centroids. If the discriminant score of the function is less than equal to the cut-off the case is classed as 0, whereas if it is above, it is classed as 1.

We consider the above set of indicators covering aspects of economic structure and access at the NSS region level. Table 5.1 provides the list of variables and their sources. The details of variable construction and data sources are provided in Chapter 3, while the logic of their selection is provided in Chapter 4. A number of related policy interventions during this time period also tie in well with the proposed indicators. With the Mahatma Gandhi National Rural Employment Guarantee Act (MGNREGA) in operation since 2004, several construction works have been taken up in the countryside absorbing workforce earlier employed in agricultural labour. The Jawaharlal Nehru National Urban Renewal Mission (JNNURM) was been launched in 2005 to build the infrastructure and service delivery capacities of key cities, followed by the Smart Cities Mission and other efforts like the Atal Mission for Rejuvination and Urban Transformation in recent years led to several investments with an urban focus. The 11th Five Year Plan document introduced a chapter on skill challenges facing the nation and saw the setting up of the National Skill Development Corporation (NSDC) in 2010 and a separate Ministry of Skills in 2014. All such policy measures are expected to have some impact on economic structure and access levels across regions. While we do not seek to attribute any observed changes to such programs, they give us a background of the prevailing policy discourse in the country. The results of the discriminant analysis are discussed in the next section.

Evidence of Divergence

The results of the statistical exercise are given in Tables 5.2 to 5.6. Table 5.2 provides the group means of all the characteristic variables used in this study across the two periods as well as the mean value of total observations. From this table, it emerges that there is a substantial difference between the characteristics exhibited by the regions in the first and second time periods. The mean differences between RVAPC, MPCE, and CRE suggest that these may be good discriminators as their separations are large. There is a strong difference in the means of regional value added, consumption expenditure, credit per branch, sectoral shares and skill levels between the two time periods.[1]

Higher Values: Greater Variation

This period has been characterized by massive growth with India being one of the most vibrant economies despite the downturn that hit the world stage in 2007–8. In our study, we find that on an average, regions almost doubled their contribution to value added over this time. The volume of finance in circulation as reflected by credit per branch has also registered a similar doubling; indicating that with a booming economy, the quantum of funds available for investment went up substantially. We expect the sectoral composition of the economy to shift in favour of the tertiary sector and find it to be so, particularly with the share of construction in the overall regional economy assuming greater importance during the post meltdown phase. This indicates that the focus on domestic infrastructure has grown in the given period, since construction feeds directly into infrastructure development.

We also find that the level of sectoral diversity has increased with the average DV value up from 0.63 to 0.69 on a scale of 0 to 1. This implies that regions have on the whole become more diversified. This may be reflective of regional economies shifting their relative focus from agriculture towards construction and service-related sectors, given the degree of

[1] For the variables MPCE, CRE and DEP, inflation could be partially responsible for this, and so we adjust for inflation to arrive at the values at constant prices. The full set of results using these adjusted values is provided in Appendix 7.

Table 7.2 Group Means of Variables

Mean	RVAPC	MPCE	DV	AGRI	MFG	CON	SVS
2004–5	26998	729	0.632	0.553	0.116	0.065	0.270
2011–12	50253	1698	0.698	0.462	0.122	0.116	0.301
% Change	86%	133%	10%	−16%	5%	79%	12%
Total	39352	1244	0.667	0.505	0.119	0.092	0.287
	OFF	**DEP**	**CRE**	**WPR**	**URB**	**REGEMP**	**SKILLIV**
2004–5	907	2155	1168	0.388	0.263	0.179	0.089
2011–12	993	3997	2541	0.367	0.291	0.205	0.108
% Change	9%	85%	118%	−5%	11%	15%	21%
Total	953	3134	1898	0.377	0.278	0.193	0.099

Source: Authors' Calculations

Table 7.3 Group Standard Deviation of Variables

Std. Deviation	RVAPC	MPCE	DV	AGRI	MFG	CON	SVS
2004	12819	245	0.14	0.17	0.06	0.04	0.12
2011	36765	576	0.13	0.18	0.07	0.07	0.13
% Change	187%	135%	-5%	4%	8%	89%	7%
Total	30431	662	0.14	0.18	0.06	0.06	0.13
	OFF	**DEP**	**CRE**	**WPR**	**URB**	**REGEMP**	**SKILLIV**
2004	772	2262	1774	0.08	0.17	0.12	0.06
2011	805	4260	3914	0.07	0.17	0.13	0.08
% Change	4%	88%	121%	-14%	-1%	8%	30%
Total	788	3580	3167	0.07	0.17	0.13	0.07

Source: Authors' Calculations

global uncertainty and the fact that manufacturing is not seen to increase very much. We also find that the increase is not simply in terms of absolute average values, but also in the variation between the regions on the given parameters, as given by the standard deviation. This implies that the divergence for these factors across regions has also increased over time. The differential in output between rich and poor regions appears to have increased, with the standard deviation of deposit per branch and also the contribution to value added having almost doubled. The variation in skill levels is also substantial between regions, which could be due to a low initial base of high-end skills to start with. The standard deviation for DV has decreased, implying that regions have moved closer together on the higher end of the diversity spectrum—thus having a more diversified sectoral mix in the regional economy.

Primary Drivers of Change

Table 7.4 presents the results of univariate test. From the F and T values given in the table, per capita consumption and value added, sectoral mix, volume of finance and access to skills emerged significant at 1 per cent and 5 per cent levels, in differentiating the characteristics of regions over time. The other five variables did not emerge significant. The univariate test clearly highlights the importance of output and expenditure (RVAPC,

Table 7.4 Results of Univariate Analysis

Variable	Wilks' Lambda	F	Sig.
RVAPC	0.85400	**27.1**	0.0000
MPCE	0.46400	**182.7**	0.0000
DV	0.94200	**9.7**	0.0020
AGRI	0.93800	**10.5**	0.0010
MFG	0.99800	0.3	0.5710
CON	0.84000	**30.2**	0.0000
SVS	0.98400	2.6	0.1110
OFF	0.99700	0.5	0.4970
DEP	0.93400	**11.2**	0.0010
CRE	0.95300	**7.8**	0.0060
WPR	0.98000	3.3	0.0730
URB	0.99300	1.1	0.3070
REGEMP	0.98900	1.7	0.1920
SKILLIV	0.98100	3.1	0.0820

Note: Figures in blocks and underlines represent significance at 1 per cent and 5 per cent respectively.

Source: Authors' Calculations

Table 7.5 Canonical Discriminant Function Coefficients

Variables	Standardised	Unstandardized
RVAPC	**−0.295**	0.000
MPCE	**−1.692**	−0.004
DV	**0.526**	**3.950**
AGRI	0.258	**1.455**
MFG	−0.070	**−1.089**
CON	**−0.336**	**−5.685**
SVS	0.154	**1.237**
OFF	0.153	0.000
DEP	−0.262	0.000
CRE	0.030	0.000
WPR	**0.333**	**4.554**
URB	0.129	**0.748**
REGEMP	**1.162**	**9.269**
SKILLIV	0.104	**1.526**
(Constant)		−1.833

Source: Authors' Calculations

MPCE), sectoral shares (CON, AGRI, DV) and access levels (CRE, DEP, WPR, SKILLIV) as major factors.

Table 7.5 shows the correlation of each variable with the discriminant function. The largest loadings give us an indication on naming of the functions. The vibrancy and size of the local economy as given by RVAPC and MPCE, along with the degree of diversification of the economy given by DV, emerge as the chief discriminants across regions between the two time periods. The share of the construction sector, workforce participation as well as the share of regular employment has high coefficient values indicating increasing divergence in the nature of jobs and opportunities accessed by various actors.

The results highlight the role of sectoral shares during the 2011–12 period over 2004–5 in differentiating between the regions. The sectoral mix of the regional economy has changed with the reduction in concentration of agriculture as the mainstay and moved in favour of construction and other service sector-oriented activities. Construction is particularly significant as it has moved from accounting for 6 per cent to 11 per cent of regional employment, and its standard deviation has increased by 90 per cent from 0.03 to 0.07. Since the base is also low, the increase and related dispersion is even more pronounced. This is to be read with the indicator DV which is also significant and is a measure of the degree of diversification of the regional economy. Regions have varied in terms of the level of diversification as well, since a few regions such as Chhattisgarh have continued to stay fairly concentrated, while others such as Maharashtra and Gujarat have encouraged the growth of additional industry sectors, either organically or to offset the fallout of the global crisis and its impact on specific products.

Output as reflected by regional value added is another significant factor that emerges as a key determinant. Here the absolute values as well as the standard deviations are very high. The same holds true for monthly consumption expenditure. Certain regions within Madhya Pradesh, Maharashtra, and so on, have experienced unprecedented growth, while output and consumption levels have grown slowly in other regions such as Kerala, Punjab, and so on. It can also be that these regions have experienced a plateau in terms of incremental opportunities for growth, resulting in the redeployment of human and financial capital. There has been a surge in disposable income in the hands of fresh graduates leading to increased demand for consumer goods, opening of malls, ecommerce, and so on. The growth of network and communications has made alternate revenue streams as well as alternate market places possible.

This brings us to the point on access to finance which is also a significant differentiator, making it clear that financial access has increased between 2004–5 and 2011–12. While banks have had stiff targets to increase the number of branches, especially in interior locations, financial inclusion has been an important buzzword in a decade that has witnessed the rise and fall of microfinance. The experience has been very different across regions, with states like Andhra Pradesh, Maharashtra being the fore-runners and states such as Assam and Northeast having very limited access to finance in terms of the volume of credits and deposits.

The skill level of the workforce is another important factor, but just falls short of being significant in our analysis. However since its value is at 0.29 and the cut-off generally considered is 0.3, we will include it since it has emerged as having a marked increase over the period both in absolute terms as also in its standard deviation. A heightened awareness of India's demographic dividend and the limited window to reap its dividends could be one of the reasons for the increasing skill levels in the workforce in certain regions. It could also be reflective of a workforce trying to keep pace with the changing economic structure of the region.

Accuracy of Prediction

These results support the view that major indicators of economic structure and access display significant divergence across regions during the two time periods of 2004–5 and 2011–12. While there is significant growth and most critical factors register an increase, this is accompanied by huge variations within regions which have got accentuated over time. The degree of overlap between the discriminant score distributions can be used as a measure of the success of the technique. It is clear from the Table 7.6 that in the current specification there is little or almost no overlap. The accuracy of prediction of the results (79 per cent) is also very high. Further nearly 97.5 per cent of cross tabulated cases (Table 7.6) are correctly classified.

While the percentage of cases correctly classified is an important indicator of the effectiveness of the discriminant function, a '"good"' discriminant function is also the one which has higher between group variability when compared to within group variability (SPSS Inc. 1999). The goodness of a discriminant function is given by its Eigen Value, where Eigen

Table 7.6 Classification Results

Actual Group	Cases	No. of Predicted Group Membership	
		2004–5	2011–12
Group 1 (2004–5)	75	75 100%	0 0%
Group 2 (2011–12)	85	2 2.60%	83 97.60%
Percent of originally grouped cases correctly classified - 98.8 per cent			

Source: Authors' Calculations

Value = between-group sum of squares/within-group sum of squares. The higher the Eigen Value is, the better is the function. In this analysis, the Eigen Value is estimated to be 3.86 which is quite high. Thus, the results presented in Tables 5.4 to 5.6 give a good indication of the differences in the characteristics of regions over different time periods in India.

The analysis was repeated adjusting by deflating MPCE, DEP and CRE to arrive at constant prices, the results of which are provided in Appendix 7. We find that the Eigen Value is 1.073 and Wilks' Lambda is 0.482. A good percentage of 82.05 per cent of the cases are correctly classified.

Moving Ahead Yet Apart

The decade of 2000-2010 witnessed a fundamental shift in the composition of economic activity in India, with the share of agriculture falling significantly and making way for sectors like construction, transport, communications, and so on. A large number of private sector firms have entered the market in sectors outside of traditional agriculture and manufacturing—a trend that is likely to increase with the growing importance of e-commerce and other sunrise sectors. Public policy interventions initiated in this period have moved into their next phases. Some of these have great potential to impact regional economic structures and access levels. MGNREGA has sought to boost construction related activity in the rural hinterland. The urban programs have been developed with the idea of boosting the productivity and performance of cities as engines of growth. Skilling has slowly but steadily emerged as an important policy agenda and needs some credible actionables to tackle jobless growth. All such efforts have an impact on regional development and hence need to be very well thought through with regional nuances. While this chapter does not attempt to assess the impact or efficiency of any government program, it underscores the nature of divergence and the importance of the related shifts in the regional economy against this policy backdrop.

The focus of this chapter is to build on the existing knowledge base for India. Earlier studies analyse output and other development indicators at a state level and look at annualized data for various periods with data up to 2003–4 to see whether regional disparity has increased or decreased. We therefore add to this body of work by carrying out our analysis at the sub-state level by considering regional units that provide a more granular understanding of regional differences.

Our analysis reveals that certain parameters of economic structure and access are the primary determinants of differences for the period in question. The key distinguishing factors between the two periods across regions are primarily with respect output and consumption at a regional level, along with sectoral composition of the regional economy. While earlier studies use sectoral shares on three parameters, primary secondary and tertiary, we break this up into a fourth adding construction, while also factoring in a composite index for sectoral diversity at the NIC 2 digit level. We clearly find evidence of a move over time towards greater diversity in the local economy, emergence of construction and other service sectors with significant shares, and increased but more unequal access to finance and skills.

Of the factors that emerge as key differentiators, further research is required to detail and analyse determinants as well as the interlinks between them. Having identified sectoral composition and regional value added as two important variables that appear to influence differences across the two time periods, we move forward now, and try to see if we can develop a typology of regions that exhibit similar characteristics. In other words, we plan to examine the possibility of NSS regions forming a 'cluster' to enable such groups of regions to be considered for specific focus of policy intervention and support to fast track the growth process.

8

Formation of Regional Clusters

We are now gradually piecing together a kaleidoscope of the country as a composite of over 75 regions. There is clearly a lot happening at the sub-state level. We find that each region within the state has its own characteristics in terms of its output, economic structure, and levels of access. This is what makes this regional dipstick valuable—it helps industry to see where the growth hubs are, and which regions are yet to reach their full potential; it also helps policy makers see which regions are low on important parameters and may need nuanced planning to trigger growth.

Unique Yet Similar?

While each region is unique, are there also similarities between regions? Are there underlying patterns across select regions which helps us classify them? Is it possible, that while regions within the state may differ from each other, they could be similar to regions in other states? In that case, we should explore if it is possible to classify the regions into 'clusters' which would be a set of regions that demonstrate similar characteristics across parameters of economic structure and access. The best way to do this is by way of a 'cluster analysis', which is a very detailed and interesting method to form groupings.

Such a typology would help planners adopt a cluster approach to get regions with similarities to learn from each other, share common challenges, identify scalable solutions, and develop strategies built on these groupings without being limited by state boundaries. The previous chapters clearly underscore the fact that there are substantial variations at the NSS region level across regions and between the two periods. We therefore carry out a cluster analysis to compare different NSS regions across parameters of economic structure and access, and to investigate which

Regional Economic Diversity. Poornima Dore and Krishnan Narayanan, Oxford University Press. © Oxford University Press India 2022. DOI: 10.1093/oso/9780190130596.003.0008

regions are grouping together to form clusters and also whether there are any changes in the groupings over the two periods.

Cluster Analysis

The objective of a cluster analysis is to form homogenous groups of objects that are described by a variety of characteristics. This method is relevant when it is not known which object (case) belongs to which group; if fact the number of groups is also unknown. The clustering method uses the dissimilarities or distances between objects (in this case regions) when forming the clusters. In this case, we seek to form groups of regions that are similar to each other based on the set of selected characteristics. No assumptions are made on the underlying distribution of the data or pre-classification of groups. We, therefore, focus on the formation of these clusters based entirely on the data on each region.

The steps involved in a cluster analysis are as follows:

- Selection of the number of cases to start with, Identification of variables on which similarity of groups is to be assessed,
- Standardization of variables so that there is parity in their contribution to similarity or distance between cases,
- Clustering procedure to be taken up,
- Distance determining statistic to be applied,
- Formation of groups (method), and
- Finalizing number of clusters.

Let us begin with the number of cases which need to be subdivided into homogenous groups. Here we have 75 NSS regions in period 1 and 85 NSS regions in period 2. It is prudent to carry out the cluster analysis for each period separately and hence arrive at a separate set of clusters for each period. This also gives us the opportunity to examine whether the clustering pattern has changed between the two periods.

Next comes the choice of parameters along which we want the groups to be similar. For this purpose, consider all the variables measuring economic structure (output levels, consumption, sectoral shares, and so on) and access (skill levels, workforce participation, access to finance, and so on) at a regional level as described in detail in Chapter 3. The list of variables is provided in Table 8.1.

We need to decide whether to standardize the variables in some way so that they all contribute equally to the similarity or differences between cases. We have some variables such as RVA, and so on that capture data in INR crores, while others such as WPR that are in percentage terms. Given the various unit scales in our variables which could lead to different weighting of the variables, it is advisable to standardize the variables using a z-transformation (Everitt 2002).

We also need to determine which clustering procedure to adopt, based on the number of cases and types of variables that we use to form the clusters. There are three different procedures that can be used: two-step cluster, k-means cluster, and hierarchical cluster analysis. The two-step procedure is used in case of large data sets greater than 1,000 cases or a mix of continuous and categorical variables. The k-means cluster method is relevant when the number of desired clusters is known and the data set is moderate in size. Since we wish to use this method to arrive at the number of clusters as well, we follow the process of agglomerative hierarchical clustering which is recommended for datasets with less than 1,000 cases, and where it is possible to examine solutions with various numbers of clusters and arrive at an optimal solution.

Here, the first step involves identifying a criterion to determine similarity or distances between cases. Of the various distance measures, Euclidean distance is the most common distance measure, and gives the geometric distance in multidimensional space. It is suitable only for continuous variables and serves to quantify how far apart two cases are. For our purpose we take the Squared Euclidean distance, which can be squared in order to place progressively greater weight on objects that are farther apart as represented by a proximity matrix.

The next step involves identifying a criterion for determining which clusters are merged at successive steps. If there is only one case in a cluster, then the distance measure selected for the proximity matrix gives us the smallest distance between cases. At subsequent steps, similar clusters are merged, and one needs to define the distance between a pair of clusters. For our analysis we select the Ward's minimum-variance method to combine clusters. In comparison with other hierarchical fusion algorithms such as nearest neighbour, centroid method, and so on, which use a minimization of the distance between clusters as the fusion criterion, several simulation studies have shown that the Ward's technique appears to be superior to alternative approaches and forms very homogenous clusters (Bacher 2000). The objective of Ward's technique is to join two clusters at each step such that the variance for the joined clusters is minimized. The step-by-step fusion of clusters is depicted by an agglomeration schedule. Each step represents a merger of clusters that result in the smallest increase in the sum of squared within-cluster distances of the variable means from respective cluster means. The coefficient in the agglomeration schedule is therefore the within-cluster sum of squares at that step, not the distance at which the clusters are joined. A tabular representation is the icicle plot where each column represents one of the objects being clustered and each row shows a cluster solution with a different number of clusters.

To determine the optimal number of clusters one needs to study the agglomeration schedule, since larger coefficients indicate that fairly homogeneous clusters are being combined, while smaller coefficients indicate that dissimilar clusters are being combined. The selection of the optimal number of clusters depends upon the characteristics of clusters at successive steps. It is advisable to stop cluster formation when the decrease in the coefficients column between two adjacent steps is large. While it is not possible to represent all the schedules and plots in this document, for a more visual representation of the distance at which clusters are combined, we refer to the Dendograms (Appendices 6 and 7) produced as a result of our analysis. A Dendogram is read from left to right with vertical lines showing joined clusters, and the position of the line on the scale indicating the distance at which clusters are joined. The grey dotted line indicates our cut-off points for cluster selection. Large distances between sequential vertical lines convey stages at which there are large distances between the clusters being combined, enabling us to select the number of clusters that appear reasonable for each period.

Regional Characteristics

We apply this method to the set of characteristics on economic structure and access, having compiled information for all NSS regions for these variables (Table 8.1). The size dimensions of the regional economy are

Table 8.1 Variables and Data Sources*

Variables	Variable Name	Measurement	Data Source
Regional Value Added per capita	RVAPC	Regional Value Added/ Total Population of the Region	Constructed based on Handbook of Statistics on Indian economy, 2004–5 and 2011–12, RBI; 61st and 68th Round NSSO Surveys
Disposable income per capita	MPCE	Monthly per capita Expenditure	61st and 68th Round NSSO Surveys
Diversity Index	DV	$DV_r = 1 - H_r$ denoting the sectoral mix scale of 0 to 1	Constructed based on sectoral shares from the 61st and 68th Round NSSO surveys
Share of Agriculture	AGRI	Proportion of total workers engaged in Agriculture	Classification based on NIC codes of industrial classification as followed by the NSSO surveys. The 14 categories at 2 digit level are collapsed into the four broad categories
Share of Manufacturing	MFG	Proportion of total workers engaged in Manufacturing	
Share of Construction	CON	Proportion of total workers engaged in Construction	
Share of Services	SVS	Proportion of total workers engaged in service sector	
Bank Branch Offices	OFF	No. of bank branch offices	Basic Statistical Returns of Scheduled Commercial Banks in India, 2005 and 2010, RBI
Bank Accounts	ACC	No of bank accounts in '000	
Credit per branch	CRE	Volume of credit outstanding (Rs. Lakhs)/ branch offices	
Deposit per branch	DEP	Volume of deposits in Rs. Lakhs/ branch offices	
Workforce Participation Rate	WPR	Proportion of population engaged in work as per usual principal status	61st and 68th Round NSSO Surveys
Urbanization share	URB	Proportion of total population living in urban areas	
Share of Regular Employment	REGEMP	Proportion of total population engaged in regular work	
Share of high-end skills	SKILLIV	Proportion of total workforce with level IV skills in occupations coded 0 to 2	61st and 68th Round NSSO Surveys based on NCO codes 2004.

*Detailed in Chapter 3, relevant variables reproduced here for ease of reference.

Source: Authors' Calculations

captured through regional value added, discussed in detail in the previous chapters. In addition, monthly per capita consumption expenditure (MPCE) as captured by NSS is used to measure consumption. We attempt to make these measures as granular as possible by taking them on per capita basis and accounting for population size in the process. Sectoral shares across agriculture, manufacturing, construction, and services reflect the way in which employment shares have changed over time, and the diversity index looks at the sectoral mix as a composite and measures the extent to which multiple sectors account for regional economic activity.

Access can differ across regions, in terms of various dimensions like access to finance, access to markets, access to employment, and so on. Access to finance is measured by bank penetration in terms of number of bank branches and accounts, and volume of finance as deposit per branch and credit per branch. This captures the ease with which finance is available at the local level and the extent to which such institutions are being used. A greater share of urbanization in a region can be linked with access to the local market both in terms of demand (based on population density) as well as supply (based on the proximity of consumers) for varied goods and services. Access to employment is governed by the proportion of the population that is being absorbed as part of the workforce (workforce participation rate), the chances of finding a regular job (share of regular employment), and the share of high-end skills, which is a clear indicator of the ability of an individual to negotiate in the job market. All these factors are assessed together for all the regions in our cluster analysis.

Typology of Clusters in India

Given that this analysis covers two periods, 2004–5 and 2011–12, we carry out a separate cluster analysis for each period. The aim is to see which regions are clustering together and whether all regions from a particular state are in the same cluster. For the period 2004–5, five clusters are identified. Similarly, for the period of 2011–12, seven clusters are identified. This increase in clusters is in itself evidence of the huge variations at the NSS region level. The region-wise composition of each cluster is provided in Tables 8.2 and 8.3 and in Maps 8.1 and 8.2.

Using these clusters, a typology of these regions has been created. We are able to clearly identify the homogeneity of select regions across the

Table 8.2 Clusters formed in 2004–5

2004–5	Frequency	Region Names
'GROWTH HUBS' Cluster A	3	Delhi, Coastal Maharashtra, Chandigarh
'DIVERSIFIED' Cluster B	11	North Punjab, Northern Plains and Dry areas of Gujarat, Inland Southern Karnataka, Tamil Nadu (except Coastal), South Kerala, Goa, Pondicherry, Andaman
'MODERATE' Cluster C	14	Jammu and Kashmir (all except Outer Hills), Eastern Haryana and Western Haryana Southern Punjab, North Eastern Rajasthan, Western Uttar Pradesh and Eastern Uttar Pradesh, Sikkim, Manipur Plains, Tripura, South Bengal Plains, Western Bengal Plains, Coastal and Ghats of Karnataka, Northern Kerala
'ASPIRATIONAL' Cluster D	22	Bihar (all regions), Assam (all regions), Central and Southern Uttar Pradesh, Himalayan West Bengal, East Bengal and Central Bengal Plains, Coastal and Southern Odisha, Arunachal, Manipur Hills, Outer Hills of Jammu and Kashmir, Southern Rajasthan and South Eastern Rajasthan Madhya Pradesh (All except Central)
'AGRARIAN' Cluster E	25	Himachal, Uttarakhand, Jharkhand, Maharashtra (except Coastal), Andhra Pradesh, Karnataka, Coastal Tamil Nadu Eastern Gujarat, Saurashtra and Southern Plains Gujarat, Nagaland, Meghalaya, Mizoram, Central Madhya Pradesh, Chhattisgarh Northern Odisha, Western Rajasthan

Source: Authors' Calculations

length and breadth of the country. One important finding is that not all regions of a particular state form part of the same cluster. Also certain regions are similar to each other, by virtue of being in the same cluster, even though they might belong to different states. We also examine whether regions continue to be in the same clusters across these two periods. Are there any common characteristics that seem to drive them to form a cluster?

Growth Hubs: Cluster A

This cluster contains coastal Maharashtra and Delhi. These regions have the highest value added, number of bank accounts, deposits per branch,

Table 8.3 Clusters formed in 2011–12

2011–12	Frequency	Region Names
'GROWTH HUBS' Cluster A (Top 2 Metros)	2	Delhi, Coastal Maharashtra
'DIVERSIFIED' Cluster B (Ports and UTs)	8	Chandigarh, Inland Southern Karnataka, Coastal Northern Tamil Nadu, Goa, Pondicherry, Andaman, South Bengal Plains, Inland North Western Andhra Pradesh
'MODERATE' Cluster C	28	Jammu and Kashmir, Eastern Haryana, Southern and Northern Punjab, North Eastern Western and Southern Rajasthan, Uttarakhand, Manipur Plains, Tripura, Eastern and Central Bengal Plains, Western Assam Plains, Hazaribagh Plateau of Jharkhand, Coastal Odisha, Mahanadi Plateau of Chhattisgarh, Coastal and Ghats of Karnataka, Northern and Southern Kerala, Coastal Northern Andhra Pradesh, Coastal Southern and Inland Tamil Nadu, Kutch and Saurashtra in Gujarat, Southern Upper Ganga Plain of Uttar Pradesh, Southern Madhya Pradesh.
'ASPIRATIONAL' Cluster D	16	Northern and Central Bihar, Central Uttar Pradesh, Northern Upper Gangetic Plains and Eastern Uttar Pradesh, Northern Odisha, Malwa and Vindhyas of Madhya Pradesh, South Eastern and Northern Plains of Gujarat, Inland West and Inland Eastern Maharashtra, Coastal Southern Andhra Pradesh and Inland Northern Karnataka
'AGRARIAN' Cluster E	24	Himachal Pradesh, Western Haryana, Inland North and Eastern Maharashtra, North and South Eastern Rajasthan, Arunachal, Nagaland, Manipur Hills, Mizoram, Meghalaya, Assam (Eastern, Cachar and Central Brahmaputra Plains), Himalayan and West Bengal Plains, Ranchi Plateau of Jharkhand, Southern Odisha, Central and Northern Madhya Pradesh, Southern Uttar Pradesh, Dry Areas of Gujarat, Inland North Eastern Andhra Pradesh
'ACUTE' Cluster F	5	Northern and Southern Chhattisgarh, South Western Madhya Pradesh, Inland Central Maharashtra, Inland Eastern Karnataka
OUTLIERS	2	Sikkim, Inland and Southern Andhra Pradesh

Source: Authors' Calculations

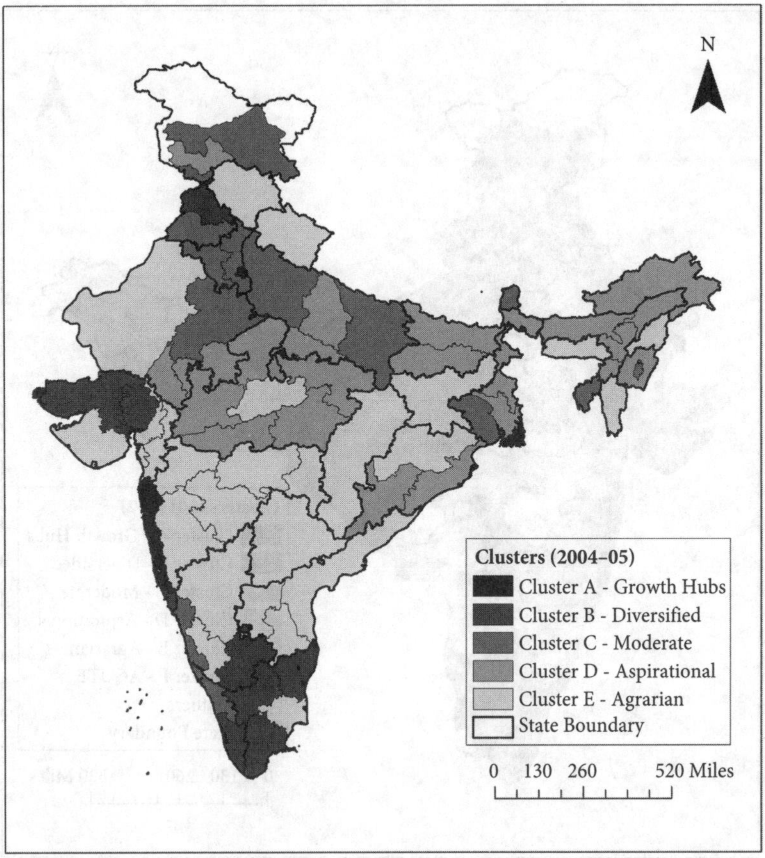

Map 8.1 Clusters of NSS regions formed for the time period 2004–05

as well as the highest share of urbanization, skills, manufacturing and service sector employment. Chandigarh, India's first planned city, is a union territory and also acts as the capital of both Punjab and Haryana. Chandigarh forms part of this cluster in period 1 but shifts to the next cluster in period 2. It is home to several automobile, pharmaceutical and related companies and houses headquarters as well as factory operations. The Delhi region covers the National Capital Region (NCR) of Delhi, and coastal Maharashtra covers Mumbai metropolitan region which is the financial capital of India. The two cities of Delhi and Mumbai are the political and financial power centres of the country, and also probably account for a large part of the Foreign Direct Investment (FDI) inflows into

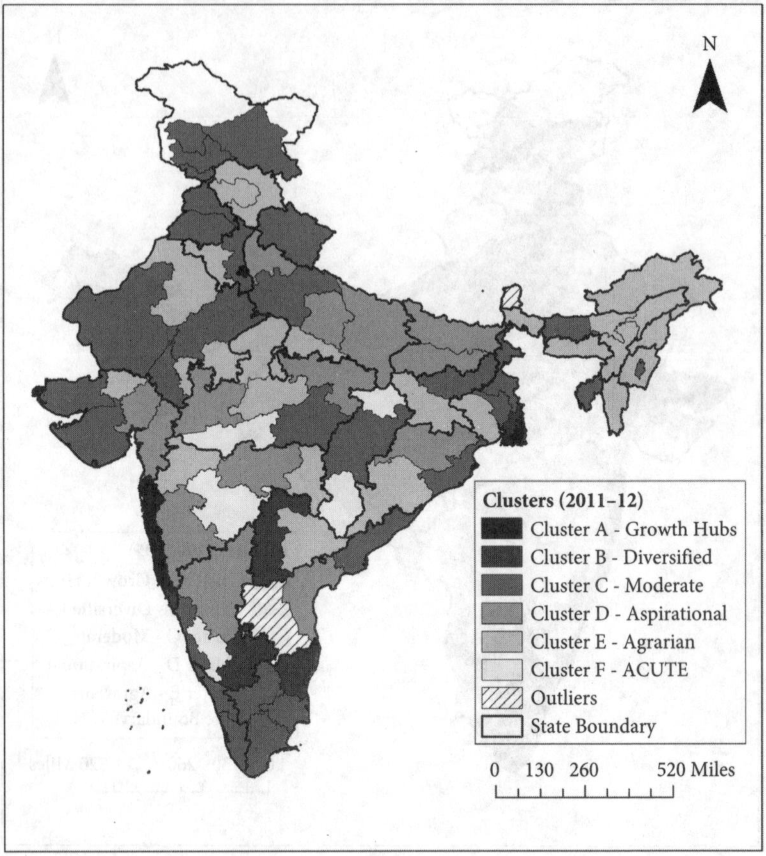

Map 8.2 Clusters of NSS regions formed for the time period 2011–12

the country. Hence we call this cluster the 'Growth Hubs'. This cluster has the highest values of output and consumption expenditure per capita. It is highly urbanized at 84 per cent, has peak diversity index values at 0.85 and exhibits very high access to finance with record values of bank accounts and deposits per branch. The fact that most Indian companies are headquartered in these cities, is reflected in terms of access to human capital in period 2, with 60 per cent employment being regular in nature and 31 per cent of the workforce being skilled at the postgraduate level. As seen in Tables 8.4 and 8.5, this cluster is starkly different from all the other regions as its mean values across parameters of economic structure and access are extremely high.

2004–5	STATISTICS	RVAPC	MPCE	OFF	ACC	DEP	DV	URB
'GROWTH HUBS' Cluster A	Mean	55340	1399	1491	16394	10389	0.85	0.84
	SD	24254	243	1163	13490	4388	0.01	0.11
'DIVERSIFIED' Cluster B	Mean	38265	974	1077	7564	2582	0.79	0.42
	SD	14367	197	815	5829	934	0.07	0.1
'MODERATE' Cluster C	Mean	23324	781	1133	8327	1910	0.74	0.24
	SD	8079	149	1093	8859	632	0.08	0.09
'ASPIRATIONAL' Cluster D	Mean	18132	559	656	3469	1641	0.53	0.14
	SD	5967	105	524	3250	2128	0.1	0.07
'AGRARIAN' Cluster E	Mean	28499	662	857	5021	1570	0.57	0.24
	SD	8017	163	644	4305	660	0.07	0.08

2004–5	STATISTICS	WPR	REGEMP	SKILL IV	AGRI	MFG	CON	SVS
'GROWTH HUBS' Cluster A	Mean	0.35	0.58	0.24	0.07	0.23	0.05	0.64
	SD	0.03	0.1	0.04	0.11	0.04	0.01	0.13
'DIVERSIFIED' Cluster B	Mean	0.41	0.29	0.12	0.37	0.18	0.09	0.36
	SD	0.07	0.08	0.04	0.11	0.05	0.03	0.1
'MODERATE' Cluster C	Mean	0.33	0.2	0.09	0.45	0.14	0.09	0.33
	SD	0.04	0.06	0.03	0.1	0.05	0.02	0.08
'ASPIRATIONAL' Cluster D	Mean	0.37	0.1	0.05	0.67	0.07	0.06	0.21
	SD	0.06	0.04	0.02	0.08	0.03	0.05	0.06
'AGRARIAN' Cluster E	Mean	0.45	0.13	0.06	0.64	0.1	0.05	0.21
	SD	0.04	0.04	0.02	0.06	0.04	0.03	0.05

Source: Authors' calculations basis Cluster Analysis.

Table 8.5 Cluster-wise Descriptive Statistics in 2011–12

2011–12	STATS	RVAPC	MPCE	OFF	ACC	DEP	DV	URB
'GROWTH HUBS' Cluster A	Mean	83725	3087	2344	29232	28643	0.86	0.86
	SD	38260	51	158	12091	7973	0.01	0.09
'DIVERSIFIED' Cluster B	Mean	64866	2602	1287	11476	6870	0.84	0.56
	SD	33475	422	1145	10382	1988	0.04	0.16
'MODERATE' Cluster C	Mean	39440	1777	999	7863	3387	0.66	0.26
	SD	18204	513	679	5183	920	0.08	0.1
'ASPIRATIONAL' Cluster D	Mean	81284	1423	1742	14642	3226	0.78	0.28
	SD	61555	398	702	8005	1115	0.06	0.12
'AGRARIAN' Cluster E	Mean	36105	1482	437	3194	2682	0.63	0.20
	SD	14314	337	270	2034	1079	0.05	0.11
'ACUTE' Cluster F	Mean	37409	1201	380	2614	1995	0.41	0.19
	SD	35067	324	229	1487	276	0.1	0.07
'OUTLIERS' Cluster G	Mean	63359	1628	573	5992	3377	0.62	0.22
	SD	14629	8	705	7985	1216	0.03	0.06

2011–12	STATS	WPR	REGEMP	SKILL IV	AGRI	MFG	CON	SVS
'GROWTH HUBS' Cluster A	Mean	0.35	0.60	0.31	0.05	0.23	0.06	0.66
	SD	0.03	0.05	0.04	0.07	0.01	0.02	0.10
'DIVERSIFIED' Cluster B	Mean	0.38	0.42	0.22	0.20	0.18	0.10	0.51
	SD	0.04	0.12	0.09	0.15	0.07	0.05	0.14
'MODERATE' Cluster C	Mean	0.35	0.21	0.11	0.36	0.15	**0.16**	0.33
	SD	0.06	0.08	0.05	0.1	0.06	0.08	0.09
'ASPIRATIONAL' Cluster D	Mean	0.36	0.16	0.09	0.54	0.12	0.1	0.24
	SD	0.07	0.08	0.04	0.1	0.06	0.05	0.05
'AGRARIAN' Cluster E	Mean	0.37	0.15	0.08	0.57	0.08	0.10	0.25
	SD	0.06	0.06	0.04	0.05	0.04	0.06	0.06
'ACUTE' Cluster F	Mean	0.43	0.08	0.08	0.76	0.05	0.04	0.15
	SD	0.06	0.02	0.07	0.07	0.01	0.03	0.06
'OUTLIERS' Cluster G	Mean	0.52	0.17	0.09	0.60	0.09	0.07	0.25
	SD	0.01	0.08	0.02	0.03	0.04	0.01	0.01

Source: Authors' calculations basis Cluster Analysis.

Diversified: Cluster B

This cluster can be said to represent regions that are performing well with high levels of value added and consumption, though not in the league of Cluster A. These regions have good access to markets as they include all the remaining metro cities of Bangalore, Chennai, Kolkata, and Hyderabad, which have been very important industrial and commercial centres, with prominence across several sectors such as information technology, automobiles, cement, textiles, and so on. This clustering reflects the reality that after Delhi and Mumbai, these are the locations of choice for companies to set up operations and for professionals to choose as base locations. This cluster also covers several ports and the compact self-sufficient Union Territories of Pondicherry, Andaman, and so on. These regions also have a high share of employment (18 per cent) in manufacturing. We find that Punjab has moved out of this cluster to the next one in period 2. This clusters' urban share increases to 56 per cent in period 2, with a high diversity index value of 0.84, both parameters showing a marked increase over the two periods. It also experiences an increase in regular employment to 42 per cent, with 22 per cent of the workforce being in the highly skilled category. Some of the best hospitals and institutes of higher learning are these regions. Financial access, while not as high as the previous cluster, is substantially higher than all other clusters.

Moderate: Cluster C

This cluster represents the regions of Jammu and Kashmir, Haryana, southern Punjab, north-eastern Rajasthan, Manipur Plains, Tripura, segments of Kerala, and Tamil Nadu. They have moderate mean values across most of the variables capturing access to finance and human capital. Many of these regions, such as the Bengal and Assam plains, are blessed with river basins and alluvial soil, and account for the cultivation of rice and other staple crops. Others such as the hilly regions of Kashmir and Uttarakhand have fruit orchards and horticulture. This cluster includes the industrial centres/tourist hubs of Ludhiana, Faridabad, Bhubaneshwar, Trivandrum, Kozhikode, Jaipur, Udaipur,

Jodhpur, Jammu, Srinagar, Leh, Dehradun, Rajkot, Jamnagar, Raipur, and so on. This also coincides with the establishment and growth of some of these cities following their announcements as new state capitals. The two periods register a significant and growing share of construction and services in this cluster. This makes for a well-rounded economic profile of this cluster with a mean diversity index around 0.7, with one third dependence on agriculture, a third on services and the balance being split almost equally between construction and manufacturing. Some of these regions are gradually emerging as educational hubs with many engineering colleges and management schools developing a good reputation in recent years. However, while these regions have several natural advantages, they have some distance to go towards attaining their full potential.

Aspirational: Cluster D

This is clearly the most backward cluster in period 1 with lowest mean values across almost all variables (indicated in light grey in Table 8.4). Several regions of the erstwhile BIMARU states find their place here, with Bihar, large tracts of Uttar Pradesh, and central India. In period 1, this cluster has the lowest mean values of output and consumption per capita, and fairly limited access to finance in terms of number of offices and bank accounts per branch. It also registered the lowest share of regular employment at 10 per cent, with only 5 per cent of the workforce having high-end skills. In period 2, the composition of this cluster changes significantly while retaining the earlier regions, but also having a mix of regions from the diversified and agrarian clusters of 2004–5. It ceases to have the lowest values across indicators and in fact shows a marked improvement across most indicators in period 2, which is why we name this cluster as 'aspirational'. There is very high population density, with the million plus cities of Patna, Lucknow, Kanpur, Varanasi, and Indore. Parts of Maharashtra and Gujarat become part of this cluster in 2011–12, which include the million-plus cities of Nagpur, Pune, Pimpri Chinchwad, Surat, Vadodara, and Ahmedabad. It is possible that these regions are pushing up the mean values of the cluster. For instance, the urban share has doubled from 14 per cent to 28 per cent, and sectoral diversity of the cluster has changed from 0.53 to 0.78. This is clearly not an organic improvement, but a change in the profile of the cluster as more urban and industrialized regions become part of it.

Agrarian: Cluster E

These are regions with a predominantly agrarian economy (64 per cent). This cluster, while having low values in terms of economic structure and access, is a notch higher than the Aspirational Cluster across most indicators in period 1. In period 2, Cluster E splits into Cluster E and F, with Cluster F being the most agrarian separating out to form a different cluster, which we will discuss next. Cluster E, that we call agrarian, includes Himachal Pradesh, and large segment of the east and North-eastern states (Assam, Mizoram, Meghalaya, and so on). Geographically most of these regions are marked by hilly terrain and dense forests, and are not very easy to navigate. Several predominantly tribal regions also find a place in this cluster—Ranchi Plateau, South Odisha, Gadchiroli, central Madhya Pradesh, and so on. It is the least industrialized cluster, with a manufacturing share of 7–8 per cent. However, the services sector accounts for over 20 per cent of economic activity, but regular employment share hovers around 13 per cent. There is only one million-plus city Nashik in this cohort. This is clearly a cluster where continued access to markets and productivity improvements in agriculture need to be prioritized. Pathways to diversify the regional economy, reduce its susceptibility to natural shocks, and develop alternative forms of livelihood which capitalize on native capabilities are very important. Access to skills and finance both require better incentives and nuanced planning.

Acute: Cluster F

This cluster emerges in period 2, as north and southern Chhattisgarh, south-western Madhya Pradesh, inland central Maharashtra, and inland eastern Karnataka come together to form a separate cluster. This cluster has lowest mean values in period 2 across parameters of economic structure and access and so we call it 'acute'. This position was occupied by the aspirational cluster in period 1. This cluster has 76 per cent of the workforce employed in agriculture, with a meagre 8 per cent having high-end skills. This is the least urbanized region at 19 per cent, with extremely low levels of financial access in terms of bank branches in the region as well as accounts and deposits per branch. This is the first NSS round where north and south Chhattisgarh were studied separately and that could also account for how these regions (which include the tribal pockets of Bastar, Dantewada, Koriya, Surguja etc.) are different from central Chhattisgarh which forms part of the aspirational cluster. The resultant creation of a fresh cluster underscores the need to tease out the details at the sub state level to understand how variations within the state can change the national narrative. Also, Karnataka, Madhya Pradesh, and Maharashtra are all states where the macro growth narrative has been very positive over the last 2 decades. The fact that the three other regions (covering districts like Shimoga, Kodagu, Sagar Damoh, Latur, Beed) are from these states, points towards the inequalities within such well-off states as well. The regions of this cluster are, therefore, in acute need of policy attention and special assistance.

Outliers—Cluster G

Sikkim and inland southern Andhra Pradesh separate to form this cluster in 2011. We treat them as outliers for our analysis.

Cluster Level Variations

The fact that certain regions cluster together in both periods is indicative of a consistent homogeneity. For instance, in both periods, Nagaland and Mizoram are in the same cluster (Agrarian) as Eastern and Inland Northern Maharashtra. Inland Western Andhra Pradesh also falls within the same cluster. Eastern Maharashtra contains the tribal districts of Gadchiroli, Chandrapur, and so on, while Inland Northern Maharashtra contains Nandurbar, Jalgaun, Dhule, and so on. This shows that neglected regions are not only in the Northeast or in the central part of India but can also be found in the so-called developed states of Maharashtra and Andhra Pradesh as well. It implies that regions come together in this analysis in terms of levels of achievement of development, irrespective of the states to which they belong. The benefit of this analysis is that we are able to identify regions that require immediate attention for development, making a case for policy action at a regional level which is more homogenous.

We also find that over the two periods, the number of clusters have expanded instead of reducing. This in itself is an indication of greater divergence between the regions. If we were to follow the convergence hypothesis, it would indicate that the regions were becoming more homogeneous and so differences between the clusters would go down, either retaining the same number of clusters or bringing it down altogether. However, the clear increase in the number of clusters and the reallocation of regions across clusters, point towards the fact those inter-regional differences have actually increased over the period under consideration. For instance, the formation of Cluster F in period 2, with a 76 per cent agrarian workforce replacing Cluster D as having the lowest values across most variables considered, and the reorganization of Cluster D is a clear indication of increasing divergence across regions.

We now turn our attention to the descriptive statistics for cluster level averages across some of the key variables analysed in the given Tables 8.4 and 8.5. To reiterate, Cluster A has the highest mean values (highlighted in dark grey) in both periods across most indicators except the share of agriculture. This is followed by Cluster B and then C in period 1. Cluster D has the lowest mean values (highlighted in light grey) in period 1, while Cluster F has the lowest values in period 2. On parameters related to economic structure and access levels, Cluster D is far behind the others in period 1. Period 2 witnesses a marked increase in mean values across clusters, but this increase is particularly sharp for Cluster D. The standard deviation is high in Cluster A and C in period 1 and in Clusters D and C in period 2. So even though regions may be part of the same cluster, if the standard deviation is high, it means there is wider disparity within the cluster as well. The variation within cluster A comes down significantly in period 2, possibly since Chandigarh moves out and becomes a part of Cluster B. So only Delhi and Coastal Maharashtra remain in Cluster A. We also witness that while the means have increased, the standard deviation for the diversity index in particular, has reduced in most regions, which could imply that regions with similar diversity scores are clustering together, or more importantly that the diversity index is a key factor influencing the formation of clusters itself.

If we look across both periods for the same cluster we find that the standard deviation has increased substantially for Cluster B and Cluster D. If the standard deviation is low, there is convergence within the cluster and if standard deviation is high, there is divergence within the cluster. While there could be some level of convergence in Cluster A, Clusters B and D witness a definite increase in variations in output levels, bank offices, accounts, deposits per branch. This is offset by reducing mean values in clusters C and E, possibly due to the reorganization of clusters and formation of new clusters in period 2, as the average number of bank branches and accounts in these clusters are also seen to drop. However, sizeable increases in standard deviation are observed in clusters B and D across variables like regular employment and high-end skills, albeit on a small base. Employment in construction and manufacturing also witnesses wide variations from 100 per cent to 150 per cent implying that even within clusters, there is a sizable variation in the values at a regional level, building a steady case for the divergence hypothesis.

The Case of Maharashtra

In order to understand the distribution of regions across clusters, it is useful to take the example of one state and study the pattern of cluster formation. This will give a flavour of what such an analysis tells us about a state and its regions, their similarities and differences. Let us take the case of Maharashtra, which is the 3rd largest State in the country and is divided into 6 NSS regions—coastal, inland western, inland northern, inland central, inland eastern, and eastern.

Table 8.6 and Figure 8.1 illustrate how the state of Maharashtra is divided into the 6 NSS regions. As can be seen from Figure 8.1, each NSS region is a set of districts in the state which are geographically contiguous and fall in similar agro-climatic zones. The cluster analysis for all NSS regions across the country distributes the regions of Maharashtra into 2 distinct clusters in 2004–5, namely 'Growth Hubs' (A) and 'Agrarian' (E).

Coastal Maharashtra, which along with Delhi is in the Growth Hubs Cluster A, includes the three million-plus cities of Greater Mumbai, Thane, and Kalyan-Dombivali. This region experiences a very high concentration of economic activity and population density. It acts as

Table 8.6 Regions of Maharashtra and Cluster Membership

Region	Name	Districts	2004–5	2011–12
R271	Coastal	Thane (21) Raigarh (24) Mumbai (22) Ratnagiri (32) Mumbai Suburban (23) Sindhudurg (33)	Growth Hubs Cluster A	Growth Hubs Cluster A
R272	Inland Western	Pune (25) Satara (31) Ahmadnagar (26) Kolhapur (34) Solapur (30) Sangli (35)	Agrarian Cluster E	Aspirational Cluster D
R273	Inland Northern	Nandurbar (01) Jalgaon (03) Dhule (02) Nashik (20)	Agrarian Cluster E	Agrarian Cluster E
R274	Inland Central	Nanded (15) Aurangabad (19) Hingoli (16) Bid (27) Parbhani (17) Latur (28) Jalna (18) Osmanabad (29)	Agrarian Cluster E	Acute Cluster F
R275	Inland Eastern	Buldana (04) Wardha (08 Akola (05) Nagpur (09) Washim (06) Yavatmal (14) Amravati (07)	Agrarian Cluster E	Aspirational Cluster D
R276	Eastern	Bhandara (10) Gadchiroli (12) Gondiya (11) Chandrapur (13)	Agrarian Cluster E	Agrarian Cluster E

Source: Authors' Calculations

the financial epicenter of the country and also accounts for a high proportion of informal sector workers and slum settlements. Real estate values are the highest in the country—both commercial and residential. A large section of Indian companies are headquartered in this region, bringing a lot of highly skilled professionals to settle here. The Indian film industry Bollywood is also based here and has huge economic and cultural influence globally.

The remaining 5 NSS regions of Maharashtra are a part of the Agrarian Cluster E. In 2011–12, the inland northern and eastern regions remain in Cluster E. Inland eastern and inland western Maharashtra move from Cluster E to Cluster D. Inland central Maharashtra moves to the acute Cluster F. As shared earlier, Cluster F is a subset of Cluster E in the previous period. The differences within Cluster E have got accentuated to a point that a separate Cluster F has been formed in 2011–12.

What categorizes these clusters and what could possibly explain these shifts in the regions of Maharashtra? Let us look at the regions that

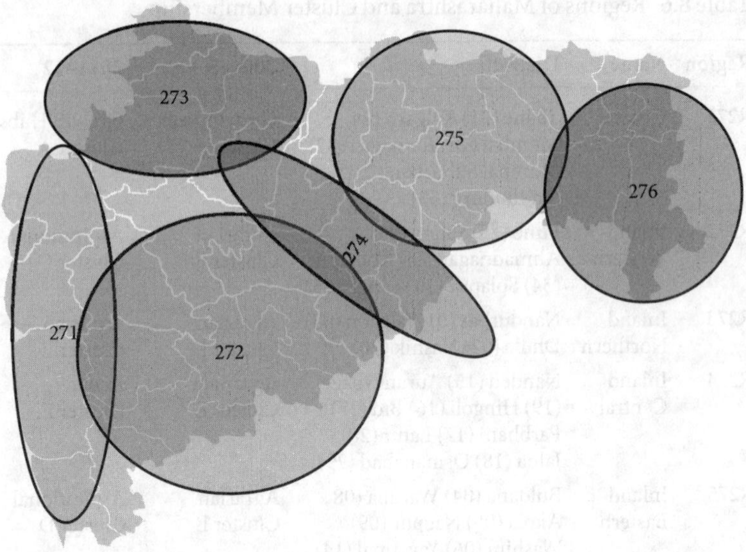

Figure 8.1 Classification of NSS Regions of Maharashtra
Source: Authors' Calculations

formed Cluster E in 2004–5 across states. This is a mix of regions with strong agrarian focus in the economic structure. If we look at the groupings in 2011–12, we find that certain regions have moved into cluster D (2011–12). These include Inland Western Maharashtra (Region No. 272, covering the districts of Pune, Solapur, and so on) and Inland Eastern Maharashtra (Region No. 275, covering Nagpur, Wardha, and so on). Let us take a closer look at some select districts of these two regions of Maharashtra that are a part of this aspiration Cluster D.

Inland western Maharashtra: Pune is the 2nd largest district after Mumbai city and is known as a manufacturing and information technology hub of India. It has the 8th highest metropolitan economy with the 6th highest per capita income across the country. In terms of industries it has 6 co-operative industrial estates with companies such as Tata Motors, Mahindra, and Volkswagen. Pimpri, Hinjewadi, and Haveli are the service hubs of the district known for automobile components, computer software, business process outsourcing, and dairy related products. At the same time agriculture occupies the highest share of employment followed by industries and service sector. Another district of the region, Solapur, which is famous for its power loom industry, has about 6,000 power loom industries operational and employing about 30,000 workers with 25,000 power looms. The district ranks 4th in industrialization in the state. The district's sugar production accounts for 8 per cent of the country and 17 per cent of the state production.

Inland eastern Maharashtra: Wardha is one of the districts of the Inland Eastern Maharashtra region and its economy is mainly agrarian. The major crops of the district are soyabean, pigeon-pea, cotton, pulses, and gram. In terms of industries it has 2 sugar factories. Nagpur which is the 3rd largest city after Mumbai and Pune is also known as the Orange City and is a major trade centre for oranges. The economy is mainly agrarian and major crops are: paddy, sorghum (jowar), and cotton. Sericulture is also concentrated in the district. In terms of infrastructure and industry, there are two major thermal power stations (Koradi and Khaparkheda).

Are there any common traits across regions of other states that make a similar transition from Cluster E (2004–5) to Cluster D (2011–12)? This would include south-eastern Gujarat (Region No. 241, covering districts of Surat, Vadodara, Bharuch, and so on) and northern plains of Gujarat (Region No. 242, covering districts of Ahmedabad , Gandhinagar, Mehsana, and so on) coastal southern Andhra Pradesh (Region No. 282, including districts of Krishna, Guntur, Nellore, and so on) and southern Ganga plain of Uttar Pradesh (Region No. 95, including districts of Bareilly, Agra, Mathura, and so on). If we follow the attributes of cluster D in Table 8.5, we find that this cluster reflects a structural mix of industry and services, fairly high literacy levels, while continuing to have a strong agrarian economy. While analysing the descriptive statistics to identify possible markers for this cluster, we find that while the share of urbanization is not particularly high as a whole, this cluster has a fair concentration of million plus cities, accounting for 13 out of the 26 million-plus cities in 2011–12 (Table 8.7). For the full list of million-plus cities considered, please refer Appendix 5.

We now turn our attention to the regions in Maharashtra which have continued to be part of cluster E over the 2 periods. These are inland northern (Region No. 273, which includes districts of Nandurbar, Nashik, and so on) and eastern (Region No. 276, which includes districts of Gadchiroli, Chandrapur, and so on) Maharashtra. Between these two regions also there are sizable differences in values as reflected by the high standard deviation across values in Cluster E.

Table 8.7 Aspirational Cluster: Composition and Million-plus Cities (2011–12)

Region	Cluster	Regions	State	No. of Million-plus Cities	City
R91	D	Northern Upper Ganga Plains,	Uttar Pradesh	1	Meerut
R92	D	Central	Uttar Pradesh	2	Kanpur, Lucknow
R93	D	Eastern	Uttar Pradesh	1	Varanasi
R95	D	Southern Ganga Plains	Uttar Pradesh	1	Agra
R101	D	Northern	Bihar	0	-
R102	D	Central	Bihar	1	Patna
R213	D	Northern	Odisha	0	-
R222	D	Chattisgarh	Chattisgarh	0	-
R231	D	Vindhyas,	Madhya Pradesh	0	-
R233	D	Malwa	Madhya Pradesh	1	Indore
R241	D	South Eastern	Gujarat	2	Surat, Vadodara
R242	D	Northern Plains	Gujarat	1	Ahmedabad
R272	D	Inland West	Maharashtra	2	Pune, Pimpri-Chinchwad
R275	D	Inland Eastern	Maharashtra	1	Nagpur
R282	D	Coastal Southern	Andhra Pradesh	0	-
R294	D	Inland Northern	Karnataka	0	-

Source: Authors' calculations and Classification of Million-plus cities basis NSSO survey 68th round.

Inland northern Maharashtra covers Nashik, which is largely agrarian and is better known as India's wine capital. It has extensive grape production and its vineyards account for over 50 per cent of India's domestic wine production. As part of the contradictions that make India interesting, this wine hub is also a religious pilgrimage centre with the Triyambakeshwar temple and Igatpuri as popular destinations and hosts the Kumbh mela once every 12 years. Nandurbar district is also part of this cluster and is one of the poorer agricultural regions in Maharashtra. It mainly grows jowar, wheat, and groundnut.

Eastern Maharashtra includes Gadchiroli, which is mostly tribal in demography and is densely covered with forests. The main occupation of people is agriculture and forestry and the major crops are paddy, wheat and linseed. Also the region is famous for bamboo and tendu leaves. Chandrapur district is well known for its reservoirs of limestone and coal, and tourism in the Pench forest sanctuary. The economy is primarily agrarian, and the major crops are paddy, cotton, and sorghum (jowar).

We find that other regions in Cluster E include Ranchi Plateau of Jharkhand and South Odisha. These regions share similar characteristics of being tribal, high on minerals, low on share of services and industry in the economy, while also consistently having low literacy and skill levels. This confirms our earlier hypothesis that Eastern Maharashtra is indeed similar to South Odisha and Ranchi Plateau by virtue of being in the same cluster.

The sixth and final NSS region of Inland Central Maharashtra has moved to the new cluster F 'Acute' in 2011–12. We take a closer look at some select districts within this region to understand the typology. Inland Central Maharashtra includes Aurangabad which is a prominent location for the IT and tourism. At the same time, the main source of employment is agriculture and major crops are sorghum (jowar), pearl millet, and cotton. The district is also a silk production centre. Nanded is another such district which is mainly agrarian and major crops are cotton, sorghum (*jowar*), and sugarcane. It has poor infrastructural facilities, even the industries are agricultural base. Beed, Latur, and Jalna are some of the poorest districts of Maharashtra. Regions from other states in this cluster are Northern and Southern Chhattisgarh, South Western Madhya Pradesh and Inland Eastern Andhra Pradesh. We find that almost all of their individual regional values are significantly below the national average across parameters of economic structure and access.

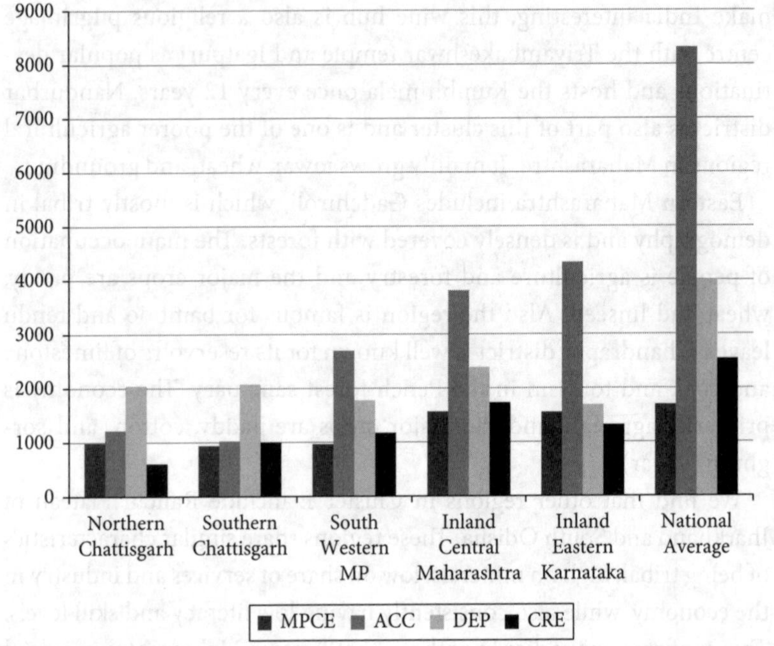

Figure 8.2 Acute Cluster Comparisons 1
Source: Authors' calculations basis cluster analysis.

It is evident from the Figure 8.2 that these regions in Cluster F are lagging behind the national average significantly in terms of access to finance and have lower consumption expenditure. On an average, these regions have a lower number of bank accounts (2,614,000) compared to the national average (8,312,000), as well as deposit values per branch which are a third of the national average as well as credit values per branch which are half the national average. The shares of urbanization (19 per cent) and regular employment (8 per cent) are much lower than the national averages 29 per cent and 20 per cent respectively.

A close look at Figure. 8.3 clearly shows that the diversity index is very low (0.41) for cluster F regions, with Chhattisgarh being as low as 0.30. This goes hand in hand with agriculture having the lion's share in employment at 70 per cent and the lowest share in manufacturing and services at 5 per cent and 15 per cent respectively. Thus, we find that in these respects, the inland central Maharashtra is closer to north and south Chhattisgarh and portions of southern Madhya

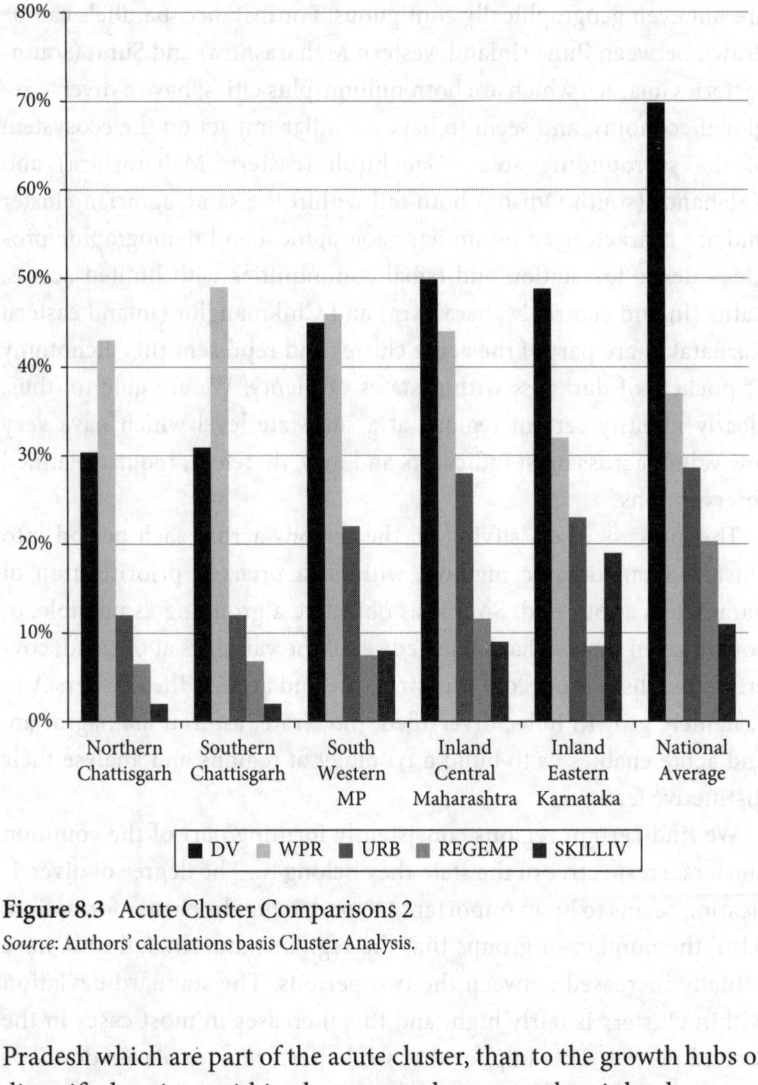

Figure 8.3 Acute Cluster Comparisons 2

Source: Authors' calculations basis Cluster Analysis.

Pradesh which are part of the acute cluster, than to the growth hubs or diversified regions within the state such as coastal or inland western Maharashtra.

Clusters to Aid Planning

The case of Maharashtra throws up specific examples that highlight similarities between regions which may be part of different states and are not even geographically contiguous. For instance, parallels can be drawn between Pune (inland western Maharashtra) and Surat (south-eastern Gujarat), which are both million-plus cities, have a diverse regional economy, and seem to have a similar impact on the ecosystem of the surrounding areas. Gadchiroli (eastern Maharashtra) and Kalahandi (south Odisha) both fall within the same agrarian cluster and are characterized by similar geographical and demographic profiles—dense forestation and tribal communities with limited access. Latur (inland central Maharashtra) and Chikmanglur (inland eastern Karnataka) are part of the acute cluster and represent this dichotomy of pockets of darkness within states of plenty. We are able to, thus, clearly identify certain regions at a sub-state level which have very low values across most indicators and may, therefore, require planned interventions.

This process of classifying all the regions across each period into clusters is an organic method, without a prefixed prioritization of parameters at our end. So it is as objective a grouping as possible, of course given that we have selected set of the variables at our end, covering dimensions of economic structure and access. The Clusters A to F, namely growth hubs, diversified, moderate, aspirational, agrarian, and acute enables us to build a typology of regions and analyse their distinctive features.

We find certain regions consistently forming part of the common clusters irrespective of the state they belong to. The degree of diversification seems to be an important factor driving the cluster formation. Also, the number of groups that the regions naturally fall into, have actually increased between the two periods. The standard deviation within clusters is fairly high, and this increases in most cases in the second period. This implies that while performance across development indicators is positive, the benefits are unevenly spread across the regions and the variation not only between, but also within regions has actually increased. Thus the state level patterns of divergence (Sachs et al. 2002) is being further accentuated at the regional level. The analysis clearly indicates that the policy focus for regional development could target NSS region as a unit for intervention, rather than a state- or district-level intervention which has been attempted thus far. There is no one size fit all policy measure, however regions with similar characteristics and forming into a cluster could benefit from similar policy interventions. The recent initiative towards 'aspirational districts' could be applied to 'aspirational regions', where by the NSS region could be an economically feasible set for planning and execution, reaping the economies of scale and economies of scope advantages.

9
Summary and Conclusions

Overview

The twin objectives of economic growth and balanced regional development are challenges often at divergence with each other and a reconciliation requires policy intervention. This book is situated in the midst of the debate on specialization and diversification. The attempt has been to analyse the extent of regional economic diversity across India in terms of the sectoral shares of employment, and regional variations in output in the context of sluggish manufacturing, skilling and urbanization, as also to offer an understanding of the determinants of such variations based on the principles of agglomeration.

Through the spatial dimensions of structural change, we have adopted a two-way classification: (*a*) benefits from the perspective of the firm, which explain concentration and locational decisions related to processes/production and (*b*) benefits from the perspective of the household which explain the concentration and locational decisions related to the population. The empirical literature is based primarily on experiences from Korea, Brazil, Indonesia, and India to understand the phenomenon of agglomeration in the context of developing economies in particular. The results of such studies reveal how agglomeration economies affect firm and household level outcomes in the form of productivity increases, cost reduction and profitability increases; while also touching briefly on the aspect of urban growth. In particular, urbanization economies represented by sectoral diversification are seen to be significant in the Indian context. We felt that it was important to look at what this means for India, and how a more detailed understanding of agglomeration can help influence regional development specifically in terms of its economic structure and access to finance, skills, and markets.

Regional Economic Diversity. Poornima Dore and Krishnan Narayanan, Oxford University Press. © Oxford University Press India 2022. DOI: 10.1093/oso/9780190130596.003.0009

From a methodological standpoint, our attempt has been to deepen the lens of regional analysis for Indian economy through five fresh aspects:

1. We began with state level analysis and have then moved ahead by considering the NSS region as the unit of analysis to examine inter-regional differences at the sub-state level for the entire country, by applying the principle of homogeneity. Also several similar 'clusters' have been found across the country.
2. Next, the inter-temporal dimension has been examined by considering the time periods 2004–5 and 2011–12. This is an upgrade, as most earlier efforts were seen to be cross sectional and typically covered only a single time period. We have now covered 75 regions in the first period and 85 regions in the second period
3. The variables on access to labour and finance are selected by using metrices, which are more direct output indicators such as skill levels and the banking outreach. These are variables which impact all segments of the population, and are reflective of all-round access, as opposed to variables like FDI, which are very specific to formal sector firms. A measure of sectoral diversity is calculated both at the state and for all regions. Our book develops and reports a measure of diversity (DV) for each region across both time periods.
4. Perhaps, for the first time in India, value added at the NSS region level has been calculated using appropriate techniques followed by international scholars adopting the UN Habitat guidelines. It is unique since this measure of value added covers both formal and informal sector output; and hence, provides a more holistic picture of regional level output.

We have used a variety of public data sources by drawing primarily from the 61st and 68th rounds of NSSO Employment and Unemployment surveys for 2004–5 and 2011–12. The NSSO follows a multi stage stratified sampling design and hence is representative of the regions under consideration. This is supplemented with data published by the Reserve Bank of India (RBI) in the Handbook of Statistics on Indian Economy for 2004–5 and 2011–12, the Basic Statistical Returns of Scheduled Commercial Banks in India for 2005 and 2010, and the Population Census of India for 2001 and 2011.

Major Findings

We began with analysing the trends of regional development by studying the changing sectoral shares in Chapter 4. An examination of the ranking of sectoral shares was carried out, both within and between regions, with specific emphasis on the top 10 and bottom 10 regions in each period. We found significant regional differences: For instance, coastal Karnataka and inland Maharashtra feature in the list of top 10 regions with a high share of manufacturing, while inland eastern Karnataka and eastern Maharashtra feature in the bottom 10 of the same list. Thus within even the same state, manufacturing looks very unevenly distributed.

Chapter 5 involves a detailed analysis of the Diversity Index (DV) as a measure of sectoral diversity. While there have been few studies (Lall and Mengistae 2005) that have underscored the importance of diversity in the Indian context, to the best of our knowledge this would be the first instance of an empirical study in India that involves construction and comparison of the diversity index at the state and the regional level. We find an increase in diversity levels over time (2004–5 to 2011–12) and across locations. We follow the literature (Sveikauskas 1975; Tabuchi 1986) and test whether the theoretical argument that diversity and size are positively associated holds true. This leads to an estimation of the relationship of sectoral diversity in India with scale economies and skill intensity. Contrary to the prevalent view that the attractiveness of states or regions to industry is governed by size, represented by geographical area, population or density of the region, the results reveal that none of these are sufficient conditions. We empirically conclude that diversity and size cannot be used as interchangeable measures of urbanization economies, as they capture different aspects and are clearly not correlated. On the other hand, we find that the diversity index is positively influenced by the availability of a highly skilled workforce. Further, a cross sectional analysis is conducted for each time period as well as a pooled analysis both at the state and at the NSS region level, having four models in all.

In all cases, we find a positive relationship between sectoral diversity and skill intensity. Skill intensity represents embodied technology and we validate the claim that the availability of a high calibre workforce with higher order skills is critical for regions to harness technology and to be competitive in a country such as India (Rajan 2006). In other words, we can say that regions which have been able to attract industries across sectors, are also observed to have access to a skilled workforce that can innovate and maximize the gains through the processes of sharing, matching and networking, all of which underlie the phenomenon of agglomeration. We also find that coastal regions are clearly more diversified, reaffirming the findings of Lall and Chakravorty (2005) on the bias of fresh investments in favour of coastal regions.

All official estimates of output in India are at the national and state level. For the first time, we provide an estimate of output at the NSS region level both in absolute and per capita terms, which can be useful for studies across various dimensions beyond the scope of this study. In Chapter 6, we conduct a deeper analysis of output levels measured in terms of contribution to regional value added (RVA). We observe the change in rankings of states as well as regions and find that trends for output at the NSS region level are much more dynamic than what one would expect purely through state level analysis, thereby justifying the choice of the region as a unit of analysis. A deeper examination of the role of agglomeration and access to finance, skills and markets and their influence on regional output, both in absolute as well as per capita terms, with a focus on the top 10 and bottom 10 regions, serves to bring out how stark the differences really are. Regions with access to strong institutional networks of finance as well as a highly skilled workforce clearly feature among the top 10 regions.

Through a cross sectional as well as pooled regression across a mix of eight models, we find that there are thresholds up to which sectoral diversity and regional value added go together. The association appears to take the form of an inverted-U shape, implying that beyond a point, excessive diversification may have a negative impact on output. We identify a point of inflexion and therefore propose that in the debate between specialisation and diversification (Beaudry and Schiffauerova 2009), while there is stronger evidence in favour of diversification in the Indian context, specialized diversification may be a better model for sustained economic development.

Next, in Chapter 7, we seek to identify critical factors that influence the variations over time and explore the inter-temporal differences by carrying out a discriminant analysis. This process identifies whether the observations across the two time periods are significantly different from each other and helps to highlight those factors from our pool of variables that cause divergence in values over 2004–5 and 2011–12. The analysis of variables related to economic structure such as sectoral shares, extent of economic diversification, per capita output and consumption, describes the size and composition of the regional economy. We also factor in differences in access to finance, based on the number of bank branches and bank accounts as well as the volume of deposits and credit, in addition to the availability of a highly skilled workforce, all of which are essential for regional economic development.

We find evidence of significant divergence across regions during the two time periods of 2004–5 and 2011–12. While there is significant growth and most indicators register an increase, this is accompanied by huge variations between regions which have got accentuated over time. Our results lead us to conclude that the indicators of economic structure and access included in our study explain 75 per cent–90 per cent of the variation between the two periods. We find that output and consumption levels along with sectoral diversity, and to some extent high-end skills, play an important role. Sectoral diversity and output levels are selected for further analysis to study the causal factors that are responsible for some of these variations.

A typology of clusters is then prepared across regions by employing a cluster analysis which highlights inter-regional differences in Chapter 8. This helps us classify regions and also observe whether they remain in the same cluster or change over time. We find that the number of clusters increase, indicative of divergence. There are huge variations between and within states and it is noted that regions within states may actually be more similar to certain regions from other states. Regions which continue to be largely agrarian reflect poorly on most indicators, while those which have a greater share of construction activity or witnessing higher urbanization have higher levels of output. Maharashtra is taken as a case in point to bring out the differences between its six constituent NSS regions. We find that the regions form 5 clusters in period 1 and 7 clusters in period 2 which we broadly classify as: Growth Hubs, Diversified, Moderate, Aspirational, Agrarian and Acute, all of which substantiate the view that the Indian economic story is characterized by diversification and divergence.

This is the first study of its kind that arrives at a specific measurable tipping point for agglomeration economies as represented by diversification. A test for the impact of the presence of million plus cities along with the rate of urbanization reveals that although urbanization plays a significant role in influencing output, the presence of a million-plus city is not a pre-requisite. In fact, million-plus cities appear to have a negative association with output in per capita terms. This underscores the potential of smaller urban centres (Mitra 2011; Denis et al. 2012) to act as growth agents with adequate policy focus. Also, the top 10 regions with the highest output both in absolute and per capita terms clearly behave differently from all the other regions, further underscoring the cumulative causation hypothesis. There is a substantial variation across regions and clusters and we find that regions across different states also tend to cluster together.

Opportunities to Delve Deeper

We have now vividly elucidated the dynamism at the regional level and described the inter-regional and inter-temporal differences in India. Emphasis has been on identifying an initial set of factors that influence these differences, while carrying out a detailed assessment of the extent of sectoral diversity and its role in impacting output levels. However, there are some limitations and scope for further research:

1. The application of the NSS region as unit of analysis has limited the kind of variables that could be studied since most aggregate data is at the state level and not all information is captured or reported at the NSS region level. Compiling more information at this unit can enhance the dimensions to understand the regional economy.
2. The pooled analysis is based on an unbalanced cross-sectional panel, since there are 10 additional NSS regions that have been created (largely from existing regions) between 2004–5 and 2011–12. Also in a few cases the composition of the NSS region has undergone a minor change through the addition or deletion of 1 or 2 districts

3. The availability of annual data for each year in the time period under consideration would have helped to create a panel and added more rigour to our empirical analysis. Timely and official estimates along such parameters will be very useful going forward to give a real picture on matters of significant policy importance.

There have been some efforts in recent years to address this. Based on the recommendation of the National Statistical Commission (NSC), a Committee was set up under the Chairmanship of Prof. Amitabh Kundu to review the nature and methodology of employment data collection in the country. Their findings were similar to some of our observations elucidated on the challenges/limitations of the current data on skills and labour markets: (*a*) There is a dire need for greater periodicity of information flows. Data that comes in once every 5 or 10 years becomes dated very quickly, given the dynamic nature of labour market changes. (*b*) There needs to be some way to factor in the level of education and skills and triangulate the same while looking at employment choice and nature of industry as captured in the NCO and NIC classifications respectively.

Subsequently a Standing Committee on Labour Force Statistics (SCLFS) was set up under the Chairmanship of Prof S.P. Mukherjee which proposed a new survey approach. It has further helped the cause, that the IMFs Special Data Dissemination Standard (which India is also a signatory to) prescribes greater frequency of labor market information. It recommended quarterly data on labour market aspects of employment, wage earnings as well as conceptual convergence with internationally acceptable standard.

As a result, from 2017-18, the Ministry of Statistics and Program Implementation has launched the Periodic Labour Force Survey (PLFS) 'with the objective of measuring quarterly changes of various statistical indicators of the labor market in urban areas as well as generating the annual estimates of different labor force indicators both in rural and urban areas.' This is therefore a new series, with a changed methodology, and differs from the EUS having a different rural and urban sampling approach. In addition, the EUS conducted till 2011–12, which we include in our analysis, used the monthly per capita expenditure of the household in the selected blocks as a basis for stratification of households; and out of 8 households in the selected blocks, 75 per cent were from the middle-income group or above in the urban areas. In the Periodic Labour Force Survey (PLFS) conducted from 2017-18, a decision was taken to use education levels as a criterion for stratification at the ultimate level, the rationale for this decision was based on the fact that the education levels in the economy have risen due to various policy interventions like the Right to Education Act and it would be important to assess the level of employment and unemployment using this as a stratification basis. Thus the PLFS is in effect as a new series for measuring employment and unemployment on an annual basis, addressing the issues of both periodicity and factoring in human capabilities.

More recent government programs such as the Smart Cities Mission and the Transforming Aspirational District Program which look at integrated urban and rural development respectively, have components that involve mechanisms to review district performance, and set up command and control centres respectively. We hope that over time, these will create a sustainable administrative system to track progress on important development indicators and over time enable measurement on parameters related to economic structure and access as well.

Insights for Economic Theory

1. This book reaffirms the value of defining the region as a homogeneous unit for analysis. Regional science literature speaks of this, and we find that the application of this principle to our analysis makes it richer and throws up several underlying patterns.
2. Several empirical studies have used population or population density as a proxy for diversity. This book questions these assumptions and indicates through state, region and city level analyses, that the general application of such proxies is incorrect and a separate index of sectoral shares like the diversity index will need to be created. We also find that for agglomeration, it is quality and not quantity alone that matters. In other words, the quality of the workforce in terms of skills plays a far greater role in determining the colocation of multiple sectors, rather than the sheer geographic size or population of the region.

3. This book also seeks to define a point of inflexion, beyond which the benefits of diversification begin to taper, taking the shape of an inverted 'U'. In other words, as more sectors begin to contribute to the employment in a region, the output levels of the region is seen to increase, This holds true upto an inflection point, beyond which as sectoral diversity increases, we find diminishing levels of output,
4. Specialization and diversification are clearly not binary choices, but a series of points on a continuum between 0 and 1, representing absolute specialisation and complete diversification respectively. In line of some of the more recent research (Kemeny and Storper 2014), this treatise proposes 'specialized diversification' as a goal that the regional economy can aspire for. This is in contrast to the single sector special economic zone (SEZ) approach that often promotes one industry of competitive advantage. This book strongly recommends 'Specialized Diversification', which would involve a policy to promote a few select sectors which harness the benefits of regional economic diversity, while also ensuring focused growth.

Implications for Policy

1. Divergence at the regional level has increased. There are clearly pockets of growth which are at a very different levels of development in comparison to other very backward segments. Given that the state level picture masks the degree of variation at the regional level, then in order to attain the planned goals of balanced development there is clearly the need for a very serious concerted effort to make the gains from development more equitable. This book clearly identifies certain regions which have very low values across most indicators and may therefore require planned interventions.
2. There is merit in using the NSS region framework to define policy or devolve the implementation protocol at the NSS region level. Given the wide variations within states and similarities across regions, the approach and targeting of government schemes and programs needs to be far more nuanced to ensure results. For instance, in deployment of any government program, say on financial inclusion, while the overall program design may be the same pan India, the way in

which outreach and opening of bank accounts as well as provision of savings facility, and so on, is provided, may require significant variations at the regional level. A one size fits all approach at the state level is unlikely to work. The district, on the other hand, is too small a unit for effective planning and for all practical purposes will result in 700 units of planning which may not be tenable at all times. The NSS region is a more manageable and representative level of disaggregation.

3. The sheer dearth of data to support region level analysis through the course of this study points towards a serious need for compilation of official data sets at NSS region level or district level across the country. For instance, our measure of RVA is an approximation and will have its limitations as it cannot substitute real data at the regional level. Compilation of data at least at the NSS region level is highly recommended as this unit is statistically sound and fulfils the principle of acting as a homogenous denominator. This will help study the underlying causal factors much better and enable more targeted solution design across departments. It is desirable to have as much granularity of information as possible so that the nuances at the micro level can be captured.
4. The smaller cities and urban centres have tremendous growth potential which need to be leveraged early on. Policy interventions are essential to prepare non-million plus cities for accelerated growth and to help census towns identify their sectors of competitive advantage and create conditions that boost the same, in addition to town planning to ensure that their communities get access to education, skills, finance and basic amenities. Programmes such as the Smart Cities Mission, and so on, require a strong data and performance oriented approach as well as forward planning to integrate the colocation of industry and people.

Lessons for Business

1. Business leaders and industry bodies should look at such parameters while planning geographic expansion and choosing locations for branches, factories etc. Diversification clearly emerges as an important driver of the regional economy. At the same time there

are thresholds to its benefits as well. Certain backward regions and states need to accelerate the process of developing specific sectors of competitive advantage beyond agriculture, in a focused manner without spreading themselves too thin. The focus needs to be on maintaining optimal levels of specialized diversification. This is an important element to be taken up at appropriate industry forums to review the approach to SEZs and fiscal incentives, many of which continue to be single sector focused.

2. There is a need for business to focus on skilling and improving the quality of the workforce if such diversified economic regions are expected to grow and multiply. One of the most differentiating factors of a region's ability to have a diversified economy is the availability of high quality workforce. A thrust on education levels and professional skills even in hitherto agrarian belts is essential. There also needs to be a mechanism to ensure that while there is a push towards quantity and numbers in terms of youth trained, the quality of skills created should not get compromised. At the same time, professional skills do not guarantee job creation and so there will need to be a specific strategy to address the same. Industry adoption of ITIs and accountability of skilling operators are steps in the right direction. Industry needs to participate actively in this process to ensure that the requisite skills get generated to plug the current demand supply gap.
3. Access to finance needs to go beyond opening of bank branches and setting up accounts, to enable more easy access to credit and other facilities. The banking correspondent model seems to have worked, but with limited success. With Jan Dhan accounts, direct benefit transfers and other digital payment formats becoming popular in recent years, payments have definitely become simplified—we will need to see if this translates into easier access to finance. In addition, differentiated products and vigilance mechanisms may be required as high collateral is difficult to arrange in regions where the population pressure on assets is high. There is need for focus on product development which enhances access to working capital, especially in the agrarian belts, savings and insurance products for construction sector workers, and small business financing to boost multi-sectoral growth in interior locations.

Actionables for Administrators

1. The clustering of regions may support National and Local Leaders (e.g. District Collectors in India) to identify patterns that need to be addressed, to ensure that the top 10 regions continue to perform well, and that other regions including the bottom 10 find pathways to improve performance. Efforts such as the Aspirational Districts Program can be successful when regional administrators take steps towards analysing the causal factors behind district rankings and plan interventions that can actually boost the socio-economic status of the regions.
2. Every cluster has its own set of challenges and opportunities; The Growth Hubs need to look at how to maximize output without compromising on quality of life. The Diversified Cluster needs to ensure that its regions continue to anchor the regional and national economy and target both domestic and export markets. The Moderate Cluster must find ways to maximize its potential and build its competitive advantage in tourism, horticulture, and so on. The Aspirational Cluster needs to identify and address the issues of job creation, harnessing the demographic dividend it is blessed with. The Agrarian Cluster has to find a way to improve agricultural productivity and access to markets. The Acute cluster must focus on all development parameters to pull itself out of poverty and neglect. A consolidated cluster level strategy in conjuction with the Centre and States will be a good starting point to help strengthen the regional economy and improve access along the twin pillars of skills and finance.
3. Most city development programs have infrastructure plans which involve construction, which has noted the highest employment growth during the period considered for the analysis. City level administrators including Municipal Commissioners, Mayors and Heads of Urban Local Bodies (ULBs), have a very important role to play. Larger cities must work to manage the movements of people and business so that diminishing returns do not set in, particularly with COVID-19 having brought to the fore, the need to factor migrants into city level plans. There is also the need to prepare the smaller cities for upcoming growth as these are clearly emerging as growth engines for the future, while maintaining a healthy balance

between specialisation and diversification. Linkages from cities to the hinterland by way of road, rail and frequent transportation will help create actual and better access to markets.

4. A forum can be created to bring together bureaucrats of regions across states that have been identified as being a part of the same cluster. As on date, interactions at a local level are either within departments, or for district or block level administration across departments, it is largely within the state. National convergence does happen, but on specific national programs. Focused cross learning opportunities across the clusters as defined in our book can enable sharing of best practices, identification of common problems and challenges, and greater interactions on matters of process and implementation of flagship programs of national importance.

This book has attempted to cover a wide canvas, especially in analysing the inter-regional and inter-temporal trends and patterns in a developing country context. All information has been brought to one common homogeneous unit of analysis, in this case - the NSS Region. The discussion presented across chapters uses data and examples to clearly highlight that the Indian regional economy is characterised by both diversification and divergence. A nuanced approach is hence required, while formulating economic strategies to foster development and business growth, given the large region-level variations. Spatial dynamics (economic geography) is an important variable which all leaders, businesses and investors must factor in - we underscore that a robust regional economy is critical for sustained growth and last mile access. This is true of most countries that have the potential to impact the global economy at scale. This book therefore makes an important contribution to regional planning and industrial development both from the perspective of methodology and findings. The future includes creating enabling conditions for the design of financial products, fixing the demand supply gap for higher order skills, making regional information accessible to foster R&D, having a common denominator like the NSS frame for public datasets, formation of regional advisory councils and avenues for industry forums and multilaterals to make specialized diversification a planned objective. We hope this book provokes such conversations, encourages our readers to look out for some of these markers while traveling, and makes a case for informed efforts to strengthen the levers of regional economic structure and access. by using a common homogeneous regional unit of analysis. The results provide greater clarity on the issues in fostering economic development at the sub-state level. It opens up the possibilities of our analysis, of our approach. The results obtained several policy implications for balanced regional development through specialised diversification of the regional economy. This book hopes to make an important contribution to regional planning and industrial development both from the perspective of methodology and findings. The discussion presented use examples to clearly highlight that there no 'one size fits all' while formulating economic policies to foster development, given the large region-level variations. The clustering of regions does point towards preparing a region-specific approach in policy making. Policy intervention applicable to regions at similar levels of development could be more focused and attract greater investment in region specific sectors and foster growth. We could think of broad-basing and identifying 'aspirational' and 'acute regions' from a public policy perspective. It is evident that not all the regions within a state are homogeneous and there are comparable regions in terms of economic development across the length and breadth of the country. We hope this book provokes a conversation, encourages our readers to look out for some of these markers while travelling, and makes a case for informed efforts to strengthen the levers of economic structure and access.

APPENDIX 1

List of NSS Regions and their Composition 2004–05

sl. no.	state/u.t. (code)	SR	detailed composition of region				
			description	name of district	code	name of district	code
(1)	(2)	(3)	(4)	(5)	(6)	(7)	(8)
1.	Andaman & Nicobar Islands (35)	351	Andaman & Nicobar Islands	Andamans	(01)	Nicobars	(02)
2.	Andhra Pradesh (28)	281	Coastal	Srikakulam	(11)	Krishna	(16)
				Vizianagaram	(12)	Guntur	(17)
				Visakhapatnam	(13)	Prakasam	(18)
				East Godavari	(14)	Nellore	(19)
				West Godavari	(15)		
3.		282	Inland	Adilabad	(01)	Rangareddi	(06)
			Northern	Nizamabad	(02)	Mahbubnagar	(07)
				Karimnagar	(03)	Nalgonda	(08)
				Medak	(04)	Warangal	(09)
				Hyderabad	(05)	Khammam	(10)
4.		283	South -Western	Kurnool	(21)	Anantapur	(22)

5.		284	Inland Southern	Cuddapah	(20)	Chittoor	(23)
6.	Arunachal Pradesh (12)	121	Arunachal Pradesh	Tawang	(01)	East Siang	(08)
				West Kameng	(02)	Upper Siang	(09)
				East Kameng	(03)	Dibang Valley	(10)
				Papum Pare	(04)	Lohit	(11)
				Lower Subansiri	(05)	Changlang	(12)
				Upper Subansiri	(06)	Tirap	(13)
				West Siang	(07)		
7.	Assam (18)	181	Plains Eastern	Lakhimpur	(12)	Jorhat	(17)
				Dhemaji	(13)	Golaghat	(18)
				Tinsukia	(14)	Cachar	(21)
				Dibrugarh	(15)	Karimganj	(22)
				Sibsagar	(16)	Hailakandi	(23)
8.		182	Plains Western	Kokrajhar	(01)	Nalbari	(07)
				Dhubri	(02)	Darrang	(08)
				Goalpara	(03)	Marigaon	(09)
				Bongaigaon	(04)	Nagaon	(10)
				Barpeta	(05)	Sonitpur	(11)
				Kamrup	(06)		
9.		183	Hills	Karbi Anglong	(19)	North Cachar Hills	(20)

sl. no.	state/u.t. (code)	SR	detailed composition of region				
			description	name of district	code	name of district	code
(1)	(2)	(3)	(4)	(5)	(6)	(7)	(8)
10.	Bihar (10)	101	Northern	Champaran(W)	(01)	Madhepura	(11)
				Champaran(E)	(02)	Saharsa	(12)
				Sheohar	(03)	Darbhanga	(13)
				Sitamarhi	(04)	Muzaffarpur	(14)
				Madhubani	(05)	Gopalganj	(15)
				Supaul	(06)	Siwan	(16)
				Araria	(07)	Saran	(17)
				Kishanganj	(08)	Vaishali	(18)
				Purnia	(09)	Samastipur	(19)
				Katihar	(10)		
11.		102	Central	Begusarai	(20)	Bhojpur	(29)
				Khagaria	(21)	Buxar	(30)
				Bhagalpur	(22)	Kaimur (Bhabua)	(31)
				Banka	(23)	Rohtas	(32)
				Munger	(24)	Jehanabad	(33)
				Lakhisarai	(25)	Aurangabad	(34)
				Sheikhpura	(26)	Gaya	(35)
				Nalanda	(27)	Nawada	(36)
				Patna	(28)	Jamui	(37)

sl. no.	state/u.t. (code)	SR	detailed composition of region				
			description	name of district	code	name of district	code
(1)	(2)	(3)	(4)	(5)	(6)	(7)	(8)
12.	Chandigarh (04)	041	Chandigarh	Chandigarh	(01)		
13.	Chhattisgarh (22)	221	Chhattis-garh	Koriya	(01)	Rajnandgaon	(09)
				Surguja	(02)	Durg	(10)
				Jashpur	(03)	Raipur	(11)
				Raigarh	(04)	Mahasamund	(12)
				Korba	(05)	Dhamtari	(13)
				Janjgir-Champa	(06)	Kanker	(14)
				Bilaspur	(07)	Bastar	(15)
				Kawardha	(08)	Dantewada	(16)
14.	Dadra & Nagar Haveli (26)	261	Dadra & Nagar Haveli	Dadra & Nagar Haveli	(01)		
15.	Daman & Diu (25)	251	Daman & Diu	Diu	(01)	Daman	(02)
16.	Delhi (07)	071	Delhi	North West	(01)	Central	(06)
				North	(02)	West	(07)
				North East	(03)	South West	(08)
				East	(04)	South	(09)
				New Delhi	(05)		

17.	Goa (30)	301	Goa	North Goa	(01)	South Goa	(02)
18.	Gujarat (24)	241	Eastern	Sabar Kantha	(05)		
				[Khedbarhma, Vijaynagar, Bhiloda, Meghraj]			
				Panch Mahals	(17)		
				[Kadana, Santrampur]			
				Dohad	(18)		
				Vadodara	(19)		
				[Jetpur Pavi, Chhota Udaipur, Kavant, Nasvadi]			
				Narmada	(20)		
				Bharuch	(21)		
				[Jhagadia, Anklesvar, Valia]			
				Surat	(22)		
				[Mangrol, Umarpada, Nizar, Uchchhal, Songadh, Mandvi, Palsana, Bardoli, Vyara, Valod, Mahuva]			
				The Dangs	(23)		
				Navsari	(24)		
				[Chikhli, Bansda]			
				Valsad	(25)		

sl. no.	state/u.t. (code)	SR	detailed composition of region				
			description	name of district	code	name of district	code
(1)	(2)	(3)	(4)	(5)	(6)	(7)	(8)
19.		242	Plains	Patan	(03)		
			Northern	[Vagdod, Siddhpur, Patan]			
				Mahesana	(04)		
				Sabar Kantha	(05)		
				[Vadali, Idar, Himatnagar, Prantij, Talod, Modasa, Dhansura, Malpur, Bayad]			
				Gandhinagar	(06)		
				Ahmedabad	(07)		
				Anand	(15)		
				Kheda	(16)		
20.		243	Plains	Panch Mahals	(17)		
			Southern	[Khanpur, Lunawada, Sehera, Morwa(hadaf), Godhra, Kalol, Ghoghamba, Halol, Jambughoda]			
				Vadodara	(19)		
				[Savli, Vadodara, Vaghodia, Sankheda, Dabhoi, Padra, Karjan, Sinor]			
				Bharuch	(21)		
				[Jambusar, Amod, Vagra, Bharuch, Hansot]			

				Surat	(22)		
				[Olpad, Kamrej, Surat City, Chorasi]			
				Navsari	(24)		
				[Navsari, Jalalpur, Gandevi]			
21.		244	Dry areas	Kachchh	(01)		
				Bans Kantha	(02)		
				Patan	(03)		
				[Santalpur, Radhanpur, Harij, Sami, Chanasma]			
				Surendranagar	(08)		
22.		245	Saurashtra	Rajkot	(09)	Junagadh	(12)
				Jamnagar	(10)	Amreli	(13)
				Porbandar	(11)	Bhavnagar	(14)
23.	Haryana (06)	061	Eastern	Panchkula	(01)	Panipat	(07)
				Ambala	(02)	Sonipat	(08)
				Yamunanagar	(03)	Rohtak	(14)
				Kurukshetra	(04)	Jhajjar	(15)
				Kaithal	(05)	Gurgaon	(18)
				Karnal	(06)	Faridabad	(19)
24.		062	Western	Jind	(09)	Bhiwani	(13)
				Fatehabad	(10)	Mahendragarh	(16)
				Sirsa	(11)	Rewari	(17)
				Hisar	(12)		

sl. no.	state/u.t. (code)	SR	detailed composition of region				
			description	name of district	code	name of district	code
(1)	(2)	(3)	(4)	(5)	(6)	(7)	(8)
25.	Himachal Pradesh (02)	021	Himachal Pradesh	Chamba	(01)	Una	(07)
				Kangra	(02)	Bilaspur	(08)
				Lahul & Spiti	(03)	Solan	(09)
				Kullu	(04)	Sirmaur	(10)
				Mandi	(05)	Shimla	(11)
				Hamirpur	(06)	Kinnaur	(12)
26.	Jammu & Kashmir (01)	011	Mountain ous	Jammu	(13)	Kathua	(14)
27.		012	Outer Hills	Doda	(09)	Punch	(11)
				Udhampur	(10)	Rajauri	(12)
28.		013	Jhelam Valley	Kupwara	(01)	Pulwama	(05)
				Baramula	(02)	Anantnag	(06)
				Srinagar	(03)	Leh* (Ladakh)	(07)
				Badgam	(04)	Kargil*	(08)

29.	Jharkhand (20)	201	Jharkhand	Garhwa	(01)	Pakaur	(10)
				Palamu	(02)	Dumka	(11)
				Chatra	(03)	Dhanbad	(12)
				Hazaribag	(04)	Bokaro	(13)
				Kodarma	(05)	Ranchi	(14)
				Giridih	(06)	Lohardaga	(15)
				Deoghar	(07)	Gumla	(16)
				Godda	(08)	Singhbhum(W)	(17)
				Sahibganj	(09)	Singhbhum (E)	(18)
30.	Karnataka (29)	291	Coastal & Ghats	Uttara Kannada	(10)	Dakshina Kannada	(24)
				Udupi	(16)		
31.		292	Inland Eastern	Shimoga	(15)	Hassan	(23)
				Chikmagalur	(17)	Kodagu	(25)
32.		293	Inland Southern	Tumkur	(18)	Mandya	(22)
				Kolar	(19)	Mysore	(26)
				Bangalore	(20)	Chamarajanagar	(27)
				Bangalore (Rural)	(21)		

* not yet covered by NSS

sl. no.	state/u.t. (code)	SR	detailed composition of region				
			description	name of district	code	name of district	code
(1)	(2)	(3)	(4)	(5)	(6)	(7)	(8)
33.	Karnataka	294	Inland	Belgaum	(01)	Gadag	(08)
	(29)		Northern	Bagalkot	(02)	Dharwad	(09)
				Bijapur	(03)	Haveri	(11)
				Gulbarga	(04)	Bellary	(12)
				Bidar	(05)	Chitradurga	(13)
				Raichur	(06)	Davanagere	(14)
				Koppal	(07)		
34.	Kerala	321	Northern	Kasaragod	(01)	Kozhikode	(04)
	(32)			Kannur	(02)	Malappuram	(05)
				Wayanad	(03)	Palakkad	(06)
35.		322	Southern	Thrissur	(07)	Alappuzha	(11)
				Ernakulam	(08)	Pathanamthitta	(12)
				Idukki	(09)	Kollam	(13)
				Kottayam	(10)	Thiruvananthapuram	(14)
36.	Lakshadweep	311	Laksha-dweep	Lakshadweep	(01)		
	(31)						
37.	Madhya Pradesh	231	Vindhya	Tikamgarh	(08)	Rewa	(14)
	(23)			Chhatarpur	(09)	Umaria	(15)
				Panna	(10)	Shahdol	(16)
				Satna	(13)	Sidhi	(17)

38.		232	Central	Sagar	(11)	Bhopal	(32)
				Damoh	(12)	Sehore	(33)
				Vidisha	(31)	Raisen	(34)
39.		233	Malwa	Neemuch	(18)	Dewas	(23)
				Mandsaur	(19)	Jhabua	(24)
				Ratlam	(20)	Dhar	(25)
				Ujjain	(21)	Indore	(26)
				Shajapur	(22)	Rajgarh	(30)
40.		234	South	Katni	(38)	Mandla	(42)
				Jabalpur	(39)	Chhindwara	(43)
				Narsimhapur	(40)	Seoni	(44)
				Dindori	(41)	Balaghat	(45)
41.		235	South Western	W. Nimar (Khargoan)	(27)	Betul	(35)
						Harda	(36)
				Barwani	(28)	Hoshangabad	(37)
				E. Nimar (Khandwa)	(29)		
42.		236	Northern	Sheopur	(01)	Datia	(05)
				Morena	(02)	Shivpuri	(06)
				Bhind	(03)	Guna	(07)
				Gwalior	(04)		
43.	Maharashtra (27)	271	Coastal	Thane	(21)	Raigarh	(24)
				Mumbai	(22)	Ratnagiri	(32)

sl. no.	state/u.t. (code)	SR	detailed composition of region				
			description	name of district	code	name of district	code
(1)	(2)	(3)	(4)	(5)	(6)	(7)	(8)
				Suburban		Sindhudurg	(33)
				Mumbai	(23)		
44.	Maharashtra	272	Inland	Pune	(25)	Satara	(31)
	(27)		Western	Ahmadnagar	(26)	Kolhapur	(34)
				Solapur	(30)	Sangli	(35)
45.		273	Inland	Nandurbar	(01)	Jalgaon	(03)
			Northern	Dhule	(02)	Nashik	(20)
46.		274	Inland	Nanded	(15)	Aurangabad	(19)
			Central	Hingoli	(16)	Bid	(27)
				Parbhani	(17)	Latur	(28)
				Jalna	(18)	Osmanabad	(29)
47.		275	Inland	Buldana	(04)	Wardha	(08)
			Eastern	Akola	(05)	Nagpur	(09)
				Washim	(06)	Yavatmal	(14)
				Amravati	(07)		
48.		276	Eastern	Bhandara	(10)	Gadchiroli	(12)
				Gondiya	(11)	Chandrapur	(13)

49.	Manipur	141	Plains	Bishnupur	(04)	Imphal West	(06)
	(14)			Thoubal	(05)	Imphal East	(07)
50.		142	Hills	Senapati	(01)	Ukhrul	(08)
				Tamenglong	(02)	Chandel	(09)
				Churachandpur	(03)		
51.	Meghalaya	171	Meghalaya	West Garo Hills	(01)	Ri Bhoi	(05)
	(17)			East Garo Hills	(02)	East Khasi Hills	(06)
				South Garo Hills	(03)	Jaintia Hills	(07)
				West Khasi Hills	(04)		
52.	Mizoram	151	Mizoram	Mamit	(01)	Serchip	(05)
	(15)			Kolasib	(02)	Lunglei	(06)
				Aizwal	(03)	Lawngtlai	(07)
				Champhai	(04)	Saiha	(08)
53.	Nagaland	131	Nagaland	Mon	(01)	Wokha	(05)
	(13)			Tuensang	(02)	Dimapur	(06)
				Mokokchung	(03)	Kohima	(07)
				Zunheboto	(04)	Phek	(08)
54.	Orissa	211	Coastal	Baleshwar	(08)	Nayagarh	(16)
	(21)			Bhadrak	(09)	Khordha	(17)
				Kendrapara	(10)	Puri	(18)
				Jagatsinghapur	(11)	Ganjam	(19)
				Cuttack	(12)	Gajapati	(20)
				Jajapur	(13)		

sl. no.	state/u.t. (code)	SR	detailed composition of region				
			description	name of district	code	name of district	code
(1)	(2)	(3)	(4)	(5)	(6)	(7)	(8)
55.		212	Southern	Kandhamal	(21)	Rayagada	(27)
				(Phoolbani)		Nabarangapur	(28)
				Baudh	(22)	Koraput	(29)
				Nuapada	(25)	Malkangiri	(30)
				Kalahandi	(26)		
56.	Orissa	213	Northern	Bargarh	(01)	Mayurbhanj	(07)
	(21)			Jharsuguda	(02)	Dhenkanal	(14)
				Sambalpur	(03)	Anugul	(15)
				Debagarh	(04)	Sonapur	(23)
				Sundargarh	(05)	Balangir	(24)
				Kendujhar	(06)		
57.	Pondicherry	341	Pondi-	Yanam	(01)	Mahe	(03)
	(34)		cherry	Pondicherry	(02)	Karaikal	(04)
58.	Punjab	031	Northern	Gurdaspur	(01)	Hoshiarpur	(05)
	(03)			Amritsar	(02)	Nawanshahr	(06)
				Kapurthala	(03)	Rupnagar	(07)
				Jalandhar	(04)	Ludhiana	(09)

59.		032	Southern	Fatehgarh Sahib	(08)	Bathinda	(14)
				Moga	(10)	Mansa	(15)
				Firozpur	(11)	Sangrur	(16)
				Muktsar	(12)	Patiala	(17)
				Faridkot	(13)		
60.	Rajasthan (08)	081	Western	Ganganagar	(01)	Jaisalmer	(16)
				Hanumangarh	(02)	Barmer	(17)
				Bikaner	(03)	Jalor	(18)
				Churu	(04)	Sirohi	(19)
				Nagaur	(14)	Pali	(20)
				Jodhpur	(15)		
61.		082	North-Eastern	Jhunjhunun	(05)	Dausa	(11)
				Alwar	(06)	Jaipur	(12)
				Bharatpur	(07)	Sikar	(13)
				Dhaulpur	(08)	Ajmer	(21)
				Karauli	(09)	Tonk	(22)
				Sawai Madhopur	(10)	Bhilwara	(24)
62.		083	Southern	Rajsamand	(25)	Dungarpur	(27)
				Udaipur	(26)	Banswara	(28)
63.		084	South-Eastern	Bundi	(23)	Baran	(31)
				Chittaurgarh	(29)	Jhalawar	(32)
				Kota	(30)		

sl. no.	state/u.t. (code)	SR	detailed composition of region				
			description	name of district	code	name of district	code
(1)	(2)	(3)	(4)	(5)	(6)	(7)	(8)
64.	Sikkim	111	Sikkim	North (Mongam)	(01)	South	(03)
	(11)			West	(02)	(Nimachai)	
				(Gyalshing)		East (Gangtok)	(04)
65.	Tamil Nadu	331	Coastal	Thiruvallur	(01)	Tiruvanamalai	(06)
	(33)		Northern	Chennai	(02)	Viluppuram	(07)
				Kancheepuram	(03)	Cuddalore	(18)
				Vellore	(04)		
66.		332	Coastal	Karur	(14)	Nagapattinam	(19)
				Tiruchirappalli	(15)	Thiruvarur	(20)
				Perambalur	(16)	Thanjavur	(21)
				Ariyalur	(17)	Pudukkottai	(22)
67.	Tamil Nadu	333	Southern	Dindigul	(13)	Ramanathapuram	(27)
	(33)			Sivaganga	(23)	Toothukudi	(28)
				Madurai	(24)	Tirunelveli	(29)
				Theni	(25)	Kanniyakumari	(30)
				Virudhunagar	(26)		
68.		334	Inland	Dharmapuri	(05)	Erode	(10)
				Salem	(08)	The Nilgiris	(11)
				Namakkal	(09)	Coimbatore	(12)

69.	Tripura (16)	161	Tripura	West Tripura	(01)	Dhalai	(03)
				South Tripura	(02)	North Tripura	(04)
70.	Uttaranchal (05)	051	Uttaranchal	Uttarkashi	(01)	Champawat	(08)
				Chamoli	(02)	Almora	(09)
				Rudraprayag	(03)	Bageshwar	(10)
				Tehri Garhwal	(04)	Nainital	(11)
				Dehradun	(05)	Udham Singh Nagar	(12)
				Garhwal	(06)		
				Pithoragarh	(07)	Hardwar	(13)
71.	Uttar Pradesh (09)	091	Western	Saharanpur	(01)	Mathura	(14)
				Muzaffarnagar	(02)	Agra	(15)
				Bijnor	(03)	Firozabad	(16)
				Moradabad	(04)	Etah	(17)
				Rampur	(05)	Mainpuri	(18)
				J Phule Nagar	(06)	Budaun	(19)
				Meerut	(07)	Bareilly	(20)
				Baghpat	(08)	Pilibhit	(21)
				Ghaziabad	(09)	Shahjahanpur	(22)
				G. Buddha Nagar	(10)	Farrukhabad	(29)
				Bulandshahr	(11)	Kannauj	(30)
				Aligarh	(12)	Etawah	(31)
				Hathras	(13)	Auraiya	(32)

sl. no.	state/u.t. (code)	SR	detailed composition of region				
			description	name of district	code	name of district	code
(1)	(2)	(3)	(4)	(5)	(6)	(7)	(8)
72.		092	Central	Kheri	(23)	Rae Bareli	(28)
				Sitapur	(24)	Kanpur Dehat	(33)
				Hardoi	(25)	Kanpur Nagar	(34)
				Unnao	(26)	Fatehpur	(42)
				Lucknow	(27)	Barabanki	(46)
73.		093	Eastern	Pratapgarh	(43)	Gorakhpur	(58)
				Kaushambi	(44)	Kushinagar	(59)
				Allahabad	(45)	Deoria	(60)
				Faizabad	(47)	Azamgarh	(61)
				Ambedkar Nag.	(48)	Mau	(62)
				Sultanpur	(49)	Ballia	(63)
				Bahraich	(50)	Jaunpur	(64)
				Shrawasti	(51)	Ghazipur	(65)
				Balrampur	(52)	Chandauli	(66)
				Gonda	(53)	Varanasi	(67)
				Siddharthnagar	(54)	S.R.Nagar(Bhadohi)	(68)
				Basti	(55)	Mirzapur	(69)
				S. Kabir Nagar	(56)	Sonbhadra	(70)
				Maharajganj	(57)		

74.	Uttar Pradesh (09)	094	Southern	Jalaun	(35)	Mahoba	(39)
				Jhansi	(36)	Banda	(40)
				Lalitpur	(37)	Chitrakoot	(41)
				Hamirpur	(38)		
75.	West Bengal (19)	191	Himalayan	Darjiling	(01)	Koch Bihar	(03)
				Jalpaiguri	(02)		
76.		192	Eastern Plains	Uttar Dinajpur	(04)	Murshidabad	(07)
				Dakshin Dinajpur	(05)	Birbhum	(08)
				Maldah	(06)	Nadia	(10)
77.		193	Central Plains	Barddhaman	(09)	Howrah	(16)
				North 24-Parganas	(11)	Kolkata	(17)
				Hugli	(12)	South 24-Parganas	(18)
78.		194	Western Plains	Bankura	(13)	Medinipur	(15)
				Puruliya	(14)		

Source: *Instructions to Field Staff*, Vol-I Appendix II: NSS 61st Round, 2004-05.

APPENDIX 2

List of NSS Regions and their Composition (2011–12)

sl. no	state/u.t. (code)	NSS region code	detailed composition of region				
			description	name of district	code	name of district	code
(1)	(2)	(3)	(4)	(5)	(6)	(7)	(8)
1.	Andaman & Nicobar Islands (35)	351	Andaman & Nicobar Islands	South Andaman	(01)	North and Middle Andaman	(03)
				Nicobars	(02)		
2.	Andhra Pradesh (28)	281	Coastal Northern	Srikakulam	(11)	East Godavari	(14)
				Vizianagaram	(12)	West Godavari	(15)
				Visakhapatnam	(13)		
3.		282	Coastal Southern	Krishna	(16)	Prakasam	(18)
				Guntur	(17)	Nellore	(19)
4.		283	Inland North Western	Adilabad	(01)	Hyderabad	(05)
				Nizamabad	(02)	Rangareddi	(06)
				Medak	(04)	Mahbubnagar	(07)
5.		284	Inland North Eastern	Karimnagar	(03)	Warangal	(09)
				Nalgonda	(08)	Khammam	(10)
6.		285	Inland Southern	Cuddapah	(20)	Anantapur	(22)
				Kurnool	(21)	Chittoor	(23)

sl. no	state/u.t. (code)	NSS region code	detailed composition of region				
			description	name of district	code	name of district	code
(1)	(2)	(3)	(4)	(5)	(6)	(7)	(8)
7.	Arunachal Pradesh (12)	121	Arunachal Pradesh	Tawang	(01)	Upper Siang	(09)
				West Kameng	(02)	Dibang Valley	(10)
				East Kameng	(03)	Lohit	(11)
				Papum Pare	(04)	Changlang	(12)
				Lower Subansiri	(05)	Tirap	(13)
				Upper Subansiri	(06)	Anjaw	(14)
				West Siang	(07)	Kurungkumey	(15)
				East Siang	(08)	Lower Dibang Valley	(16)
8.	Assam (18)	181	Plains Eastern	Lakhimpur	(12)	Sibsagar	(16)
				Dhemaji	(13)	Jorhat	(17)
				Tinsukia	(14)	Golaghat	(18)
				Dibrugarh	(15)		
9.		182	Plains Western	Kokrajhar	(01)	Kamrup rural	(06)
				Dhubri	(02)	Nalbari	(07)
				Goalpara	(03)	Chirang	(24)
				Bongaigaon	(04)	Baksa	(25)
				Barpeta	(05)	Kamrup metro	(26)
10.		183	Cachar Plain	Karbi Anglong	(19)	Karimganj	(22)
				North Cachar Hills	(20)	Hailakandi	(23)
				Cachar	(21)		

11.		184	Central Brahamputra Plains	Darrang	(08)	Sonitpur	(11)
				Marigaon	(09)	Udalguri	(27)
				Nagaon	(10)		
12.	Bihar (10)	101	Northern	Champaran(W)	(01)	Saharsa	(12)
				Champaran(E)	(02)	Darbhanga	(13)
				Sheohar	(03)	Muzaffarpur	(14)
				Sitamarhi	(04)	Gopalganj	(15)
				Madhubani	(05)	Siwan	(16)
				Supaul	(06)	Saran	(17)
				Araria	(07)	Vaishali	(18)
				Kishanganj	(08)	Samastipur	(19)
				Purnia	(09)	Begusarai	(20)
				Katihar	(10)	Khagaria	(21)
				Madhepura	(11)		
13.		102	Central	Bhagalpur	(22)	Kaimur (Bhabua)	(31)
				Banka	(23)	Rohtas	(32)
				Munger	(24)	Jehanabad	(33)
				Lakhisarai	(25)	Aurangabad	(34)
				Sheikhpura	(26)	Gaya	(35)
				Nalanda	(27)	Nawada	(36)
				Patna	(28)	Jamui	(37)
				Bhojpur	(29)	Arwal	(38)
				Buxar	(30)		

sl. no	state/u.t. (code)	NSS region code	detailed composition of region				
			description	name of district	code	name of district	code
(1)	(2)	(3)	(4)	(5)	(6)	(7)	(8)
14.	Chandigarh (04)	041	Chandigarh	Chandigarh	(01)		
15.	Chhattisgarh (22)	221	Northern Chhattisgarh	Koriya	(01)	Surguja	(02)
16.		222	Mahanadi Basin	Jashpur	(03)	Rajnandgaon	(09)
				Raigarh	(04)	Durg	(10)
				Korba	(05)	Raipur	(11)
				Janjgir-Champa	(06)	Mahasamund	(12)
				Bilaspur	(07)	Dhamtari	(13)
				Kawardha	(08)		
17.		223	Southern Chhattisgarh	Kanker	(14)	Narayanpur	(17)
				Bastar	(15)	Bijapur	(18)
				Dantewada	(16)		
18.	Dadra & Nagar Haveli (26)	261	Dadra & Nagar Haveli	Dadra & Nagar Haveli	(01)		
19.	Daman & Diu (25)	251	Daman & Diu	Diu	(01)	Daman	(02)
20.	Delhi (07)	071	Delhi	North West	(01)	Central	(06)
				North	(02)	West	(07)
				North East	(03)	South West	(08)
				East	(04)	South	(09)
				New Delhi	(05)		

21.	Goa (30)	301	Goa	North Goa	(01)	South Goa	(02)
22.	Gujarat (24)	241	South Eastern	Panch Mahals	(17)	Surat	(22)
				Dohad	(18)	The Dangs	(23)
				Vadodara	(19)	Navsari	(24)
				Narmada	(20)	Valsad	(25)
				Bharuch	(21)		
23.		242	Plains Northern	Mahesana	(04)	Ahmedabad	(07)
				Sabar Kantha	(05)	Anand	(15)
				Gandhinagar	(06)	Kheda	(16)
24.		243	Dry areas	Bans Kantha	(02)	Patan	(03)
25.		244	Kachchh	Kachchh	(01)		
26.		245	Saurashtra	Surendranagar	(08)	Junagadh	(12)
				Rajkot	(09)	Amreli	(13)
				Jamnagar	(10)	Bhavnagar	(14)
				Porbandar	(11)		
27.	Haryana (06)	061	Eastern	Panchkula	(01)	Sonipat	(08)
				Ambala	(02)	Rohtak	(14)
				Yamunanagar	(03)	Jhajjar	(15)
				Kurukshetra	(04)	Gurgaon	(18)
				Kaithal	(05)	Faridabad	(19)
				Karnal	(06)	Mewat	(20)
				Panipat	(07)	Palwal	(21)

sl. no	state/u.t. (code)	NSS region code	detailed composition of region				
			description	name of district	code	name of district	code
(1)	(2)	(3)	(4)	(5)	(6)	(7)	(8)
28.		062	Western	Jind	(09)	Bhiwani	(13)
				Fatehabad	(10)	Mahendragarh	(16)
				Sirsa	(11)	Rewari	(17)
				Hisar	(12)		
29.	Himachal Pradesh (02)	021	Central	Kangra	(02)	Hamirpur	(06)
				Kullu	(04)	Una	(07)
				Mandi	(05)		
30.		022	Trans Himalayan & Southern	Chamba	(01)	Sirmaur	(10)
				Lahul & Spiti	(03)	Shimla	(11)
				Bilaspur	(08)	Kinnaur	(12)
				Solan	(09)		
31.	Jammu & Kashmir (01)	011	Mountainous	Jammu	(13)	Kathua	(14)
				Samba	(15)		
32.		012	Outer Hills	Doda	(09)	Punch	(11)
				Udhampur	(10)	Rajauri	(12)
				Kishtwar	(16)	Reasi	(17)
				Ramban	(18)		

33.		013	Jhelam Valley	Kupwara	(01)	Badgam	(04)
				Baramula	(02)	Pulwama	(05)
				Srinagar	(03)	Anantnag	(06)
				Ganderbal	(19)	Kulgam	(20)
				Shopian	(21)	Bandipora	(22)
34.		014	Ladakh	Leh (Ladakh)	(07)	Kargil	(08)
35.	Jharkhand (20)	201	Ranchi Plateau	Garhwa	(01)	Singhbhum(W)	(17)
				Palamu	(02)	Singhblnun (E)	(18)
				Ranchi	(14)	Latehar	(19)
				Lohardaga	(15)	Simdega	(20)
				Gumla	(16)	Saraikela Khareswan	(22)
36.		202	Hazaribagh Plateau	Chatra	(03)	Sahibganj	(09)
				Hazaribag	(04)	Pakaur	(10)
				Kodarma	(05)	Dumka	(11)
				Giridih	(06)	Dhanbad	(12)
				Deoghar	(07)	Bokaro	(13)
				Godda	(08)	Jamtara	(21)
37.	Karnataka (29)	291	Coastal & Ghats	Uttara Kannada	(10)	Dakshina Kannada	(24)
				Udupi	(16)		
38.		292	Inland Eastern	Shimoga	(15)	Hassan	(23)
				Chikmagalur	(17)	Kodagu	(25)

sl. no	state/u.t. (code)	NSS region code	detailed composition of region				
			description	name of district	code	name of district	code
(1)	(2)	(3)	(4)	(5)	(6)	(7)	(8)
39.		293	Inland Southern	Tumkur	(18)	Mysore	(26)
				Kolar	(19)	Chamarajanagar	(27)
				Bangalore	(20)	Ramanagara	(28)
				Bangalore (Rural)	(21)	Chikkaballapura	(29)
				Mandya	(22)		
40.		294	Inland Northern	Belgaum	(01)	Gadag	(08)
				Bagalkot	(02)	Dharwad	(09)
				Bijapur	(03)	Haveri	(11)
				Gulbarga	(04)	Bellary	(12)
				Bidar	(05)	Chitradurga	(13)
				Raichur	(06)	Davanagere	(14)
				Koppal	(07)		
41.	Kerala (32)	321	Northern	Kasaragod	(01)	Kozhikode	(04)
				Kannur	(02)	Malappuram	(05)
				Wayanad	(03)	Palakkad	(06)
42.		322	Southern	Thrissur	(07)	Alappuzha	(11)
				Ernakulam	(08)	Pathanamthitta	(12)
				Idukki	(09)	Kollam	(13)
				Kottayam	(10)	Thiruvananthapuram	(14)

43.	Lakshadweep (31)	311	Lakshadweep	Lakshadweep	(01)		
44.	Madhya Pradesh (23)	231	Vindhya	Tikamgarh	(08)	Umaria	(15)
				Chhatarpur	(09)	Shandol	(16)
				Panna	(10)	Sidhi	(17)
				Satna	(13)	Anuppur	(47)
				Rewa	(14)	Singrauli	(50)
45.		232	Central	Sagar	(11)	Bhopal	(32)
				Damoh	(12)	Sehore	(33)
				Vidisha	(31)	Raisen	(34)
46.	Madhya Pradesh (23)	233	Malwa	Neemuch	(18)	Dewas	(23)
				Mandsaur	(19)	Jhabua	(24)
				Ratlam	(20)	Dhar	(25)
				Ujjain	(21)	Indore	(26)
				Shajapur	(22)	Rajgarh	(30)
				Alirajpur	(49)		
47.		234	South	Katni	(38)	Mandla	(42)
				Jabalpur	(39)	Chhindwara	(43)
				Narsimhapur	(40)	Seoni	(44)
				Dindori	(41)	Balaghat	(45)
48.		235	South Western	W. Nimar (Khargoan)	(27)	Betul	(35)
				Barwani	(28)	Harda	(36)
				E Nimar (Khandwa)	(29)	Hoshangabad	(37)
						Burhampur	(48)

sl. no	state/u.t. (code)	NSS region code	detailed composition of region				
			description	name of district	code	name of district	code
(1)	(2)	(3)	(4)	(5)	(6)	(7)	(8)
49.		236	Northern	Sheopur	(01)	Datia	(05)
				Morena	(02)	Shivpuri	(06)
				Bhind	(03)	Guna	(07)
				Gwalior	(04)	Ashoknagar	(46)
50.	Maharashtra (27)	271	Coastal	Thane	(21)	Raigarh	(24)
				Mumbai	(22)	Ratnagiri	(32)
				Suburban Mumbai	(23)	Sindhudurg	(33)
51.		272	Inland Western	Pune	(25)	Satara	(31)
				Ahmadnagar	(26)	Kolhapur	(34)
				Solapur	(30)	Sangli	(35)
52.		273	Inland Northern	Nandurbar	(01)	Jalgaon	(03)
				Dhule	(02)	Nashik	(20)
53.		274	Inland Central	Nanded	(15)	Aurangabad	(19)
				Hingoli	(16)	Bid	(27)
				Parbhani	(17)	Latur	(28)
				Jalna	(18)	Osmanabad	(29)

54.		275	Inland Eastern	Buldana	(04)	Wardha	(08)
				Akola	(05)	Nagpur	(09)
				Washim	(06)	Yavatmal	(14)
				Amravati	(07)		
55.		276	Eastern	Bhandara	(10)	Gadchiroli	(12)
				Gondiya	(11)	Chandrapur	(13)
56.	Manipur (14)	141	Plains	Bishnupur	(04)	Imphal West	(06)
				Thoubal	(05)	Imphal East	(07)
57.		142	Hills	Senapati	(01)	Ukhrul	(08)
				Tamenglong	(02)	Chandel	(09)
				Churachandpur	(03)		
58.	Meghalaya (17)	171	Meghalaya	West Garo Hills	(01)	Ri Bhoi	(05)
				East Garo Hills	(02)	East Khasi Hills	(06)
				South Garo Hills	(03)	Jaintia Hills	(07)
59.	Mizoram (15)	151	Mizoram	Mamit	(01)	Serchip	(05)
				Kolasib	(02)	Lunglei	(06)
				Aizwal	(03)	Lawngtlai	(07)
				Champhai	(04)	Saiha	(08)
60.	Nagaland (13)	131	Nagaland	Mon	(01)	Kohima	(07)
				Tuensang	(02)	Phek	(08)
				Mokokchung	(03)	Kiphire	(09)
				Zunheboto	(04)	Longleng	(10)
				Wokha	(05)	Peren	(11)
				Dimapur	(06)		

sl. no	state/u.t. (code)	NSS region code	detailed composition of region				
			description	name of district	code	name of district	code
(1)	(2)	(3)	(4)	(5)	(6)	(7)	(8)
61.	Odisha (21)	211	Coastal	Baleshwar	(08)	Jajapur	(13)
				Bhadrak	(09)	Nayagarh	(16)
				Kendrapara	(10)	Khordha	(17)
				Jagatsinghapur	(11)	Puri	(18)
				Cuttack	(12)		
62.		212	Southern	Ganjam	(19)	Nuapada	(25)
				Gajapati	(20)	Kalahandi	(26)
				Kandhamal (Phoolbani)	(21)	Rayagada	(27)
				Baudh	(22)	Nabarangapur	(28)
				Sonapur	(23)	Koraput	(29)
				Balangir	(24)	Malkangiri	(30)
63.		213	Northern	Bargarh	(01)	Kendujhar	(06)
				Jharsuguda	(02)	Mayurbhanj	(07)
				Sambalpur	(03)	Dhenkanal	(14)
				Debagarh	(04)	Anugul	(15)
				Sundargarh	(05)		
64.	Puducherry (34)	341	Pondicherry	Yanam	(01)	Mahe	(03)
				Pondicherry	(02)	Karaikal	(04)

65.	Punjab (03)	031	Northern	Gurdaspur	(01)	Hoshiarpur	(05)
				Amritsar	(02)	Nawanshahr	(06)
				Kapurthala	(03)	Rupnagar	(07)
				Jalandhar	(04)	S.A.S. nagar (Mohali)	(18)
				Taran Taran	(20)		
66.		032	Southern	Fatehgarh Sahib	(08)	Bathinda	(14)
				Ludhiana	(09)	Mansa	(15)
				Moga	(10)	Sangrur	(16)
				Firozpur	(11)	Patiala	(17)
				Muktsar	(12)	Barnala	(19)
				Faridkot	(13)		
67.	Rajasthan (08)	081	Western	Bikaner	(03)	Jalor	(18)
				Jodhpur	(15)	Sirohi	(19)
				Jaisalmer	(16)	Pali	(20)
				Barmer	(17)		
68.	Rajasthan (08)	082	North Eastern	Alwar	(06)	Dausa	(11)
				Bharatpur	(07)	Jaipur	(12)
				Dhaulpur	(08)	Ajmer	(21)
				Karauli	(09)	Tonk	(22)
				Sawai Madhopur	(10)	Bhilwara	(24)
69.		083	Southern	Rajsamand	(25)	Dungarpur	(27)
				Udaipur	(26)	Banswara	(28)
70.		084	South Eastern	Bundi	(23)	Baran	(31)
				Chittaurgarh	(29)	Jhalawar	(32)
				Kota	(30)	Pratapgarh	(33)

sl. no	state/u.t. (code)	NSS region code	detailed composition of region				
			description	name of district	code	name of district	code
(1)	(2)	(3)	(4)	(5)	(6)	(7)	(8)
71.		085	Northern	Ganganagar	(01)	Jhunjhunun	(05)
				Hanumangarh	(02)	Sikar	(13)
				Churu	(04)	Nagaur	(14)
72.	Sikkim (11)	111	Sikkim	North (Mongam)	(01)	South (Nimachai)	(03)
				West (Gyalshing)	(02)	East (Gangtok)	(04)
73.	Tamil Nadu (33)	331	Coastal Northern	Thiruvallur	(01)	Tiruvanamalai	(06)
				Chennai	(02)	Viluppuram	(07)
				Kancheepuram	(03)	Cuddalore	(18)
				Vellore	(04)		
74.		332	Coastal	Karur	(14)	Nagapattinam	(19)
				Tiruichirappalli	(15)	Thiruvarur	(20)
				Perambalur	(16)	Thanjavur	(21)
				Ariyalur	(17)	Pudukkottai	(22)
75.		333	Southern	Dindigul	(13)	Ramanathapuram	(27)
				Sivaganga	(23)	Toothukudi	(28)
				Madurai	(24)	Tirunelveli	(29)
				Theni	(25)	Kanniyakumari	(30)
				Virudhunagar	(26)		

76.		334	Inland	Dharmapuri	(05)	The Nilgiris	(11)
				Salem	(08)	Coimbatore	(12)
				Namakkal	(09)	Krishnagiri	(31)
				Erode	(10)		
77.	Tripura (16)	161	Tripura	West Tripura	(01)	Dhalai	(03)
				South Tripura	(02)	North Tripura	(04)
78.	Uttarakhand (05)	051	Uttarakhand	Uttarkashi	(01)	Bageshwar	(08)
				Chamoli	(02)	Almora	(09)
				Rudraprayag	(03)	Champawat	(10)
				Tehri Garhwal	(04)	Nainital (P)	(11)
				Dehradun (P)	(05)	Udham Singh Nagar	(12)
				Garhwal	(06)	Hardwar	(13)
				Pithoragarh	(07)		
79.	Uttar Pradesh (09)	091	Northern Upper Ganga Plains	Saharanpur	(01)	J Phule Nagar	(06)
				Muzaffarnagar	(02)	Meerut	(07)
				Bijnor	(03)	Baghpat	(08)
				Moradabad	(04)	Ghaziabad	(09)
				Rampur	(05)	G. Buddha Nagar	(10)
80.	Uttar Pradesh (09)	092	Central	Sitapur	(24)	Kanpur Dehat	(33)
				Hardoi	(25)	Kanpur Nagar	(34)
				Unnao	(26)	Fatehpur	(42)
				Lucknow	(27)	Barabanki	(46)
				Rae Bareli	(28)		

sl. no	state/u.t. (code)	NSS region code	detailed composition of region				
			description	name of district	code	name of district	code
(1)	(2)	(3)	(4)	(5)	(6)	(7)	(8)
81.		093	Eastern	Pratapgarh	(43)	Gorakhpur	(58)
				Kaushambi	(44)	Kushinagar	(59)
				Allahabad	(45)	Deoria	(60)
				Faizabad	(47)	Azamgarh	(61)
				Ambedkar Nag.	(48)	Mau	(62)
				Sultanpur	(49)	Ballia	(63)
				Bahraich	(50)	Jaunpur	(64)
				Shrawasti	(51)	Ghazipur	(65)
				Balrampur	(52)	Chandauli	(66)
				Gonda	(53)	Varanasi	(67)
				Siddharthnagar	(54)	S.R.Nagar(Bhadohi)	(68)
				Basti	(55)	Mirzapur	(69)
				S. Kabir Nagar	(56)	Sonbhadra	(70)
				Maharaj ganj	(57)		
82.		094	Southern	Jalaun	(35)	Mahoba	(39)
				Jhansi	(36)	Banda	(40)
				Lalitpur	(37)	Chitrakoot	(41)
				Hamirpur	(38)		

83.		095	Southern Upper Ganga Plains	Bulandshahr	(11)	Bareilly	(20)
				Aligarh	(12)	Pilibhit	(21)
				Hathras	(13)	Shahjahanpur	(22)
				Mathura	(14)	Kheri	(23)
				Agra	(15)	Farrukhabad	(29)
				Firozabad	(16)	Kannauj	(30)
				Etah	(17)	Etawah	(31)
				Mainpuri	(18)	Auraiya	(32)
				Budaun	(19)	Kanshiram Nagar	(71)
84.	West Bengal (19)	191	Himalayan	Darjiling	(01)	Koch Bihar	(03)
				Jalpaiguri	(02)		
85.		192	Eastern Plains	Uttar Dinajpur	(04)	Murshidabad	(07)
				Dakshin Dinajpur	(05)	Birbhum	(08)
				Maldah	(06)	Nadia	(10)
86.		193	Southern Plains	North 24-Parganas	(11)	South 24-Parganas	(18)
				Kolkata	(17)		
87.		194	Central Plains	Barddhaman	(09)	Howrah	(16)
				Hugli	(12)		
88.		195	Western Plains	Bankura	(13)	Paschim Midnapur	(15)
				Puruliya	(14)	Purba Midnapur	(19)

Source: *Instructions to Field Staff*, Vol-I Appendix II: NSS 68th Round, 2011–12.

APPENDIX 3

Regional Sector-wise Shares 2004–05

Region 2004-05		Within-Region Shares				Between-Region Shares			
Region	State	AGRI	MFG	CON	SVS	AGRI	MFG	CON	SVS
11	Jammu and Kashmir	35%	13%	11%	41%	0.10%	0.15%	0.28%	0.26%
12	Jammu and Kashmir	57%	5%	16%	21%	0.05%	0.02%	0.14%	0.04%
13	Jammu and Kashmir	42%	21%	10%	27%	0.27%	0.59%	0.58%	0.39%
21	Himachal Pradesh	60%	8%	12%	20%	0.79%	0.47%	1.48%	0.59%
31	Punjab	26%	22%	13%	40%	0.55%	2.03%	2.55%	1.93%
32	Punjab	53%	9%	8%	30%	0.76%	0.58%	1.04%	0.98%
41	Chandigarh	1%	19%	5%	75%	0.00%	0.12%	0.07%	0.25%
51	Uttarakhand	61%	6%	8%	25%	0.88%	0.37%	1.06%	0.79%
61	Haryana	36%	20%	11%	34%	0.78%	1.89%	2.19%	1.67%
62	Haryana	55%	10%	8%	28%	0.61%	0.48%	0.84%	0.70%
71	Delhi	0.46%	25%	6%	68%	0.01%	2.01%	1.09%	2.81%
81	Rajasthan	60%	12%	9%	19%	1.98%	1.79%	2.74%	1.44%
82	Rajasthan	54%	12%	10%	24%	2.25%	2.28%	4.01%	2.24%
83	Rajasthan	55%	7%	22%	16%	0.78%	0.45%	2.90%	0.50%
84	Rajasthan	71%	8%	4%	17%	0.71%	0.34%	0.36%	0.38%

Region 2004-05		Within-Region Shares				Between-Region Shares			
Region	State	AGRI	MFG	CON	SVS	AGRI	MFG	CON	SVS
91	Uttar Pradesh	47%	18%	7%	28%	4.07%	6.82%	5.87%	5.43%
92	Uttar Pradesh	59%	12%	5%	24%	2.73%	2.39%	2.15%	2.47%
93	Uttar Pradesh	63%	11%	6%	19%	6.09%	4.83%	5.40%	4.18%
94	Uttar Pradesh	63%	7%	14%	16%	0.76%	0.36%	1.57%	0.43%
101	Bihar	75%	5%	3%	17%	4.22%	1.14%	1.42%	2.18%
102	Bihar	67%	9%	4%	20%	2.80%	1.64%	1.40%	1.91%
111	Sikkim	54%	5%	8%	32%	0.06%	0.02%	0.08%	0.07%
121	Arunachal Pradesh	76%	1.49%	4%	18%	0.13%	0.01%	0.07%	0.07%
131	Nagaland	60%	4%	2%	34%	0.09%	0.02%	0.03%	0.11%
141	Manipur	39%	15%	6%	39%	0.08%	0.13%	0.11%	0.17%
142	Manipur	#####	2%	0.4%	12%	0.12%	0.01%	0.01%	0.04%
151	Mizoram	70%	2%	2%	25%	0.11%	0.01%	0.03%	0.08%
161	Tripura	38%	5%	11%	46%	0.18%	0.11%	0.50%	0.50%
171	Meghalaya	74%	5%	3%	19%	0.36%	0.12%	0.11%	0.20%
181	Assam	65%	3%	2%	29%	1.04%	0.24%	0.27%	1.04%
182	Assam	65%	5%	4%	25%	1.50%	0.54%	0.89%	1.31%
183	Assam	62%	0.71%	0.14%	37%	0.09%	0.00%	0.00%	0.11%
191	West Bengal	67%	6%	3%	23%	0.75%	0.31%	0.31%	0.58%
192	West Bengal	54%	15%	5%	25%	1.82%	2.25%	1.70%	1.87%
193	West Bengal	31%	21%	6%	41%	1.87%	5.61%	3.32%	5.49%

194	West Bengal	64%	10%	3%	23%	1.66%	1.16%	0.64%	1.35%
201	Jharkhand	59%	12%	11%	18%	2.50%	2.26%	4.28%	1.65%
211	Odisha	56%	11%	8%	26%	1.49%	1.28%	1.91%	1.57%
212	Odisha	71%	7%	8%	14%	0.99%	0.42%	0.98%	0.44%
213	Odisha	61%	16%	5%	17%	1.65%	1.94%	1.35%	1.02%
221	Chattisgarh	77%	6%	4%	13%	3.69%	1.20%	1.86%	1.39%
231	Chattisgarh	76%	8%	3%	13%	1.71%	0.83%	0.62%	0.64%
232	Chattisgarh	57%	16%	5%	22%	0.82%	1.00%	0.69%	0.73%
233	Madhya Pradesh	68%	9%	4%	19%	2.10%	1.24%	1.02%	1.33%
234	Madhya Pradesh	67%	9%	5%	19%	1.40%	0.88%	1.04%	0.88%
235	Madhya Pradesh	75%	5%	3%	17%	1.13%	0.34%	0.42%	0.57%
236	Madhya Pradesh	65%	6%	9%	20%	0.90%	0.37%	1.18%	0.63%
241	Gujarat	68%	14%	5%	12%	1.45%	1.34%	1.03%	0.59%
242	Gujarat	46%	18%	5%	30%	1.04%	1.80%	1.04%	1.53%
243	Gujarat	45%	20%	5%	29%	0.96%	1.87%	1.07%	1.39%
244	Gujarat	63%	14%	2%	20%	0.70%	0.69%	0.24%	0.49%
245	Gujarat	57%	18%	2%	22%	1.16%	1.63%	0.44%	0.99%
271	Maharashtra	20%	25%	5%	50%	0.84%	4.54%	1.80%	4.64%
272	Maharashtra	57%	12%	6%	25%	2.81%	2.54%	2.53%	2.79%
273	Maharashtra	66%	9%	4%	21%	1.51%	0.96%	0.82%	1.08%
274	Maharashtra	73%	5%	5%	17%	2.63%	0.87%	1.63%	1.35%
275	Maharashtra	65%	7%	5%	23%	2.11%	1.02%	1.49%	1.67%
276	Maharashtra	66%	12%	6%	16%	0.83%	0.69%	0.71%	0.44%

Region 2004-05		Within-Region Shares				Between-Region Shares			
Region	State	AGRI	MFG	CON	SVS	AGRI	MFG	CON	SVS
281	Andhra Pradesh	59%	9%	5%	27%	4.39%	3.06%	3.26%	4.40%
282	Andhra Pradesh	58%	14%	5%	23%	3.74%	3.96%	2.74%	3.27%
283	Andhra Pradesh	61%	14%	4%	21%	1.06%	1.10%	0.62%	0.83%
284	Andhra Pradesh	58%	14%	5%	24%	0.77%	0.82%	0.58%	0.72%
291	Karnataka	46%	17%	7%	29%	0.41%	0.67%	0.60%	0.57%
292	Karnataka	74%	5%	3%	19%	0.82%	0.24%	0.29%	0.47%
293	Karnataka	53%	13%	5%	29%	2.14%	2.29%	2.00%	2.62%
294	Karnataka	72%	8%	3%	18%	3.66%	1.68%	1.29%	2.00%
301	Goa	22%	14%	11%	54%	0.04%	0.10%	0.17%	0.20%
321	Kerala	37%	14%	11%	38%	0.67%	1.07%	1.87%	1.53%
322	Kerala	29%	18%	12%	41%	0.93%	2.49%	3.60%	2.94%
331	Tamil Nadu	41%	19%	7%	33%	1.73%	3.60%	2.76%	3.15%
332	Tamil Nadu	60%	10%	6%	24%	1.30%	0.92%	1.16%	1.17%
333	Tamil Nadu	43%	24%	7%	26%	1.28%	3.19%	1.83%	1.75%
334	Tamil Nadu	46%	25%	5%	24%	1.53%	3.65%	1.67%	1.79%
341	Pondicherry	30%	21%	11%	39%	0.04%	0.14%	0.14%	0.13%
351	Andaman and Nicobar Islands	27%	9%	13%	51%	0.01%	0.02%	0.06%	0.06%

APPENDIX 4

Regional Sector-wise Shares 2011–12

Region 2011–12		Within-Region Shares				Between-Region Shares			
Region	State	AGRI	MFG	CON	SVS	AGRI	MFG	CON	SVS
11	Jammu and Kashmir	17%	14%	23%	45%	0.08%	0.22%	0.47%	0.33%
12	Jammu and Kashmir	35%	8%	35%	22%	0.15%	0.11%	0.64%	0.16%
13	Jammu and Kashmir	25%	17%	20%	38%	0.18%	0.40%	0.62%	0.45%
21	Himachal Pradesh	57%	9%	15%	20%	0.96%	0.49%	1.09%	0.55%
31	Punjab	23%	18%	18%	41%	0.45%	1.24%	1.59%	1.32%
32	Punjab	31%	21%	14%	34%	0.82%	1.89%	1.60%	1.50%
41	Chandigarh	1%	15%	8%	77%	0.00%	0.10%	0.07%	0.24%
51	Uttarakhand	44%	11%	14%	32%	0.71%	0.61%	0.98%	0.85%
61	Haryana	29%	18%	16%	37%	0.77%	1.67%	1.91%	1.64%
62	Haryana	55%	10%	11%	24%	0.80%	0.49%	0.71%	0.58%
71	Delhi	0.19%	22%	4%	74%	0.00%	1.78%	0.42%	2.89%
81	Rajasthan	51%	13%	16%	20%	2.27%	1.90%	3.16%	1.50%
82	Rajasthan	44%	13%	15%	28%	1.84%	1.85%	2.68%	1.91%
83	Rajasthan	43%	6%	37%	13%	0.65%	0.31%	2.44%	0.33%

Region 2011–12		Within-Region Shares				Between-Region Shares			
Region	State	AGRI	MFG	CON	SVS	AGRI	MFG	CON	SVS
84	Rajasthan	52%	8%	23%	17%	0.79%	0.39%	1.48%	0.42%
91	Uttar Pradesh	43%	17%	13%	26%	4.93%	6.67%	6.72%	4.95%
92	Uttar Pradesh	48%	13%	17%	23%	2.46%	2.20%	3.73%	1.93%
93	Uttar Pradesh	51%	13%	13%	23%	5.53%	4.70%	6.27%	3.98%
94	Uttar Pradesh	54%	9%	21%	17%	0.81%	0.47%	1.36%	0.42%
101	Bihar	62%	5%	11%	22%	5.05%	1.39%	3.95%	2.95%
102	Bihar	62%	7%	9%	22%	3.00%	1.12%	1.99%	1.77%
111	Sikkim	62%	6%	6%	26%	0.09%	0.03%	0.04%	0.06%
121	Arunachal	68%	1.42%	6%	25%	0.14%	0.01%	0.05%	0.08%
131	Nagaland	55%	4%	3%	38%	0.10%	0.03%	0.03%	0.11%
141	Manipur	32%	15%	13%	40%	0.08%	0.13%	0.14%	0.16%
142	Manipur	57%	5%	12%	26%	0.09%	0.02%	0.08%	0.07%
151	Mizoram	57%	3%	5%	35%	0.12%	0.02%	0.05%	0.12%
161	Tripura	30%	8%	33%	30%	0.19%	0.17%	0.90%	0.31%
171	Meghalaya	57%	5%	6%	32%	0.34%	0.10%	0.14%	0.31%
181	Assam	58%	8%	10%	24%	0.81%	0.39%	0.60%	0.56%
182	Assam	51%	6%	7%	35%	1.34%	0.57%	0.82%	1.50%
183	Assam	57%	5%	0.61%	38%	0.40%	0.11%	0.02%	0.44%
191	West Bengal	51%	7%	11%	31%	0.73%	0.34%	0.69%	0.74%
192	West Bengal	50%	18%	12%	20%	2.14%	2.65%	2.14%	1.43%

193	West Bengal	27%	28%	6%	39%	2.08%	7.54%	2.09%	4.95%
194	West Bengal	55%	12%	8%	25%	1.50%	1.08%	0.90%	1.13%
201	Jharkhand	45%	11%	20%	24%	2.01%	1.70%	3.96%	1.79%
211	Odisha	45%	10%	12%	33%	1.14%	0.86%	1.30%	1.36%
212	Odisha	60%	6%	17%	17%	1.55%	0.51%	1.93%	0.72%
213	Odisha	53%	14%	10%	23%	1.28%	1.19%	1.10%	0.90%
221	Chattisgarh	73%	6%	6%	14%	4.02%	1.18%	1.50%	1.31%
231	Madhya Pradesh	57%	7%	21%	15%	1.20%	0.47%	1.94%	0.53%
232	Madhya Pradesh	51%	16%	10%	22%	0.89%	0.98%	0.79%	0.65%
233	Madhya Pradesh	61%	8%	7%	25%	1.94%	0.85%	0.92%	1.29%
234	Madhya Pradesh	46%	8%	19%	27%	0.99%	0.57%	1.78%	0.97%
235	Madhya Pradesh	73%	4%	7%	15%	1.42%	0.26%	0.62%	0.49%
236	Madhya Pradesh	58%	7%	15%	20%	1.03%	0.43%	1.18%	0.59%
241	Gujarat	50%	25%	4%	20%	2.54%	4.32%	0.86%	1.68%
242	Gujarat	39%	22%	5%	34%	1.19%	2.27%	0.68%	1.68%
243	Gujarat	55%	15%	4%	26%	0.39%	0.35%	0.13%	0.30%
244	Gujarat	40%	7%	12%	41%	0.22%	0.14%	0.28%	0.37%
245	Gujarat	49%	22%	5%	25%	1.47%	2.22%	0.59%	1.20%
271	Maharashtra	10%	24%	7%	59%	0.55%	4.68%	1.81%	5.55%
272	Maharashtra	49%	15%	7%	30%	2.74%	2.83%	1.71%	2.72%
273	Maharashtra	60%	11%	5%	24%	1.65%	1.01%	0.61%	1.10%
274	Maharashtra	70%	6%	5%	19%	2.76%	0.83%	0.86%	1.23%
275	Maharashtra	60%	6%	7%	27%	2.23%	0.69%	1.13%	1.65%

Region 2011–12		Within-Region Shares				Between-Region Shares			
Region	State	AGRI	MFG	CON	SVS	AGRI	MFG	CON	SVS
276	Maharashtra	69%	5%	8%	17%	0.95%	0.25%	0.49%	0.38%
281	Andhra Pradesh	49%	12%	9%	29%	1.94%	1.65%	1.62%	1.88%
282	Andhra Pradesh	49%	10%	8%	32%	4.42%	3.16%	2.99%	4.76%
283	Andhra Pradesh	60%	13%	5%	22%	2.01%	1.52%	0.69%	1.18%
284	Andhra Pradesh	58%	11%	7%	24%	2.16%	1.42%	1.16%	1.50%
291	Karnataka	31%	22%	9%	38%	0.31%	0.73%	0.37%	0.62%
292	Karnataka	71%	4%	2%	23%	0.62%	0.13%	0.09%	0.33%
293	Karnataka	37%	17%	6%	40%	1.84%	2.81%	1.31%	3.27%
294	Karnataka	60%	10%	6%	24%	3.56%	1.95%	1.61%	2.31%
301	Goa	4%	23%	8%	65%	0.01%	0.21%	0.09%	0.28%
321	Kerala	23%	13%	21%	42%	0.53%	1.03%	2.08%	1.59%
322	Kerala	19%	16%	16%	48%	0.67%	1.94%	2.48%	2.74%
331	Tamil Nadu	28%	21%	11%	41%	1.33%	3.40%	2.21%	3.21%
332	Tamil Nadu	48%	11%	9%	32%	1.22%	0.95%	0.96%	1.32%
333	Tamil Nadu	37%	24%	11%	29%	1.32%	2.95%	1.67%	1.70%
334	Tamil Nadu	33%	29%	9%	28%	1.43%	4.21%	1.75%	1.99%
341	Pondicherry	13%	19%	16%	52%	0.03%	0.14%	0.16%	0.19%
351	Andaman and Nicobar Islands	20%	7%	19%	54%	0.01%	0.02%	0.05%	0.06%

APPENDIX 5

List of Million-plus Cities

List of cities (million plus population in census 2001) treated as individual stratum in NSS 68th round

Sl. no.	City	State/ UT	State code	Stratum no.
1	Ludhiana	Punjab	3	20
2	Faridabad	Haryana	6	21
3	Delhi Municipal Corporation	Delhi	7	10
4	Jaipur	Rajasthan	8	33
5	Meerut	Uttar Pradesh	9	72
6	Agra	Uttar Pradesh	9	73
7	Lucknow	Uttar Pradesh	9	74
8	Kanpur	Uttar Pradesh	9	75
9	Varanasi	Uttar Pradesh	9	76
10	Patna	Bihar	10	39
11	Howrah	West Bengal	19	20
12	Kolkata	West Bengal	19	21
13	Indore	Madhya Pradesh	23	49
14	Bhopal	Madhya Pradesh	23	50
15	Ahmedabad	Gujarat	24	26
16	Vadodara	Gujarat	24	27
17	Surat	Gujarat	24	28
18	Nagpur	Maharashtra	27	36
19	Nashik	Maharashtra	27	37
20	Kalyan-Dombivali	Maharashtra	27	38
21	Thane	Maharashtra	27	39
22	Greater Mumbai	Maharashtra	27	40
23	Pimpri-Chinchwad	Maharashtra	27	41
24	Pune	Maharashtra	27	42
25	Hyderabad	Andhra Pradesh	28	24
26	Bangalore	Karnataka	29	30
27	Chennai	Tamil Nadu	33	32

Source: *Note on Sample Design and Estimation Procedure*, NSS 68th round, 2011-12

APPENDIX 6

Dendogram (Cluster Analysis) 2004–05

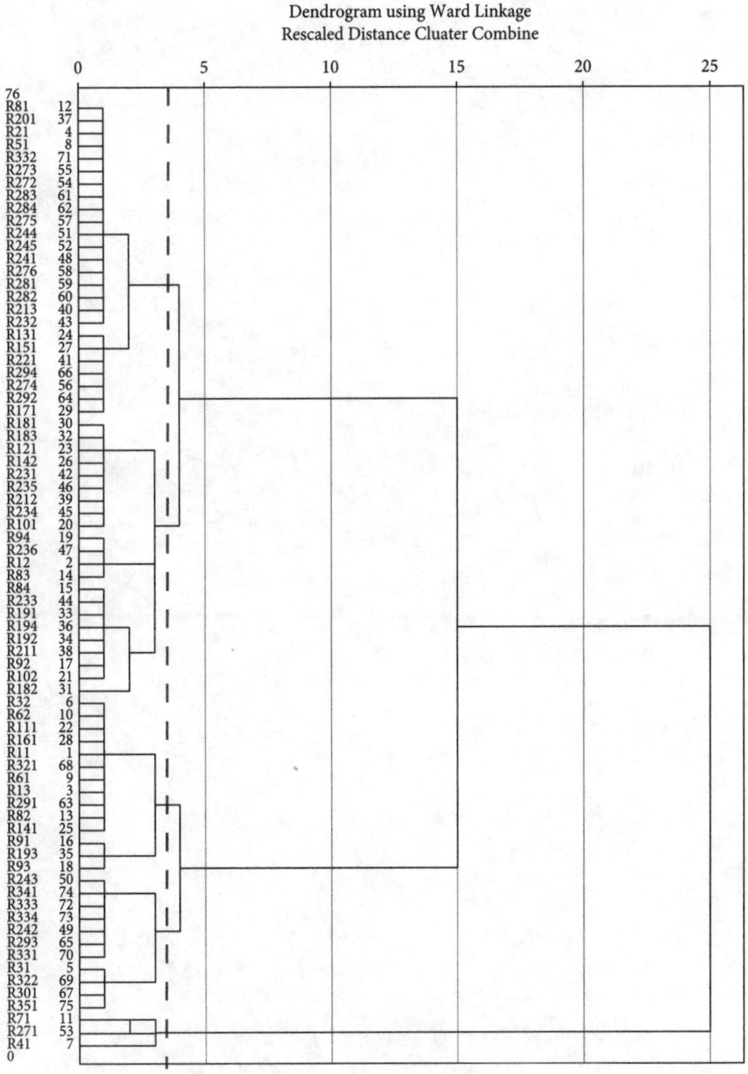

APPENDIX 7

Dendogram (Cluster Analysis) 2011–12

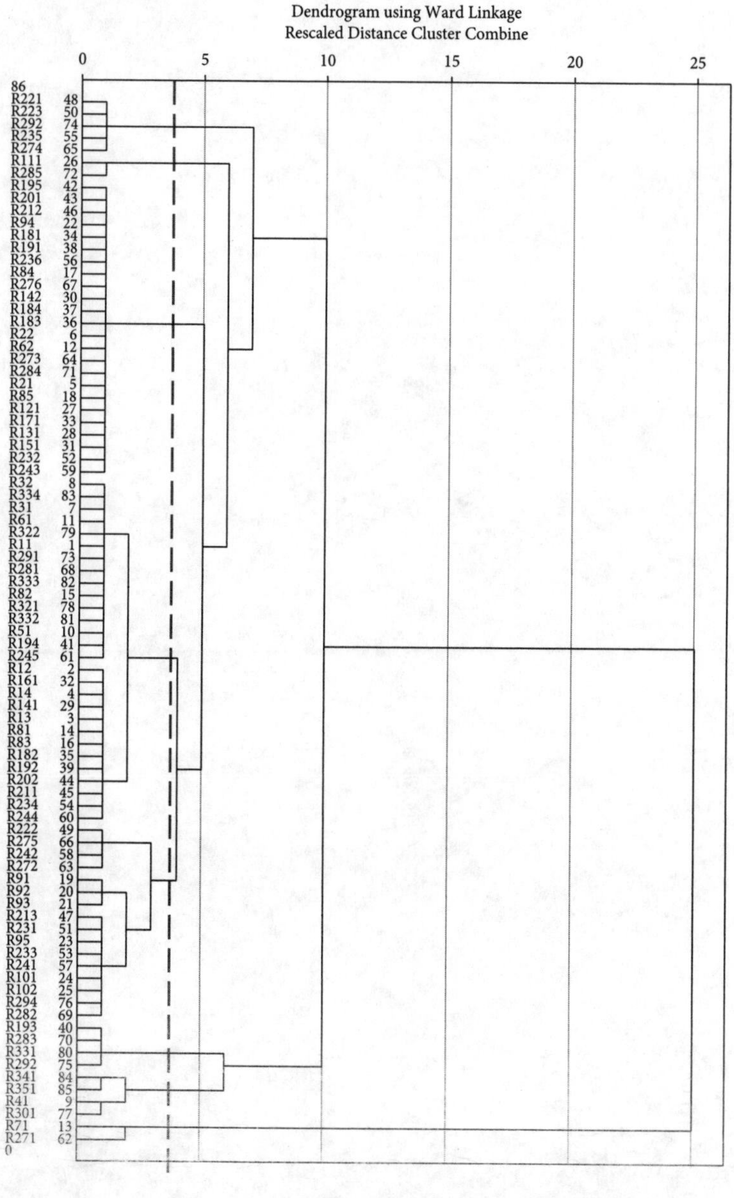

APPENDIX 8

Discriminant Analysis Results (constant prices)

Tests of Equality of Group Means			
Variable	Wilks' Lambda	F	Sig.
RVAPC	0.854	27.085	0.000
MPCE	0.848	28.388	0.000
DV	0.94	10.174	0.002
AGRI	0.939	10.289	0.002
MFG	0.998	0.323	0.571
CON	0.84	30.189	0.000
SVS	0.984	2.57	0.111
OFF	0.997	0.464	0.497
DEP	0.999	0.153	0.696
CRE	0.995	0.833	0.363
WPR	0.971	4.745	0.031
URB	0.995	0.779	0.379
REGEMP	0.987	2.065	0.153
SKILL IV	0.945	9.183	0.003

Eigenvalues			
Function	Eigenvalue	% of Variance	Canonical Correlation
1	1.073	100	0.719

Wilks' Lambda			
Test of Function(s)	Wilks' Lambda	Chi-square	Sig.
1	0.482	110.445	0.000

Canonical Discriminant Function Coefficients		
Variables	**Standardised**	**Unstandardized**
RVAPC	**0.633**	0.000
MPCE	**1.478**	0.006
DV	−0.281	**−2.182**
AGRI	0.148	0.844
MFG	0.261	**4.062**
CON	**0.596**	**10.085**
OFF	−0.257	0.000
DEP	−0.276	0.000
CRE	**0.582**	0.000
WPR	**−0.421**	**−6.45**
URB	−0.265	−1.555
REGEMP	**−1.501**	**−12.35**
SKILL IV	**0.338**	**5.478**
(Constant)		−0.69

Classification Results

Type	**Value**	**Year**	**Predicted Group Membership**		**Total**
			2004	**2011**	
Original	Count	2004	65	10	75
		2011	12	73	85
	%	2004	86.7	13.3	100.0
		2011	14.1	85.9	100.0
Cross-validated	Count	2004	65	10	75
		2011	18	67	85
	%	2004	86.7	13.3	100.0
		2011	21.2	78.8	100.0

APPENDIX 9

Region-wise Diversity Index (DV) Values for 2004-05 and 2011-12

Region	State	Year	DV	Region	State	Year	DV
11	Jammu and Kashmir	2004-05	0.8180	11	Jammu and Kashmir	2011-12	0.8588
12	Jammu and Kashmir	2004-05	0.6321	12	Jammu and Kashmir	2011-12	0.7422
13	Jammu and Kashmir	2004-05	0.7564	13	Jammu and Kashmir	2011-12	0.8374
21	Himachal Pradesh	2004-05	0.6131	14	Jammu and Kashmir	2011-12	0.85
31	Punjab	2004-05	0.8430	21	Himachal Pradesh	2011-12	0.6246
32	Punjab	2004-05	0.6875	22	Himachal Pradesh	2011-12	0.6589
41	Chandigarh	2004-05	0.8611	31	Punjab	2011-12	0.8587
51	Uttarakhand	2004-05	0.6008	32	Punjab	2011-12	0.823
61	Haryana	2004-05	0.8019	41	Chandigarh	2011-12	0.8522
62	Haryana	2004-05	0.6698	51	Uttarakhand	2011-12	0.7549
71	Delhi	2004-05	0.8412	61	Haryana	2011-12	0.8328
81	Rajasthan	2004-05	0.6187	62	Haryana	2011-12	0.6665
82	Rajasthan	2004-05	0.6795	71	Delhi	2011-12	0.8502
83	Rajasthan	2004-05	0.6383	81	Rajasthan	2011-12	0.7203
84	Rajasthan	2004-05	0.4797	82	Rajasthan	2011-12	0.7533
91	Uttar Pradesh	2004-05	0.7232	83	Rajasthan	2011-12	0.6656
92	Uttar Pradesh	2004-05	0.6222	84	Rajasthan	2011-12	0.6643

Region	State	Year	DV	Region	State	Year	DV
93	Uttar Pradesh	2004-05	0.5763	85	Rajasthan	2011-12	0.6674
94	Uttar Pradesh	2004-05	0.5702	91	Uttar Pradesh	2011-12	0.8211
101	Bihar	2004-05	0.4251	92	Uttar Pradesh	2011-12	0.7155
102	Bihar	2004-05	0.5310	93	Uttar Pradesh	2011-12	0.6935
111	Sikkim	2004-05	0.6742	94	Uttar Pradesh	2011-12	0.6605
121	Arunachal Pradesh	2004-05	0.4120	95	Uttar Pradesh	2011-12	0.6945
131	Nagaland	2004-05	0.6134	101	Bihar	2011-12	0.5892
141	Manipur	2004-05	0.8004	102	Bihar	2011-12	0.5951
142	Manipur	2004-05	0.2698	111	Sikkim	2011-12	0.6006
151	Mizoram	2004-05	0.4836	121	Arunachal	2011-12	0.5177
161	Tripura	2004-05	0.8018	131	Nagaland	2011-12	0.6634
171	Meghalaya	2004-05	0.4523	141	Manipur	2011-12	0.8215
181	Assam	2004-05	0.5555	142	Manipur	2011-12	0.6394
182	Assam	2004-05	0.5621	151	Mizoram	2011-12	0.6414
183	Assam	2004-05	0.5770	161	Tripura	2011-12	0.7785
191	West Bengal	2004-05	0.5256	171	Meghalaya	2011-12	0.6436
192	West Bengal	2004-05	0.6669	181	Assam	2011-12	0.637
193	West Bengal	2004-05	0.8348	182	Assam	2011-12	0.7753
194	West Bengal	2004-05	0.5747	183	Assam	2011-12	0.626
201	Jharkhand	2004-05	0.6192	184	Assam	2011-12	0.5364
211	Odisha	2004-05	0.6750	191	West Bengal	2011-12	0.7033
212	Odisha	2004-05	0.4758	192	West Bengal	2011-12	0.6944
213	Odisha	2004-05	0.5960	193	West Bengal	2011-12	0.8366

221	Chattisgarh	2004-05	0.3973	194	West Bengal	2011-12	0.7653
231	Madhya Pradesh	2004-05	0.4139	195	West Bengal	2011-12	0.6618
232	Madhya Pradesh	2004-05	0.6435	201	Jharkhand	2011-12	0.6749
233	Madhya Pradesh	2004-05	0.5198	202	Jharkhand	2011-12	0.7728
234	Madhya Pradesh	2004-05	0.5403	211	Odisha	2011-12	0.7446
235	Madhya Pradesh	2004-05	0.4301	212	Odisha	2011-12	0.6003
236	Madhya Pradesh	2004-05	0.5634	213	Odisha	2011-12	0.6848
241	Gujarat	2004-05	0.5129	221	Chattisgarh	2011-12	0.3036
242	Gujarat	2004-05	0.7320	222	Chattisgarh	2011-12	0.5014
243	Gujarat	2004-05	0.7324	223	Chattisgarh	2011-12	0.3091
244	Gujarat	2004-05	0.5725	231	Madhya Pradesh	2011-12	0.621
245	Gujarat	2004-05	0.6323	232	Madhya Pradesh	2011-12	0.6998
271	Maharashtra	2004-05	0.8542	233	Madhya Pradesh	2011-12	0.6061
272	Maharashtra	2004-05	0.6421	234	Madhya Pradesh	2011-12	0.7298
273	Maharashtra	2004-05	0.5522	235	Madhya Pradesh	2011-12	0.4499
274	Maharashtra	2004-05	0.4577	236	Madhya Pradesh	2011-12	0.63
275	Maharashtra	2004-05	0.5640	241	Gujarat	2011-12	0.6712
276	Maharashtra	2004-05	0.5521	242	Gujarat	2011-12	0.7696
281	Andhra Pradesh	2004-05	0.6378	243	Gujarat	2011-12	0.6532
282	Andhra Pradesh	2004-05	0.6310	244	Gujarat	2011-12	0.7697
283	Andhra Pradesh	2004-05	0.6051	245	Gujarat	2011-12	0.7172
284	Andhra Pradesh	2004-05	0.6354	271	Maharashtra	2011-12	0.8695
291	Karnataka	2004-05	0.7498	272	Maharashtra	2011-12	0.7214
292	Karnataka	2004-05	0.4475	273	Maharashtra	2011-12	0.6154

Region	State	Year	DV	Region	State	Year	DV
293	Karnataka	2004-05	0.6873	274	Maharashtra	2011-12	0.4986
294	Karnataka	2004-05	0.4680	275	Maharashtra	2011-12	0.6157
301	Goa	2004-05	0.8681	276	Maharashtra	2011-12	0.503
321	Kerala	2004-05	0.8107	281	Andhra Pradesh	2011-12	0.7206
322	Kerala	2004-05	0.8589	282	Andhra Pradesh	2011-12	0.6237
331	Tamil Nadu	2004-05	0.7759	283	Andhra Pradesh	2011-12	0.7785
332	Tamil Nadu	2004-05	0.6165	284	Andhra Pradesh	2011-12	0.6085
333	Tamil Nadu	2004-05	0.7408	285	Andhra Pradesh	2011-12	0.6402
334	Tamil Nadu	2004-05	0.7159	291	Karnataka	2011-12	0.8244
341	Pondicherry	2004-05	0.8455	292	Karnataka	2011-12	0.4882
351	Andaman and Nicobar Islands	2004-05	0.8776	293	Karnataka	2011-12	0.7945
				294	Karnataka	2011-12	0.6133
				301	Goa	2011-12	0.8912
				Region	State	Year	DV
				321	Kerala	2011-12	0.8454
				322	Kerala	2011-12	0.8677
				331	Tamil Nadu	2011-12	0.8418
				332	Tamil Nadu	2011-12	0.7267
				333	Tamil Nadu	2011-12	0.7826
				334	Tamil Nadu	2011-12	0.7857
				341	Pondicherry	2011-12	0.8714
				351	Andaman and Nicobar Islands	2011-12	0.8672

APPENDIX 10

Region-wise Values for Regional Value Added (RVA) and Regional Value Added Per Capita (RVAPC) 2004-05

Region	State	RVA in Rs.	RVA in Rs. Cr	RVAPC in Rs.
11	Jammu and Kashmir	38,707,533,422	3,871	20,586
12	Jammu and Kashmir	13,887,193,849	1,389	24,060
13	Jammu and Kashmir	92,572,120,730	9,257	21,941
21	Himachal Pradesh	202,156,743,180	20,216	33,348
31	Punjab	472,375,370,192	47,238	34,277
32	Punjab	305,627,335,716	30,563	31,472
41	Chandigarh	65,190,798,046	6,519	74,173
51	Uttarakhand	194,322,502,925	19,432	24,725
61	Haryana	549,021,064,597	54,902	39,343
62	Haryana	267,669,945,497	26,767	35,497
71	Delhi	744,108,410,914	74,411	63,877
81	Rajasthan	343,394,476,733	34,339	18,464
82	Rajasthan	407,814,002,289	40,781	16,386
83	Rajasthan	179,748,089,712	17,975	27,708
84	Rajasthan	105,753,695,378	10,575	19,384
91	Uttar Pradesh	722,484,687,142	72,248	11,595
92	Uttar Pradesh	412,308,256,063	41,231	13,384
93	Uttar Pradesh	881,573,394,279	88,157	14,011
94	Uttar Pradesh	109,708,308,716	10,971	13,981
101	Bihar	320,066,465,805	32,007	7,809
102	Bihar	242,420,690,614	24,242	8,059
111	Sikkim	13,009,480,010	1,301	26,690
121	Arunachal Pradesh	22,435,192,089	2,244	26,721
131	Nagaland	23,187,456,920	2,319	30,440
141	Manipur	17,753,824,317	1,775	14,432
142	Manipur	18,512,615,075	1,851	27,845

Region	State	RVA in Rs.	RVA in Rs. Cr	RVAPC in Rs.
151	Mizoram	16,859,979,004	1,686	24,662
161	Tripura	78,459,763,870	7,846	24,394
171	Meghalaya	49,408,069,434	4,941	24,086
181	Assam	171,946,812,287	17,195	18,709
182	Assam	230,242,715,003	23,024	15,822
183	Assam	12,788,841,267	1,279	13,654
191	West Bengal	154,945,242,501	15,495	23,244
192	West Bengal	440,771,556,859	44,077	20,645
193	West Bengal	830,171,594,210	83,017	23,247
194	West Bengal	366,647,481,315	36,665	23,872
201	Jharkhand	433,819,254,083	43,382	18,509
211	Odisha	220,808,849,284	22,081	13,039
212	Odisha	151,412,036,634	15,141	23,095
213	Odisha	285,214,886,015	28,521	21,720
221	Chattisgarh	400,377,427,098	40,038	18,559
231	Madhya Pradesh	179,489,999,737	17,949	15,930
232	Madhya Pradesh	104,870,367,880	10,487	13,097
233	Madhya Pradesh	259,692,747,044	25,969	17,699
234	Madhya Pradesh	176,093,362,645	17,609	17,438
235	Madhya Pradesh	120,383,636,852	12,038	15,835
236	Madhya Pradesh	91,851,980,452	9,185	10,983
241	Gujarat	366,421,502,991	36,642	38,093
242	Gujarat	324,509,248,409	32,451	26,806
243	Gujarat	346,860,581,493	34,686	34,537
244	Gujarat	161,896,071,214	16,190	27,787
245	Gujarat	324,451,984,146	32,445	33,129
271	Maharashtra	619,324,936,223	61,932	27,972
272	Maharashtra	846,725,812,965	84,673	37,189
273	Maharashtra	386,899,180,737	38,690	35,569
274	Maharashtra	659,234,173,727	65,923	41,905
275	Maharashtra	570,191,719,740	57,019	38,561
276	Maharashtra	240,243,646,070	24,024	45,478
281	Andhra Pradesh	780,688,510,120	78,069	24,225
282	Andhra Pradesh	702,488,068,671	70,249	26,309
283	Andhra Pradesh	201,053,413,131	20,105	28,856
284	Andhra Pradesh	137,950,828,938	13,795	22,991
291	Karnataka	93,318,397,336	9,332	22,076

Region	State	RVA in Rs.	RVA in Rs. Cr	RVAPC in Rs.
292	Karnataka	143,572,039,069	14,357	32,078
293	Karnataka	476,054,489,289	47,605	27,143
294	Karnataka	592,176,582,841	59,218	26,634
301	Goa	79,839,023,605	7,984	76,967
321	Kerala	309,581,379,524	30,958	24,868
322	Kerala	670,562,991,145	67,056	37,217
331	Tamil Nadu	539,105,668,862	53,911	27,854
332	Tamil Nadu	263,725,167,157	26,373	26,050
333	Tamil Nadu	395,903,074,524	39,590	30,463
334	Tamil Nadu	482,773,954,610	48,277	36,434
341	Pondicherry	40,229,999,502	4,023	48,301
351	Andaman and Nicobar Islands	11,390,319,429	1,139	40,921

APPENDIX 11

Region-wise Values for Regional Value Added (RVA) and Regional Value Added Per Capita (RVAPC) 2011-12

Region	State	RVA in Rs.	RVA in Rs. Cr.	RVAPC in Rs.
11	Jammu and Kashmir	91,893,678,325	9,189	37,831
12	Jammu and Kashmir	74,926,003,289	7,493	28,438
13	Jammu and Kashmir	110,571,387,157	11,057	24,746
14	Jammu and Kashmir	5,558,484,678	556	27,021
21	Himachal Pradesh	164,739,387,437	16,474	47,599
22	Himachal Pradesh	145,007,899,203	14,501	51,197
31	Punjab	492,813,231,157	49,281	43,594
32	Punjab	692,746,724,879	69,275	48,546
41	Chandigarh	80,086,940,000	8,009	80,800
51	Uttarakhand	492,106,131,695	49,211	52,607
61	Haryana	978,242,620,496	97,824	62,830
62	Haryana	514,052,715,180	51,405	59,726
71	Delhi	1,422,965,781,994	142,297	110,779
81	Rajasthan	295,055,771,150	29,506	25,218
82	Rajasthan	581,761,565,098	58,176	26,124
83	Rajasthan	271,615,625,519	27,162	43,811
84	Rajasthan	240,923,559,300	24,092	34,600
85	Rajasthan	321,698,011,880	32,170	25,712
91	Uttar Pradesh	504,201,818,063	50,420	17,921
92	Uttar Pradesh	617,571,246,696	61,757	20,696
93	Uttar Pradesh	1,162,840,338,455	116,284	16,688
94	Uttar Pradesh	195,043,378,004	19,504	23,664
95	Uttar Pradesh	767,483,949,045	76,748	17,338
101	Bihar	731,634,164,267	73,163	12,838
102	Bihar	449,669,979,918	44,967	13,695
111	Sikkim	38,377,815,427	3,838	73,703

Region	State	RVA in Rs.	RVA in Rs. Cr.	RVAPC in Rs.
121	Arunachal Pradesh	36,392,801,380	3,639	35,230
131	Nagaland	51,526,094,760	5,153	46,340
141	Manipur	29,579,493,162	2,958	20,105
142	Manipur	22,120,903,739	2,212	28,095
151	Mizoram	33,696,394,560	3,370	37,920
161	Tripura	132,787,888,137	13,279	39,381
171	Meghalaya	85,037,799,250	8,504	34,217
181	Assam	201,619,421,066	20,162	29,574
182	Assam	184,871,536,127	18,487	20,099
183	Assam	83,401,667,867	8,340	19,948
184	Assam	126,963,839,858	12,696	20,405
191	West Bengal	245,600,448,046	24,560	33,651
192	West Bengal	721,818,079,849	72,182	32,475
193	West Bengal	799,168,439,588	79,917	34,822
194	West Bengal	536,996,220,943	53,700	32,694
195	West Bengal	410,453,889,394	41,045	26,791
201	Jharkhand	333,873,687,791	33,387	27,840
202	Jharkhand	342,372,112,971	34,237	23,258
211	Odisha	285,209,090,847	28,521	19,752
212	Odisha	333,844,464,619	33,384	27,724
213	Odisha	306,703,470,430	30,670	26,363
221	Chattisgarh	74,739,843,123	7,474	27,200
222	Chattisgarh	457,959,534,347	45,796	26,109
223	Chattisgarh	92,556,691,110	9,256	34,518
231	Madhya Pradesh	599,034,302,681	59,903	53,971
232	Madhya Pradesh	507,060,333,926	50,706	55,739
233	Madhya Pradesh	961,575,338,808	96,158	60,798
234	Madhya Pradesh	642,305,229,670	64,231	58,845
235	Madhya Pradesh	738,226,351,975	73,823	97,421
236	Madhya Pradesh	506,937,588,309	50,694	52,529
241	Gujarat	1,464,349,252,058	146,435	72,012
242	Gujarat	668,498,564,493	66,850	41,507
243	Gujarat	158,919,059,998	15,892	43,662
244	Gujarat	152,378,698,709	15,238	65,684
245	Gujarat	795,273,580,166	79,527	59,980
271	Maharashtra	1,448,584,649,420	144,858	51,838
272	Maharashtra	1,521,275,309,694	152,128	59,515

Region	State	RVA in Rs.	RVA in Rs. Cr.	RVAPC in Rs.
273	Maharashtra	764,957,214,059	76,496	62,198
274	Maharashtra	1,190,628,524,773	119,063	74,039
275	Maharashtra	1,031,699,487,555	103,170	63,483
276	Maharashtra	434,549,789,460	43,455	80,756
281	Andhra Pradesh	631,141,092,948	63,114	36,824
282	Andhra Pradesh	682,349,933,104	68,235	44,439
283	Andhra Pradesh	803,889,172,137	80,389	37,386
284	Andhra Pradesh	594,001,191,921	59,400	47,327
285	Andhra Pradesh	709,560,870,524	70,956	53,014
291	Karnataka	190,432,151,742	19,043	45,407
292	Karnataka	121,646,552,208	12,165	24,686
293	Karnataka	1,168,275,726,728	116,828	57,152
294	Karnataka	1,326,056,782,982	132,606	51,949
301	Goa	172,891,860,595	17,289	129,397
321	Kerala	584,968,658,332	58,497	43,151
322	Kerala	1,051,986,857,865	105,199	59,526
331	Tamil Nadu	1,071,887,217,082	107,189	46,075
332	Tamil Nadu	632,079,993,112	63,208	54,770
333	Tamil Nadu	921,591,282,438	92,159	58,722
334	Tamil Nadu	1,209,477,727,555	120,948	75,252
341	Pondicherry	96,904,790,252	9,690	80,516
351	Andaman and Nicobar Islands	22,556,056,320	2,256	68,355

Bibliography

Abdel-Rahman, H. M. 1988. 'Product Differentiation, Monopolistic Competition and City Size'. *Regional Science and Urban Economics* 18 (1): 69–86.

Arrow, K. 1962. 'The Economic Implications of Learning by Doing'. *American Economic Review* 29 (3): 155–73.

Attaran, M. 1986. Industrial Diversity and Economic Performance in US Areas'. *The Annals of Regional Science* 20 (2): 44–54.

Au, C. C., and J. V. Henderson. 2006. 'Are Chinese Cities Too Small?' *Review of Economic Studies* 73 (3): 549–76.

Awasthi, D. N. 1991. *Regional Patterns of Industrial Growth in India*. New Delhi: Concept Publishing Co.

Bacher, J. 2000. 'A Probabilistic Clustering Model for Variables of Mixed Type'. *Quality and Quantity* 34 (3): 223–35.

Bairoch, P. 1998. *Cities and Economic Development: From the Dawn of History to the Present*. Chicago: University of Chicago Press.

Bajpai, N., and J. D. Sachs. 1996. 'Trends in Inter-state Inequalities of Income in India'. Development Discussion Paper No. 528. Cambridge, Massachusetts.

Baltagi, B. H., and J. M. Griffin. 1997. 'Pooled Estimators vs. Their Heterogeneous Counterparts in the Context of Dynamic Demand for Gasoline'. *Journal of Econometrics* 77 (2): 303–27.

Basu, K., and A. Maertens. 2007. 'The pattern and causes of economic growth in India'. *Oxford Review of Economic Policy*, 23(2), 143–67.

Basu, P., and P. Srivastava. 2004. 'Scaling-up Access to Finance for India's Rural Poor'. Policy Research Working Paper Series No. 3646, The World Bank, Washington DC.

Beaudry, C., and A. Schiffauerova. 2009. 'Who's Right, Marshall or Jacobs? The Localization versus Urbanization Debate'. *Research Policy* 38 (2): 318–37.

Beeson, P. E., D. N. DeJong, and W. Troesken. 2001. 'Population Growth in U.S. Counties, 1840–1990'. *Regional Science and Urban Economics* 31 (6): 669–99.

Berman, E., J. Bound, and S. Machin. 1998. 'Implications of Skill-Biased Technological Change: International Evidence'. *The Quarterly Journal of Economics* 113 (4): 1245–79.

Bhat, S., and N. Siddharthan. 2012. 'Human capital, Labour Productivity and Employment'. In *Human Capital and Development: The Indian Experience*, edited by N. Siddharthan and K. Narayanan. New Delhi: Springer Science and Business Media.

Black, D., and V. Henderson. 1999. 'A Theory of Urban Growth'. *Journal of Political Economy* 107 (2): 252–84.

Cashin, P., and R. Sahay. 1996. 'Regional Economic Growth and Convergence in India'. *Finance and Development* 33 (1): 49–52.

Central Statistical Organization (CSO). 2008. National Industrial Classification (All Economic Activities). *Ministry of Statistics and Programme Implementation*.

Chandrasekhar, S., and A. Sharma. 2014. 'On the Spatial Concentration of Employment in India'. *Economic and Political Weekly* 49 (21): 16–18.

Chinitz, B. 1961. 'Contrasts in Agglomeration: New York and Pittsburg'. *The American Economic Review* 51 (2): 279–89.

Christaller, W. 1966. *Central Places in Southern Germany*. London: Prentice-Hall.

Ciccone, A., and R. E. Hall. 1996. 'Productivity and the Density of Economic Activity'. *The American Economic Review* 86 (1): 54–70.

Cobb, C. W., and P. H. Douglas. 1928. 'A Theory of Production'. *American Economic Review* 18 (1): 139–65.

Combes, P. 2000. 'Economic Structure and Local Growth: France, 1984–1993'. *Journal of Urban Economics* 47 (3): 329–55.

da Mata, D., U. Deichmann, J. V. Henderson, S. V. Lall, and H. G. Wang. 2007. 'Determinants of City Growth in Brazil'. *Journal of Urban Economics* 62 (2): 252–72.

Dasgupta, D., P. Maiti, R. Mukherjee, S. Sarkar, and S. Chakrabarti. 2000. 'Growth and Inter-State Disparities in India'. *Economic and Political Weekly* 35 (27): 2413–22.

Dehejia, R. H., and V. H. Dehejia. 1993. 'Religion and Economic Activity in India: An Historical Perspective'. *American Journal of Economics and Sociology* 52 (2): 145–53.

Deichmann, U., K. Kaiser, S. V. Lall, and Z. Shalizi. 2005. 'Agglomeration, Transport, and Regional Development'. Policy Research Working Paper Series 3477, The World Bank, Washington DC.

Deichmann, U., S. V. Lall, S. J. Redding, and A. J. Venables. 2008. 'Industrial Location in Developing Countries'. *World Bank Research Observer* 23 (2): 219–46.

Denis, E., P. Mukhopadhyay, and M. H. Zérah. 2012. 'Subaltern Urbanisation in India'. *Economic and Political Weekly* 47 (30): 52–62.

Dholakia, R. H. 2009. 'Regional Sources of Growth Acceleration in India'. *Economic and Political Weekly* 44 (47): 67–74.

Dixit, A., and J. E. Stiglitz. 1977. 'Monopolistic Competition and Optimum Product Diversity'. *The American Economic Review* 67 (3): 297–308.

Drèze, J., and A. Sen. 2013. *An Uncertain Glory: India and Its Contradictions*. Princeton: Princeton University Press.

Dunford, M., Y. Aoyama, C. C. Diniz, A. Kundu, L. Limonov, G. Lin, W. Liu, S. O. Park, and I. Turok. 2016. 'Area Development and Policy: An Agenda for the 21st Century'. *Area Development and Policy* 1 (1): 1–14.

Duranton, G., and D. Puga. 2004. 'Micro-foundations of Urban Agglomeration Economies'. In *Handbook of Urban and Regional Economics*, volume 4, edited by J. V. Henderson and J. Thisse, 2063–117. Amsterdam: Elsevier.

Economic Survey, 2005–2006. Ministry of Finance, Government of India.

Elizondo, R. L., and P. Krugman. 1992. 'Trade Policy and the Third World Metropolis'. NBER Working Paper Series No. 4238, National Bureau of Economic Research, Cambridge.

Everitt, B. S. 2002. *Applied Multivariate Data Analysis*. New York: Oxford University Press.

Farhauer, O., and A. Kröll. 2012. 'Diversified Specialisation—One Step Beyond Regional Economics' Specialisation-Diversification Concept'. *Jahrbuch Fur Regionalwissenschaft* 32 (1): 63–84.

Fisher, A. G. 1939. 'Production: Primary, Secondary and Tertiary'. *Economic Record* 15 (1): 24–38.

Fujita, M., and P. Krugman. 1995. 'When is the Economy Monocentric?: von Thunen and Chamberlin Unified'. *Regional Science and Urban Economics* 25 (4): 505–28.

Fujita, M., and J. F. Thisse. 1996. 'Economics of Agglomeration'. *Journal of the Japanese and International Economies* 10 (4): 339–78.

Fujita, M., and J. F. Thisse. 2002. Agglomeration and market interaction. Available at SSRN: https://ssrn.com/abstract=315966

Ghani, E., W. R. Kerr, and I. Tewari. 2014. 'Regional Diversity and Inclusive Growth in Indian Cities'. Policy Research Working Paper Series 6919, The World Bank, Washington DC.

Goldar, B. N. 1986. *Productivity Growth in Indian Industry*. New Delhi: Allied Publishers Pvt. Ltd.

Government of India (GoI). 1980. National Committee on Development of Backward Areas, Report on Industrial Dispersal, Government of India, Planning Commission, New Delhi, October.

———. 2006a. Employment and Unemployment Situation in India 2004–05, Parts I and II, 61st Round (July 2004–June 2005), National Sample Survey Organisation, Ministry of Statistics and Programme Implementation, New Delhi.

———. 2006b. Instructions to Field Staff, Volume 1, 61st Round (July 2004–June 2005), Appendix II, National Sample Survey Organisation, Ministry of Statistics and Programme Implementation, New Delhi.

———. 2013a. Employment and Unemployment Situation in India, 2011–12, Parts I and II, 68th Round (July 2011–June 2012), National Sample Survey Organisation, Ministry of Statistics and Programme Implementation, New Delhi.

———. 2013b. Instructions to Field Staff, Volume 1, 68th Round (July 2011–June 2012), Appendix II, National Sample Survey Organisation, Ministry of Statistics and Programme Implementation, New Delhi.

———. 2013c. Note on Sample Design and Estimation Procedure, 68th Round (July 2011–June 2012), National Sample Survey Organisation, Ministry of Statistics and Programme Implementation, New Delhi.

Gupta, S. 1973. 'The Role of the Public Sector in Reducing Regional Income Disparity in Indian Plans'. *The Journal of Development Studies* 9 (2): 243–60.

Hasan, R., Y. Jiang, and R. M. Rafols. 2017. 'Urban agglomeration effects in India: evidence from town-level data'. *Asian Development Review*, 34(2), 201–28.

Helsley, R. W., and W. C. Strange. 1990. 'Matching and Agglomeration Economies in a System of Cities'. *Regional Science and Urban Economics* 20 (2): 189–212.

Henderson, J. V., T. Lee, and Y. Lee. 2001. 'Scale Externalities in Korea'. *Journal of Urban Economics* 49 (3): 479–504.

Henderson, J. V., and A. J. Venables. 2009. 'The Dynamics of City Formation'. *Review of Economic Dynamics* 12 (2): 233–54.

Hirschman, A. O. 1958. *The Strategy of Economic Development*. New Haven, Connecticut: Yale University Press.

Hirway, I. 2012. 'Missing Labour Force: An Explanation'. *Economic and Political Weekly* 47 (37): 67–72.

Jacobs, J. 1969. 'Strategies for Helping Cities'. *The American Economic Review* 59 (4): 652–6.

Johnson, E. A. J. 1970. *The Organization of Space in Developing Countries*. Cambridge, Massachusetts: Harvard University Press.

Kaldor, N. 1957. 'A Model of Economic Growth'. *The Economic Journal* 67 (268): 591–624.

———. 1967. *Strategic Factors in Economic Development*. Ithaca: Cornell University Press.

———. 1970. 'A Case for Regional Policies'. *Scottish Journal of Political Economy* 17 (3): 337–48.

Kathuria, V., N. S. Rajesh Raj, and K. Sen. 2010. 'Organised versus Unorganised Manufacturing Performance in the Post-Reform Period'. *Economic and Political Weekly* 45 (24): 55–64.

Kemeny, T., and M. Storper. 2014. 'Is Specialization Good for Regional Economic Development?' *Regional Studies* 49 (6): 1003–18.

Klecka, W. R. 1980. *Discriminant Analysis*. Beverly Hills, CA: Sage Publications.

Krishnamurty, J., and G. Raveendran. 2008. *Measures of Labour Force Participation and Utilization*. New Delhi: National Commission for Enterprises in the Unorganized Sector.

Krugman, P. 1991. 'Increasing Returns and Economic Geography'. *The Journal of Political Economy* 99 (3): 483–99.

Krugman, P., and A. J. Venables. 1995. 'Globalization and the Inequality of Nations'. NBER Working Paper Series 5098, National Bureau of Economic Research, Cambridge, Massachusetts.

Kundu, A. 1997. 'Trends and Structure of Employment in the Implications for Urban Growth'. *Economic and Political Weekly* 32 (24): 1399–405.

———. 2011. 'Method in Madness: Urban Data from 2011 Census'. *Economic and Political Weekly* 46 (40): 13–16.

Kurian, N. J. 2000. 'Widening Regional Disparities in India: Some Indicators'. *Economic and Political Weekly* 35 (7): 538–50.

Kuznets, S. 1955. 'Economic Growth and Income Inequality'. *The American Economic Review* 45 (1): 1–28.

Lall, S. V., and S. Chakravorty. 2005. 'Industrial Location and Spatial Inequality: Theory and Evidence from India'. *Review of Development Economics* 9 (1): 47–68.

———. 2007. *Made in India: The Economic Geography and Political Economy of India's Industrialization*. New Delhi: Oxford University Press.

Lall, S. V., R. Funderburg, and T. Yepes. 2004. 'Location, Concentration and Performance of Economic Activity in Brazil'. Policy Research Working Paper No. 3268, The World Bank, Washington DC, 1–43.

Lall, S. V., and T. Mengistae. 2005. 'The Impact of Business Environment and Economic Geography on Plant-Level Productivity: An Analysis of Indian Industry'. Policy Research Working Paper No. 3664, The World Bank, Washington DC.

Lall, S. V., Z. Shalizi, and U. Deichmann. 2004. 'Agglomeration Economies and Productivity in Indian Industry'. *Journal of Development Economics* 73 (2): 643–73.

Lampard, E. 1955. 'The History of Cities in the Economically Advanced Areas'. *Economic Development and Cultural Change* 3 (2): 81–136.

Lewis, A. 1954. 'Economic Development with Unlimited Supplies of Labour'. *The Manchester School* 22 (2): 139–91.

Maddala, G. S. 1991. 'To Pool or Not to Pool: That is the Question'. *Journal of Quantitative Economics* 7 (2): 255–64.

Maiti, D. S., and A. Mitra. 2010. 'Skills, Informality and Development'. IEG Working Paper No. 306, Institute for Economic Growth, New Delhi.

Marshall, A. 1890. *Principles of Economics*. London: MacMillan.

Mathur, A. 1983. 'Regional Development and Income Disparities in India: A Sectoral Analysis'. *Economic Development and Cultural Change* 31 (3): 475–505.

Mehrotra, S., S. Sinha, J. K. Parida, and A. Gandhi. 2014. 'Why A Jobs Turnaround Despite Slowing Growth?' Occasional Paper No. 1, Institute of Applied Manpower Research, Delhi.

Meyer, D. 1977. 'Agglomeration Economies and Urban-Industrial Growth: Clarification and Review of Concepts'. *Regional Science Perspectives* 7 (1): 80–91.

Meyer, J. R. 1963. 'Regional Economics: A survey'. *The American Economic Review* 53 (1): 19–54.

Mills, E. S., and B. W. Hamilton. 1997. *Urban Economics*, fifth edition. Upper Saddle River: Prentice Hall.

Mitra, A. 2011. *Urbanization in India: Evidence on Agglomeration Economies*. New Delhi: Institute for Economic Growth.

Mitra, A., and B. Mehta. 2011. 'Cities as the Engine of Growth: Evidence from India'. *Journal of Urban Planning and Development* 137 (2): 171–83.

Moomaw, R. L. 1981. 'Productivity and City Size: A Critique of the Evidence'. *The Quarterly Journal of Economics* 96 (4): 675–88.

Mukim, M., and P. Nunnenkamp. 2012. 'The Location Choices of Foreign Investors: A District-Level Analysis in India'. *World Economy* 35 (7): 886–918.

Myrdal, G. 1957. *Economic Theory and Under-Developed Regions*. London: Gerald Duckworth and Co. Ltd.

Nair, K. R. G. 2004. *Economic Reforms and Regional Disparities in Economic and Social Development in India*. New Delhi: Centre for Policy Research.

Nourse, H. O. 1968. *Regional Economics: A Study in the Economic Structure, Stability and Growth of Regions*. New York: McGraw Hill.

OECD Directorate of Science, Technology and Industry. 2011. 'ISIC Rev. 3 Technology Intensity Definition', Economic Analysis and Statistics Division, OECD Publishing, Paris.

Panagariya, A., P. Chakraborty, and M. G. Rao. 2014. *State Level Reforms, Growth, and Development in Indian States*. Oxford: Oxford University Press.

Papola, T. S., and N. Jena. 2011. *Inter-Regional Disparities in Industrial Growth and Structure*. New Delhi: Institute for Studies in Industrial Development.

Papola, T. S., and P. P. Sahu. 2012. *Growth and Structure of Employment in India: Long-Term and Post-Reform Performance and the Emerging Challenge*. New Delhi: Institute for Studies in Industrial Development.

Parr, J. B. 1965. 'Specialization, Diversification and Regional Development'. *The Professional Geographer* 17 (6): 21–5.

Pearce, D., and J. Davis. 2000. 'The Role of the Non-farm Rural Sector in the Reconstruction of the Balkans', Discussion Paper No. 2000/02, Markets, Finance and Enterprise Group, Natural Resources Institute, Kent.

Pesaran, M. H., and S. Ron. 1995. Estimating Long-Run Relationships from Dynamic Heterogeneous Panels. *Journal of Econometrics* 68 (1): 79–113.

Phelps, N., and T. Ozawa. 2003. Contrasts in Agglomeration: Proto-industrial, Industrial and Post-Industrial Forms Compared. *Progress in Human Geography* 27 (5): 583–604.

Puga, D., and A. J. Venables. 1996. 'The Spread of Industry: Spatial Agglomeration in Economic Development'. *Journal of the Japanese and International Economies* 10: 440–64.

Quigley, J. M. 1998. 'Urban Diversity and Economic Growth'. *Journal of Economic Perspectives* 12 (2): 127–38.

Rajan, R. G. 2006. 'India: The Past and Its Future'. *Asian Development Review* 23 (2): 36–52.

Rangarajan, C., Seema, B. M. Vibheesh. 2014. 'Developments in the Workforce between 2009–10 and 2011–12'. *Economic and Political Weekly* 49 (23): 117–21.

Rao, M. F., G. R. T. Shand, and K. P. Kaliranjan. 1999. 'Convergence of Income across Indian States: A Divergent View'. *Economic and Political Weekly* 34 (13): 769–78.

Registrar General and Census Commissioner. 2001. *Primary Census Abstract, Series I, Census of India 2001*, Ministry of Home Affairs, New Delhi.

———. 2011. *Primary Census Abstract, Series I, Census of India 2011*. New Delhi: Registrar General and Census Commissioner, Ministry of Home Affairs.

Reserve Bank of India. 2005a. *Basic Statistical Returns of Scheduled Commercial Banks in India 2005*, Volume 34, Reserve Bank of India, Mumbai. Retrieved from https://rbi.org.in/Scripts/AnnualPublications.aspx?head=Basic+Statistical+Returns on 30 May 2015.

———. 2005b. *Handbook of Statistics on Indian Economy 2004–05*, Part I: *Annual Series National Income, Saving And Employment*, Reserve Bank of India, Mumbai. Retrieved from https://rbi.org.in/Scripts/AnnualPublications.aspx?head=Handbook+of+Statistics+on+Indian+Economy on 10 May 2015.

———. 2010. *Basic Statistical Returns of Scheduled Commercial Banks in India 2010*, Volume 39, Reserve Bank of India, Mumbai. Retrieved from https://rbi.org.in/Scripts/AnnualPublications.aspx?head=Basic+Statistical+Returns on 30 May 2015.

———. 2012. *Handbook of Statistics on Indian Economy 2011–12*, Part I: *Annual Series National Income, Saving And Employment*, Reserve Bank of India, Mumbai. Retrieved from https://rbi.org.in/Scripts/AnnualPublications.aspx?head=Handbook+of+Statistics+on+Indian+Economy on 10 May 2015.

Robertson, D., and J. Symons. 1992. 'Some Strange Properties of Panel Data Estimators'. *Journal of Applied Econometrics* 7 (2): 175–89.

Rodgers, A. 1957. 'Some Aspects of Industrial Diversification in the United States'. *Economic Geography* 33 (1): 16–30.

Romer, P. M. 1986. 'Increasing Returns and Long-Run Growth'. *The Journal of Political Economy* 94 (5): 1002–37.

Rosenthal, S. S., and W. C. Strange. 2001. 'The Determinants of Agglomeration'. *Journal of Urban Economics* 50 (2): 191–229.

SPSS Inc. 1999. *SPSS Base 10.0 for Windows User's Guide*. Chicago, IL: SPSS Inc.

Sachs, J. D., N. Bajpai, and A. Ramiah. 2002. 'Understanding Regional Economic Growth in India', Centre for International Development (CID) Working Papers 88, Harvard University Press, Cambridge, Massachusetts.

Saradamoni, K. 1969. 'Inter-state Differences in Manufacturing and Workers' Earnings'. *Economic and Political Weekly* 4 (22): 911–15.

Segal, D. 1976. 'Are There Returns to Scale in City Size?' *The Review of Economics and Statistics* 58 (3): 339–50.

Smith, A. 1776. *The Wealth of Nations*, edited by E. Cannan. New York: Bantam Dell.

Sridhar, K. S. 2017. 'Economic Change and Specialization in India's Cities'. *Review of Urban and Regional Development Studies* 29 (1): 63–87.

Sveikauskas, L. 1975. 'The Productivity of Cities'. *The Quarterly Journal of Economics* 89 (3): 393–413.

Tabuchi, T. 1986. 'Urban Agglomeration, Capital Augmenting Technology, and Labor Market Equilibrium'. *Journal of Urban Economics* 20 (2): 211–28.

Thomas, J. J. 2012. 'India's Labour Market in the 2000s: Surveying the Changes'. *Economic and Political Weekly* 47 –51): 39–51.

———. 2013. 'Explaining the "Jobless" Growth in Indian Manufacturing'. *Journal of the Asia Pacific Economy* 18 (4): 673–92.

United Nations Population Division. 2010. World Urbanization Prospects: The 2009 Revision (POP/DB/WUP/Rev.2007) United Nations Department of Economic and Social Affairs, New York.

Veeramani, C., and B. N. Goldar. 2005. 'Manufacturing Productivity in Indian States: Does Investment Climate Matter'. *Economic And Political Weekly* 40 (24): 2413–20.

Venables, A. J. 1996. 'Equilibrium Locations of Vertically Linked Industries'. *International Economic Review* 37 (2): 341–59.

Von Thünen, J. 1826. Isolated State. Translated by Carla M. Wartenberg.

Wagner, J. E., and S. C. Deller. 1998. 'Measuring the Effects of Economic Diversity on Growth and Stability'. *Land Economics* 74 (4): 541–56.

Weber, A. 1909. *Theory of the Location of Industries*, translated by Carl Friedrich in 1929. Chicago: University of Chicago Press.

Williamson, J. G. 1965. 'Regional Inequality and the Process of National Development: A Description of the Patterns'. *Economic Development and Cultural Change* 13 (4): 1–84.

Young, A. A. 1928. 'Increasing Returns and Economic Progress'. *The Economic Journal* 38 (152): 527–42.

Index

Tables and figures are indicated by *t* and *f* following the page number

About the Authors

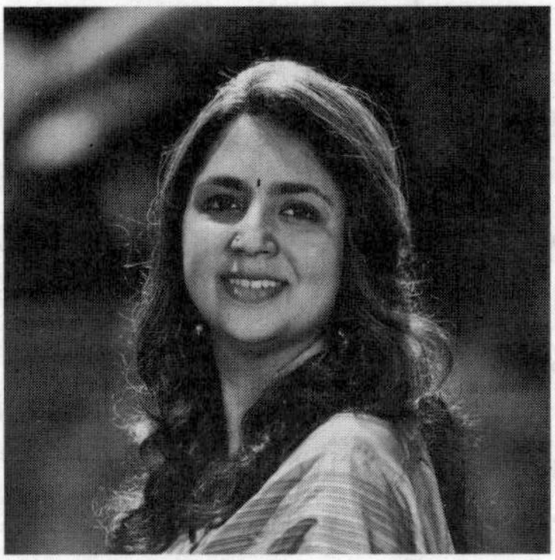

Poornima Dore

Dr. Poornima Dore is an Economist and Business Leader with deep experience in digital transformation, corporate and development finance, and currently works as Director - Analytics, Insights and Impact (AI&I) at the Tata Trusts, one of India's largest philanthropic institutions, also a major stakeholder in the salt to manufacturing conglomerate. She has earlier led the Structural Investments vertical at Tata Capital Ltd, where she anchored investments in automotive, pharma, technology, insurance and other sectors. She has been associated with investors and promoters in the driving and setting up of Commercial Finance and S.M.E. businesses, apart from assessing venture funding structures, identifying viable growth drivers, and mentorship/creation of a social venture fund. She has emerged as a strong advocate of harnessing risk capital for sustainable development, with her exposure ranging from villages to board rooms.

Over the years, she has contributed to the private sector's role in the public discourse through investments in digital goods, urban planning, skilling, migration and livelihoods, while designing special institutional programs on impact financing and employment creation. Under her leadership, her unit at the Trust has been a pioneer in Data Driven Governance, developing the concepts and tools relevant to Government departments, businesses, citizen groups and start-ups, with the objective of leveraging data and technology to achieve Sustainable Development Goals (SDGs). A specially curated approach named D.E.L.T.A (Data, Evaluation, Learning, Technology and Analysis) has been offered successfully on a large scale across 26 State Governments and 100 Cities across India, to foster systemic change and measurable results.

In addition, she is currently on the Advisory Boards of select Universities and Associations. Recognised as one of the top 100 Analytics Leaders in South Asia, she has served as a Committee member of the National Consumption Expenditure Survey, Data Smart Cities, Aspirational Districts of India, and several Ministerial Committees of Govt. Of India, and the Niti Aayog. She teaches at premiere management and technical institutes, where she curates and offers modules periodically. Her skill-sets include creating innovative solutions and structures, harnessing the synergy of ideas and people for both wealth creation and public good.

Her journey with the regional economy began with helping businesses to make investment and growth choices. The inter-play of investment preferences and regional factors stoked her curiosity to delve deeper, and engage with the concept of geographic agglomeration. This became the theme for her Doctoral dissertation at I.I.T.Bombay, alongside her extensive work travels. This book is a natural off-shoot of the above.

Dr. Dore has a number of peer reviewed publications in the field of regional growth, access to finance, and planning for development in journals like Millennial Asia, India International Centre Quarterly, Area Development and Policy. She has several publications as case studies, SOPs (standard operating practices), frameworks and policy guidelines developed by her unit for practitioners including the DELTA modules for local area development (panchayat) microplanning, Open Data guidelines for India, and edited volumes on the availability of district level finances namely 'The Budget Trails'. She has also anchored research consortiums in partnership with several multilateral agencies.

She graduated as a Principal's Award holder in economics from Lady Shri Ram College, New Delhi, studied management from XLRI Jamshedpur and came into the world of business as part of the TAS (Tata Administrative Services) Leadership cadre. She is a Life Member of the Institute of Directors (I.O.D). She is also a member of the international forums 'Women in Data' and 'Initiatives of Change', and has enlisted others. She draws inspiration from reading, poetry and spirituality. At a personal level, she is a trained vocalist in Carnatic Music, and a western percussionist (drummer) of the band Bodhi Tree. She actively enjoys composing and performing music in various genres, encouraging artistes and following her inner rhythm. She is married to Sourav and has a daughter Devika.

Dr. Dore believes that game-changing answers come from the intersection of diverse disciplines and actors. Her demonstrated strengths rest in catalysing such action through innovative financial and institutional structures, building high performing teams and driving meaningful partnerships across companies, academia, citizens and policy makers. She looks forward to working on high impact solutions, leveraging the power of economics, finance, data, people and global networks, for both equity and growth.

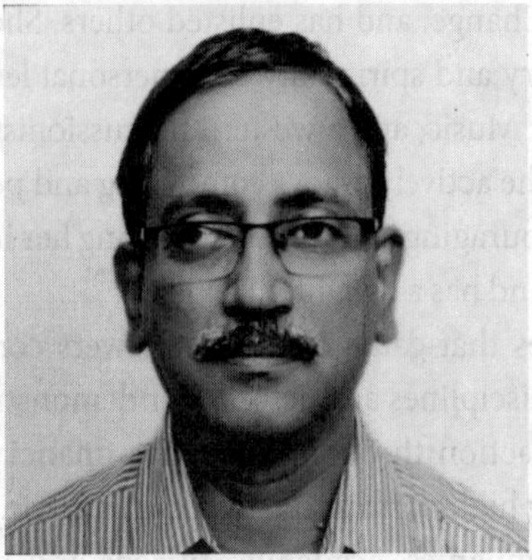

K. Narayanan

Dr. K. Narayanan obtained his Ph.D in Economics from the Delhi School of Economics, University of Delhi, India, and carried out Post-doctoral research at Institute of Advanced Studies United Nations University, Tokyo, Japan. His research interests span the areas of industrial economics, international business, Socio-economic empowerment through ICT, Environmental Economics, Economic impacts of Climate Change and Development Economics. He has a number of publications in the field of industrial competitiveness, technology transfer, ICT, international trade and socio-economic impacts of Climate Change. The research journals in which he has published include Research Policy, Studies in Regional Science, Technovation, Oxford Development Studies, Journal of Industry, Competition and Trade, International Journal of Energy Economics and Policy, Water Policy, Foreign Trade Review, Current Science, and Economic and Political Weekly.

Few of his recent publications include edited books on (i) Indian and Chinese Enterprises: Global Trade, Technology, and Investment Regimes, (ii) Human Capital and Development: The Indian Experience, (iii) Innovation and Global Competitiveness: Case of India's Manufacturing Sector, (iv) Technology: Corporate and Social Dimensions, and (v) Globalisation of Technology, (vi) FDI, Technology and Innovation [all of them were jointly edited with N.S. Siddharthan] published by Routledge & Springer. His seventh book published in 2016 by Springer titled "Globalisation of Indian Industries: Productivity, Exports and Investment" was edited jointly with Filip De Beule of KU Leuven, Belgium. He also guest edited a Special Issue of the IASSI Quarterly on the theme "Human Capital and Development", a Special Issue of the Sage published international journal, Science, Technology and Society on the theme "Agglomeration, technology clusters and networks", and a Special Issue of "Innovation and Development", published by Taylor and Francis. He is actively engaged in a web based research group, Forum for Global Knowledge Sharing, which interfaces Scientists, Technologists and Economists. He is currently Honorary Secretary of this forum. He is also a member of the study team which helps prepare India's National Communication to the UNFCCC. He also serves in the editorial board of journals like Springer Nature Business and Economics, Sarvekshana [a journal of the CSO, Government of India], and Asia Pacific Journal of Regional Sciences [edited from Japan].

His teaching and research career span a period of 31 years - 1989 to 2001 at the University of Delhi and since December 2001 at Indian Institute of Technology Bombay.

He had been an Institute Chair Professor during 2012-2018 and Head of the Department of Humanities and Social Sciences, IIT Bombay during 2010-14. He is a connoisseur of classical music and lives in Mumbai with his wife Parvati and has two sons Arvind and Arihant.

Dr. Narayanan is currently the India Value Fund Chair Professor at the Department of Humanities and Social Sciences, Indian Institute of Technology Bombay, Mumbai, INDIA.